EXPLORING COMMODITIES

EXPLORING COMMODITIES

An Anthropologist on the Trails of Malinowski and Traven in Mexico

SCOTT COOK

Peter Lang

Oxford · Bern · Berlin · Bruxelles · New York · Wien

Bibliographic information published by Die Deutsche Nationalbibliothek
Die Deutsche Nationalbibliothek lists this publication in the Deutsche Nationalbibliografie;
detailed bibliographic data is available on the Internet at http://dnb.d-nb.de.

A catalogue record for this book is available from the British Library.

Library of Congress Cataloging-in-Publication Data
Names: Cook, H. Scott, 1937- author.
Title: Exploring commodities : an anthropologist on the trails of
  Malinowski and Traven in Mexico / Scott Cook.
Description: Oxford ; New York : Peter Lang, [2021] | Includes
  bibliographical references and index.
Identifiers: LCCN 2021011264 (print) | LCCN 2021011265 (ebook) | ISBN
  9781800794016 (paperback) | ISBN 9781800794023 (ebook) | ISBN
  9781800794030 (epub) | ISBN 9781800794047 (mobi)
Subjects: LCSH: Economic anthropology--Mexico--Oaxaca (State) | Economic
  anthropology--Mexico--Tamaulipas (State) | Commercial
  products--Mexico--Oaxaca (State) | Commercial
  products--Mexico--Tamaulipas (State) |
  Anthropology--Fieldwork--Mexico--Oaxaca (State) |
  Anthropology--Fieldwork--Mexico--Tamauilpas (State) | Malinowski,
  Bronislaw, 1884-1942--Influence. | Traven, B.--Influence.
Classification: LCC GN564.M6 C63 2021 (print) | LCC GN564.M6 (ebook) |
  DDC 306.3--dc23
LC record available at https://lccn.loc.gov/2021011264
LC ebook record available at https://lccn.loc.gov/2021011265

Cover design: Brian Melville for Peter Lang
Cover images: Author photos.

ISBN   978-1-80079-401-6 (print) • ISBN   978-1-80079-402-3 (ePDF)
ISBN   978-1-80079-403-0 (ePub) • ISBN   978-1-80079-404-7 (mobi)

© Peter Lang Group AG 2021

Published by Peter Lang Ltd, International Academic Publishers,
52 St Giles, Oxford, OX1 3LU, United Kingdom
oxford@peterlang.com, www.peterlang.com

H. Scott Cook has asserted his right under the Copyright, Designs and Patents Act, 1988,
to be identified as Author of this Work.

This publication has been peer reviewed.

Contents

List of Photographs

Acknowledgments

This project had modest beginnings several years ago when I wrote a brief statement for the Society of Economic Anthropology newsletter regarding my role in establishing that organization. At the time it occurred to me that a broader initiative leading to a series of memoirs might be in order to stimulate intergenerational communication among the field's practitioners. Mike Chibnik was supportive of the idea which was then floated among a few members of the American Anthropological Association but it was stillborn possibly due to a consensus that was expressed by one of my well-known senior colleagues that "Nobody gives a rat's ass about the history of economic anthropology." Yet, somehow as I reviewed some of my early contributions to the field – especially the critique of substantivism (Cook 1966) and a review of the development of the field that included an exploration of epistemological issues (Cook 1974a) – I decided to forge ahead with my own project, if only for my own engagement and possible enlightenment. Thanks to Leigh Binford's recommendation I read Peter Worsley's memoir-autobiography (2008) and was provided with a model of how one might undertake such an endeavor – admittedly, with regard to a much different career, subject matter, and a more limited agenda. I was privileged to meet Worsley when he was a visiting speaker at the UConn Department of Anthropology during his "Three Worlds" period when he was in residency in New York City and relied on his textbook in my undergraduate teaching.

Many other persons, in addition to those already mentioned, read parts or all of many previous versions of this writing project, and made useful comments for fixes or new avenues to explore. Davydd Greenwood and Eileen Kane who were members of my graduate student cohort at Pitt standout in this regard, as do Yvan Breton since his days as my doctoral student at Michigan State and afterwards through collegial and friendly relationships in Quebec and Mexico, and Jorge Hernández Díaz my doctoral student at UConn and a long-standing colleague, friend, and communicant in Mexican and Oaxacan studies. Also, Manuel Esparza, my longtime friend, colleague, and communicant on things Mexican and Oaxacan, was kind enough to read and comment on my project which overlapped with his own (Esparza 2020).

I owe special thanks to my wife Hilda for tolerating my obsessive devotion to this project during the past five years and for regularly drawing upon her memory bank to confirm facts about people, places, and events. She patiently did her best to help. Also, all three of my offspring – my daughters Dana Lyn and Lisa Veronica, both school teachers living and working in Austin, and my son, Scott Allen, a public health officer in Connecticut, did the same – and also were especially helpful in evaluating the Introduction and Conclusion. My two grandkids, Alexandra and Andrew, now undergraduates at Trinity University and the University of Texas, respectively, were very helpful in that regard as well. Also, my sister, Beverly Ann Newell, confirmed some of my recollections regarding family relationships and experiences.

Finally, I am indebted to the publisher's anonymous reviewers who appreciated the difficulty of one of the hardest narrative challenges one can take on namely, as one of them expressed it, "how to craft an academic memoir that's a good story that distills people, events, and insights into a narrative that will illuminate the power and importance of a ubiquitous economic pursuit for a broader audience of literate non-specialists." My hope is that I have benefitted from their constructive critiques enough to have fashioned a narrative that has merit in meeting the formidable challenge.

For the record, having completed this book as a Covid-19 'long-hauler', I am entitled to commiserate with all those whose lives have been impacted by this global pandemic.

Introduction

Some of my fondest memories involve things that were given to me. When I was 2 and 3 years old living in Pittsburgh it was a wagon and a big red fire truck given to me on my birthday by my parents which enabled me to say, "Oh boy, I'm a fireman!" When I was 5 years old wintering with my grandmother in Florida to escape the punishing Pennsylvania climate which was damaging my health, it was a set of chrome cap-firing cowboy six-shooters. Later on my sixth birthday in San Antonio, Texas where my parents had relocated, it was my dream present, a Daisy Red Ryder carbine-style BB rifle given to me by a business associate of my dad. That rifle, like the six-shooters, put me right in there with all the cowboys, outlaws, and Indians fighting it out in the Wild West especially my heroes, the Lone Ranger and Tom Mix, that I listened to with rapt attention on the radio. What adult doesn't remember the thrill of opening a gift-wrapped box and being transported by what in economics parlance is known as a "commodity."

My parents certainly did. From those days to the present, my life has been associated with useful, satisfying, and valuable products which either I or someone else paid for and which had meanings beyond their material forms.

The list went on and became imposing if not overwhelming as my life-cycle progressed from childhood to adulthood. The range and type of commodities multiplied to encompass everything from prosaic items like food, clothing, equipment, books, furniture, appliances, and vehicles to more substantial items like dwellings. Most of us remember when we came into possession of our first vehicle, either a tricycle or bicycle – I remember getting my first bike, a Roadmaster, in San Antonio when I was 7 or 8, and graduating to a Schwinn around my eleventh or twelfth birthday in Austin. Even more etched in our memories is to transition from renting to taking out a mortgage for our principal dwelling – and, as a consequence, being forced to deal with money market rates, investment depreciation and appreciation, property taxes, homeowner's insurance, and so on. Those of us who produce documents for a living are apt to remember favorite type-writers (in my case a portable and wide carriage Swiss-made Hermes) and, of course, the computerized word processors that replaced them (mine was a Texas Instruments Pro, an IBM PC clone) and greatly simplified and amplified document production. Once they enter our lives many com-modities generate subsequent economic involvements (e.g., buying car or home insurance policies), evoke memories, or have cultural implications.

I remember my first vehicle, a well-used 1940 Ford coupe, which I drove from Texas to Oklahoma and back again in 1952, and the first new vehicle I purchased, a 1962 Volkswagen beetle. Then there was the Volkswagen minibus that took my family and I from Connecticut to Oaxaca and back again in the 1960s, and the four-wheel drive Jeep Cherokee that did the same in the 1970s. Today, I drive a Toyota RAV-4 hybrid SUV, a fuel-efficient, high-tech marvel compared to all the other vehicles I have owned. All of these vehicle-commodities carry associations with important relocations at crucial times in my life – the Ford to an unwelcome change of schools during my high school years; the VW Beetle to a career-altering period, following my marriage to Hilda Almenas, a teacher from Puerto Rico who I met at American University in 1958, that involved graduate study and re-search work in her native island; and the Toyota RAV 4 to my late period of retirement in Texas when this book was written.

The VW minibus and the Jeep Cherokee evoke years of fieldwork in the Oaxaca Valley, Mexico – one of the key areas in the development of Mesoamerican civilization and its world-historically unique peasant-artisan market economy. These latter two vehicles carried me in both periods to and from numerous communities of indigenous peasant-artisans, and with peasant-artisans and their craft commodities back and forth to market-places where their commodities were sold. Thus, commodities of modern industrial high-tech origin provided me with the means to observe the production and circulation of low-tech craft industrial commodities.

My office and the walls, shelves and other spaces throughout our home in San Marcos are adorned, and storage facilities stuffed, with craft com-modities my wife and I acquired in Oaxaca over the years – wooden masks and figurines elaborately carved and painted; ceramics of various sizes, shapes, colors, and textures; textiles woven on backstrap and treadle looms of handspun wool and cotton threads, some (dresses, skirts, and shawls) worn by indigenous women as ethnic identifiers; and with metates, manos, mortars and pestles cut from quarried stone. Also, on display are varieties of handmade brick, and the hand-crafted wooden molds used to mold and position them on the drying floor, and two commissioned landscape portraits of brickworks on the Texas-Mexico border.

Hidden away under lock and key in a storage closet in my home office is my extensive collection of precision airguns and target pistols displaying the skilled craftsmanship of twentieth-century manufacturing in Germany and Connecticut (Colt and High Standard factories in Hartford and New Haven) – all of them with machine-crafted and hand-polished wooden stocks and grips and highly polished blued and case-hardened steel receivers, barrels, triggers, and hand-polished and fitted internal steel parts. On the shelves and spaces of the walls to the right, left and above my computer desk and intermixed with a wide assortment of pre-Hispanic and later Mexican craft products, are several late nineteenth- and early twentieth-century weight-driven and mechanical clocks manufactured by the Seth Thomas factory in Connecticut, and a series of photographs and paintings. I feel attached to them all equally but with different associations.

Artistic work such as oil paintings intended for aesthetic appreciation, like common handmade brick or grindstones or machine-made pistols or clocks intended for utilitarian purposes, share a commodity identity as products of work embodying use, exchange, and symbolic value-realization potentials. Temporally they can be sold or purchased, gifted or not gifted, or retained for a lifetime of enjoyment only to become heirlooms transferred to a new generation of users. Some commodities are perishable; others are more durable, and may last for several generations. Their value component may change over time – utilitarian ends, for example, being replaced by purely aesthetic or sentimental ones. But until being discarded or destroyed, commodities retain cultural significance and the potential for subsequent realization of use, exchange, or symbolic value that each one embodies.

In short, my life is and has been associated with a veritable cornucopia of handmade and machine-made commodities all embodying a varied combination of differing raw materials, tools, and skilled craft labor, and the realization of economic value and symbolic content through transfer and use. It is tempting to rhapsodize about our favorite commodities, and even to romanticize those which embody low-tech craft labor. In anthropology the tendency has been to rhapsodize and romanticize most about commodities produced by ethnic others – and the older their origins the better. The received anthropological wisdom is that such commodities have probably been transferred from their actual makers to others through relations of reciprocity, redistribution (including tribute), or barter (perhaps in a marketplace) and embody unique cultural knowledge and have passed through distinctive circuits of symbolic-ritual practice.

These ideas were popularized in early twentieth-century anthropology through the work of Bronislaw Malinowski (1921, 1922) in the Trobriand Islands of Melanesia. At the same time in Mexico, the work of Geraldo Murillo (Dr Atl) (1922/1980) highlighted the aesthetic or artistic quality of craft commodities. B. Traven, who surely was familiar with Dr Atl's work, shared the view that each and every product of artisanal labor is unique not only in design and appearance but also because it embodies a piece of the cultural soul or essence of the artisan. However, he also had a broad comparative vision of commodity economy, and probed into the structural features of peasant-artisan life that limited craft production for the market and favored subsistence agriculture (Cook 2004b:46–47).

There are many visitors to Oaxaca with its impressive landscape, filled with pre-Hispanic archaeological sites of Zapotec and Mixtec civilizations and villages of peasant-artisans of pre-Hispanic or colonial origin, who contract the disease known as "pot fever." That malady's main symptom is the desire to acquire exotic ancient artifacts for one's own personal enjoyment. To satisfy this desire there is a thriving replica antique-ceramic cottage industry in Oaxaca, its representatives typically plying their wares in the vicinity of major archaeological sites like Monte Alban, Yagul, Zaachila, and Mitla (Brulotte 2012).

Anthropologists, not archaeologists who are professionally and legally sanctioned and inoculated, are susceptible to this disease, and are presented with opportunities during fieldwork to succumb to it. In every peasant-artisan community I worked in, cultivators plowing in their fields regularly turn up ancient pottery shards or, on occasion, intact pieces providing evidence of habitation or evoking the practice of ancient ceremonies and ritual. These peasant cultivators are sometimes prone to further explore such matters under the cover of darkness, not necessarily to profit from a potential find of a figurine (*ídolo*) or decorative clay pot but to place it on their home altar. I visited many dwellings with such ancient ceramic pieces on display in that sacred domestic space.

Antiquities (*antigüedades*) were offered to me on several occasions when I accompanied the *metateros* (metate-makers) into regional market-places, especially in Tlacolula and Ocotlán, and in many of the communities in which I conducted fieldwork. I admit to having acquired a few pieces over the years. Also, on two occasions, I witnessed clandestine night-time digs by villagers around mounds (*montículos* or *mogotes*) that had telltale signs of residence or ceremonial use by their Zapotec ancestors (*gentiles*). I do not remember any such expeditions leading to finds of burial goods such as those I reported for San Juan Teitipac involving *metateros* excavating stone in a quarry (Cook 1973b; cf. 2014:65–68).

During my years in Oaxaca I was privileged to become acquainted with Kent Flannery, an archaeologist whose publications (e.g., 1968a and 1968b) included the application of the concepts of seasonality and sched-uling and his analysis of the latter as "cultural activity which resolves conflict between procurement system" in the context of Oaxaca Valley prehistory (1968:74). On one occasion in 1979–1980 my son and I accompanied Kent from Rancho San Felipe (located in San Felipe del Agua on the northern outskirts of Oaxaca City) where we both were residing to the municipality of Mitla to visit an area of caves that Kent and his wife, Joyce Marcus, were excavating. The site was the Guilá Naquitz Cave located some 3 miles NW of the town of Mitla at the base of a cliff about 300 meters above the Valley floor. It was clearly a spectacular early prehistoric site with all kinds of lithic artifacts (scrapers, hammer stones, axe blades) lying around together with small dried up corn cobs (*teosinte*, an early ancestor of maize) indicating early domestication. I still have some lithic artifacts and *teosinte* cobs re-trieved that day by my son and I on display in my home office. At that site, Flannery and Marcus also found evidence of early domestication of several cultigens including *cucurbita* (squash), bottle gourds, and beans with the earliest being dated from ca. 8000 BP.

During 1980–1981 after I had closed my project office in downtown Oaxaca City and moved it to Rancho San Felipe on the city's outskirts, Kent and Joyce were neighbors driving daily to their work site in the Zapotec community of San José Mogote in Etla district. One evening as we both had returned from our separate field sites, Kent (or Joyce) knocked on my door and invited me over to their apartment to see something of interest. I immediately went and, upon entering their apartment, saw two newspaper-wrapped packages on their coffee table. I sat down and they proceeded to carefully unwrap one of them. It was a striking jade statue of a standing male figure, a foot or so tall, found that very day in their excavations. I coveted that statue but knew that the two archaeologists who found it were conscientious and dedicated professionals, strictly beholden to the rules of conduct of their profession, and always monitored by the watchful eye of the official guardians of Mexican national cultural patrimony (as they should be). That culture-historically significant jade statue ended up shortly thereafter as the "piece of the month" in the state museum in Oaxaca City where I saw it prominently displayed in a separate glass-enclosed showcase. "Pot fever" is indeed a powerful malady that more often than not leads to frustration or disappointment either because the piece coveted could not be acquired or turned out to be fake.[1]

I will not claim that my relationship with commodities during the pre-economics and pre-anthropology periods of my life determined my eventual specialization in their scientific study. The cultural studies literature launched in the mid-1980s (e.g., Appadurai, ed. 1986; cf. Appadurai 2013:Ch. 1), however, stimulated me to appreciate more the linkage between commodities and social life in my own biography and in all of our lives. Culturalist discourse, when not digressing into ethereal pedantry, raised thought-provoking issues that I had either neglected or rejected and stimulated me to belatedly address them (Cook 2003, 2004b). My experiences related to my dad's jobs, and my temporary job experiences as a teenager and young adult, predisposed me to think critically about the nature of work and its role in the making, exchanging and uses of commodities in our daily lives. Cumulatively, these experiences made me unenthusiastic about later seeking permanent involvement in a conventional, business-oriented occupation. As will be detailed in Chapter 1, this resulted in a somewhat erratic educational and job trajectory before the pathway to an academic career opened up.[2]

Despite how we relate to or think about commodities in our lives, most of us who participate in our respective societies' divisions labor as tenured university faculty are relatively privileged in terms of social class but not endowed by heredity as geniuses. We share the same range of genotypes and phenotypes characterizing the populations of our various societies. It stands to reason, then, that our academic careers mostly reflect the social circumstances of our upbringing and education which are inevitably influenced by our participation and immersion in our commodity economy.

As a background exercise for writing this book, I constructed a retrospective chronology of life events based upon my own memories and those of family and friends, cross-checked by available documentary sources including the internet, with the belief that it should cast some light on how and why, in my particular case, I became an academic researcher specializing, during most of my career, in a rather esoteric discipline identified as economic anthropology with a focus on commodities. And, how and why I practiced it in a particular part of the world, namely, Mexico – or more specifically, in the Central Valleys region of the state of Oaxaca and, during a few years more recently, in the northern border area of the state of Tamaulipas. These two quite contrasting areas of Mexico served as my chosen sites for data collection through fieldwork which requires prolonged and intense interaction with the particular people and sites selected as empirical objects of study.

With regard to the Oaxaca and Tamaulipas connection in my work, the explanation is straightforward: Prior research in Oaxaca on the handmade brick industry gave me an incentive to do research in Tamaulipas, once I learned such an industry was located there. I did not realize when that latter project was initiated, however, that Mexican brick culture also extended across the Rio Bravo into the Texas side of the border. So, the project necessarily became bi-national and trans-border in scope and provided me with an opportunity to expand my anthropological knowledge of the border region through fieldwork.

As for the matter of particular specialization in economic anthropology and my radical theoretical orientation, my autobiographical excursion suggested that these were formed during the period of my undergraduate and graduate education and modified later in an ongoing interaction with other specialists and their works, and with my research subjects and the accumulated data about their activities. The motive of the interaction was to explain and understand those activities in a coherent way attuned to both sides of the interaction.

I am not inclined to think that the connections and activities specified in the preceding paragraphs developed randomly, fortuitously, or haphazardly. Rather, there are logical and identifiable causes or explanations for them buried in the different life stages comprising my biography and reflecting choices that I made at different existential moments during my life-cycle sometimes under circumstances not of my own choosing. As a working anthropologist I was in places where I wanted to be and engaged in activities I chose, but my agency was more indirectly and diffusely involved in the story of how I became an anthropologist in the first place.

A selective review of my biographical narrative in Chapter 1 points to how a childhood move from Pennsylvania to Texas greatly impacted my life. There can be no clearer illustration of this than the fact that seven decades later this memoir is being written where I reside in San Marcos, Texas located midway between San Antonio and Austin, the two cities where our family lived in the 1940s and 1950s. Specific memories related in this narrative may not strike some readers as having foundational import in shaping my thought and career. I will counter by arguing that they are illustrative of the broader sociocultural milieu in which these were shaped – and also add an element of local color to the narrative.

My undergraduate education began in 1955 at the University of Texas and was completed in 1959 at American University in Washington, DC. Subsequently, I studied at the graduate level and/or worked in Wisconsin (Madison), New York (New York City), Puerto Rico (Rio Piedras and Caguas), Pennsylvania (Pittsburgh), Mexico (Oaxaca and Tamaulipas), Michigan (East Lansing), and Connecticut (Storrs and Willimantic) before retirement in Texas (Austin and San Marcos) in 2000.

My first trip to the Mexican interior in the summer of 1965 was to participate in a Stanford University field school in Oaxaca where I conducted fieldwork in the Zapotec village of San Sebastian Teitipac and wrote a report on its resident group of peasant-artisan stoneworkers. Between 1966 and 1990 I devoted some five years to additional research on the metate industry and on many other craft industries in the Oaxaca Valley. From 1993 to 1995 I did fifteen months of fieldwork on the Texas-Mexico border in a study of the handmade brick industry. In sum: What I have observed, thought, and written about over the years, and the commodities I used or collected, reflect where I have been and the human relationships I developed and experienced in those places.

One matter not yet addressed is why the title of this manuscript refers to B. Malinowski and B. Traven. Addressing it will return us to the opening topic of the world of commodities. Malinowski, of course, was a pioneering figure in the history of anthropology, and Traven was an enigmatic European anarchist revolutionary and writer exiled in Mexico. Malinowski's work first became familiar to me when I was introduced to the field of anthropology at the University of Puerto Rico in the early 1960s, twenty years after his death. It was there that I read for the first time his fascinating study of the Kula trade and barter in the Trobriand Islands of Melanesia (Malinowski 1961). Buried in detailed descriptions of kinship, rituals, and beliefs were equally detailed descriptions of the manufacture and/or cultivation of an impressive array of exotic commodities ranging from shell necklaces, clay pots, and canoes to garden crops. In this non-market setting Malinowski emphasized reciprocal and redistributive exchanges and their sociocultural, ritual, and political ramifications.

His work became more familiar to me as I developed my interest in economic anthropology during my doctoral studies at the University of Pittsburgh and, especially so, for his pioneering study with Julio de la Fuente of the market system and economy in the Oaxaca Valley. Malinowski's pointed, if fleeting, references to metates (querns or grindstones) as ancient Mesoamerican artifacts persisting in twentieth-century markets, and their ritual role in marriage gifting caught my attention and stimulated my interest in the production and exchange of those craft commodities (Malinowsky and de la Fuente 1957:19–20, 154–155; Malinowski and de la Fuente 1982:61, 189–170).

The work of B. Traven, who approached the world of commodities from a different perspective than Malinowski, became familiar to me first as an occasional reader of fiction and viewer of the John Huston film *The Treasure of the Sierra Madre* with a script based on the novel of that title written by Traven. During my initial period of residence and research in Oaxaca in the 1960s I acquired some of Spanish-language editions of Traven's work published in Mexico and was especially impressed by a collection of short stories *Canasta de cuentos mexicanos* (Traven 1956). One of them, in particular, was especially well-crafted and provocative: "*Canastitas en serie*" (1956:8–28).

It is a brilliantly written tale in which the main protagonists were a peasant-artisan basket maker from Oaxaca and a New York City businessman. It describes an ill-fated negotiation between them to supply a mass market demand for a special category of craft commodities, colorful little baskets hand-woven from strips of palm but produced only seasonally for local markets to provide cash income to supplement subsistence agriculture.

Given the conflicting dynamics of two forms of commodity economy, the simple (peasant-artisan) and the advanced (capitalism), insightfully laid bare through the interactions of the two protagonists, Traven displayed knowledge befitting an economic anthropologist – which he was not trained to be. I was so intrigued by Traven's story at the time that I considered incorporating it into my work but somehow never got around to doing so – after all it was fiction and I had enough of my own fieldwork data and ethnographic materials to address.

Strangely enough, and quite fortuitously in an unlikely setting, the Traven Oaxaca tale was referred to years later by a *ladrillero* (brick maker) in an informal conversation we had during my first of many visits to his brickworks (*ladrillera*) in Reynosa, Tamaulipas – far from Oaxaca. I have written in detail about this incident and its ramifications in previous publications (Cook 1995, 2004b:Ch.2), and in this one (see below pp. 165–166).

A decade after this 1993 encounter with Traven in Reynosa, another unexpected turn of events reinvigorated my interest in Malinowski and metates. I submitted a manuscript on Malinowski's economics to a journal editor for possible publication and one of the editor's sympathetic anonymous manuscript readers, recognizing that there were gaps in my data sources, identified himself to me and offered to provide assistance. That generous and collegial offer initiated a collaboration between me and

Professor Michael Young of Australian National University which gave me access to his still unpublished second volume of Malinowski's biography that covers Malinowski's period in Mexico and Oaxaca. It also facilitated my access to Malinowski's previously unavailable fieldwork notebooks from 1940 and 1941, together with an unpublished review by Malinowski of Melville Herskovits' *The Economic Life of Primitive Peoples* (1940).

My collaboration with Young resulted in our publication of a jointly authored article comparing the contributions of Herskovits and Malinowski to economic anthropology (Cook and Young 2016), and to a two-part article by me on Malinowski in Oaxaca (Cook 2017b, 2017c). But, most importantly, I was able to confirm a hunch that I had held since my first reading of Malinowski's Oaxaca markets study – that perhaps he also had a special interest in metates. Not only did his ethnographic field notes reveal that he initiated a study of the metate industry in San Juan Teitipac, where I had done fieldwork in the 1960s, but that he interviewed Inocencio Morales at work in his father's quarry. Don Inocencio, who later in life moved to Tlacolula but was still in the metate business, was one of my own key informants. For this reason alone I feel a special tie that binds me to Malinowski's pioneering interest in metates.

The lesson that readers should take from this account is that perseverance in ethnographic research can yield eventual rewards. Properly done, data collection and analysis in economic ethnography require a longtime commitment in one setting by the researcher. When talented knowledge producers like B. Malinowski and B. Traven are attracted to particular places and topics there is almost certainly going to be sufficient subject matter there to sustain generations of future inquiry. That is surely the case with the lives and livelihood of rural Oaxacans. Besides, the Oaxaca Valley is about as hospitable and vibrant a place to linger in and explore as there is in North America.

Aside from research, my roles as a teacher and as an academic program administrator were also an integral part of my career. Between 1987 and 1992 I was Director of the Center for Latin American and Caribbean Studies at the University of Connecticut in a Title VI-funded consortium with the University of Massachusetts-Amherst and Brown University. Between 1996 and 2000 I directed UConn's Institute for Puerto Rican and Latino

Studies. A condensed account of relationships and experiences in these roles will be discussed in Chapter 4.

The remembrance of things past is not only an entirely subjective and selective process but one with gaps and conflations, so a memory bank's retrieved contents must be carefully filtered and examined through disciplined retrospection before becoming part of a written record. The process of recall, especially when dealing with anthropological work, must be dependent upon the published record in every case where relevant materials exist. I have been as forthright as possible in writing this memoir. Regarding biographical background, some material has been included that is not relevant to my career development but may prove of interest to the reader. In sections addressing anthropological content, difficult or stilted language is inherent in the genre but I have attempted to simplify it when possible. The reader is encouraged to proceed perseveringly and selectively.

Chapter 1 summarizes relevant facts and recollections from my life between 1937, the date of my birth, and 1961, the year I began formal training that would lead to a career in anthropology. It suggests that there were causal linkages between my life before 1961 and the choice of anthropology as a career. Chapter 2 summarizes my experiences as a graduate student in anthropology beginning in 1961. Chapter 3 reviews my experiences as a faculty member at Michigan State University (1968–1971). Chapter 4 does the same for my three decades, 1971–2000, at the University of Connecticut. Chapters 5–10 present a chronological and critical review of my research record (from recollections and publications) with a particular emphasis on continuities and discontinuities in my work about themes, issues, and subject matter, critically review selected contributions to the recent literature and, especially in Chapters 9 and 10, suggest possible future research directions.[3]

CHAPTER I

From Pennsylvania to Texas, Places in Between, and Back Again

I was born in Oil City, Pennsylvania on June 16, 1937. My parents, Howard Allen Cook and Anna Lucille McKelvey, were also natives of Pennsylvania but in 1944 we moved to San Antonio, Texas where my dad had been promoted to assistant branch manager for the meat packer, Armour and Company. After graduation from high school in 1929, the year of the GREAT CRASH, he became a full-time employee of Armour and Co., slowly working his way up the ladder in jobs like running smoking operations and route salesman. He was promoted from Oil City to the Pittsburgh branch in 1939–1940, prior to Pearl Harbor, where he was in charge of fresh beef operations.

Regarding class-background and income-status, my dad probably was more 'working class' early on but moved quickly into middle-class managerial ranks when still in his 20s. He was never a union member – although his stepfather, John H. Cook, as a Pennsylvania Railroad engineer, was. My biological paternal grandfather, Howard E. Huff, died of an apparent aneurism before my dad was born, and dad later assumed his stepfather's surname. Life circumstances have a way of blurring the idealized boundaries between consanguinity and affinity. After his stepfather's death in a railroad accident, a union pension helped to support my widowed grandmother, Margaret Mary Blackburn, and her five offspring – but dad still had to work to help supplement her widow's pension. She had immigrated to the US in 1904 from her birthplace in Enniscorthy, Ireland (arriving at Ellis Island on a ship out of Liverpool, England).

My mother was born and raised in middle-class circumstances in Clearfield, Pennsylvania where her dad, Scott W. McKelvey, owned a candy company in the 1920s before the Wall Street "Crash" in 1929. She (and certainly her dad) never liked unions and seemed to accept the view that they were mob-affiliated. As my dad moved stepwise, if peripatetically, up the corporate ladder, mom was increasingly pleased with their upward mobility into an upper-middle-class income and lifestyle. She and my maternal grandmother, Isabelle Kauffelt Eaton born in York, Pennsylvania, were excellent cooks and bakers. I fondly remember my Pennsylvania Dutch grandma's sticky buns – and have only occasionally found matches for them later in life. In the early 1950s they were featured (and pictured) in a "family section" article in the Austin-American Statesman for their "New England boiled dinner" made, of course, with "Armour Star" corned beef brisket.

Mother had secretarial training in high school and secretarial school classes; she knew shorthand and was an expert typist. She was employed as a secretary/stenographer of the manager of the Knox Glass Bottle factory in Oil City, and in Pittsburgh worked for the Dravo Corporation during WWII which manufactured naval landing crafts known as LSTs. She taught me how to type and did a much better job typing a final draft of my doctoral dissertation that I could have done. In the early 1950s she worked for a time in the secretarial pool on the University of Texas campus in Austin.

She was proud of the fact that at Dravo, which was located on Neville Island in the Allegheny River just northwest of our Bellevue neighborhood in Pittsburgh, after a period of training, she rose to be an assembly-line supervisor and, as such, exercised supervisory authority over many college-educated engineers. She was a sort of "Rosy the Riveter" overseer. She was also the family disciplinarian and had quite a temper, and the family bookkeeper and archivist. She was always very status-conscious, upwardly-aspiring, an avid card and board-game player who did not like to lose. Much to my dad's discomfort, she and I had many a tiff over the years. But she also knew how to relax, entertain family and friends, enjoy her mixed drinks, and her many trips with the family. She was also an inventive and gifted cook. Both she and my dad were clothes-conscious, fashionable dressers – and as the family income grew they were able to participate in a bit of conspicuous consumption in that regard.

I remember going with my mom on many occasions to the large department stores, Gimbels and Hornes, in downtown Pittsburgh, where we would always have lunch in their elegant lunchrooms. Among other things during that period, I remember nighttime viewing of fiery slag from the steel mills rolling down a distant hillside after being dumped from railcars mimicking the flow of lava from an active volcano; and the nightly air raid practices (buckets of sand under the bed and my dad in an air raid warden's outfit).[4]

The reason why my parents left Pittsburgh during WWII had to do with my poor health. I caught measles and pneumonia in 1942 and then was diagnosed by doctors at Allegheny General Hospital as probably having rheumatic fever. This led to my being sent to Daytona Beach, Florida with my maternal grandmother McKelvey in the winter of 1943 where we lived for a time in a cottage owned by a contact of hers. I thrived in Florida, and especially enjoyed fishing, and going to the beach with my sand bucket to search for cucuna (little bi-valves) and sea shells. Most of the time there were marching groups of uniformed WAAC's (Women's Army Auxiliary Corps) there using the beach as a parade ground (a training center had just been established). They found me to be cute and I enjoyed their attention – much to the dismay of my grandma. At home I would listen a lot to the radio – my favorite programs being Tom Mix, the Lone Ranger, and Jack Armstrong, the All-American boy. I still remember the ditty Tom Mix sang to us: "Take a tip from Tom, go and tell your Mom, hot Ralston can't be beat." I consumed hot Ralston regularly.

Appropriately, my parents somehow managed to send me a deluxe set of chromed six-shooter-style cap pistols, complete with holster, for the Christmas of 1943. I loved to play "cowboys and Indians" and to shoot the cap pistols until I ran out of caps, which were difficult to procure during WW II. My grandma was pleased about the scarcity of caps, but I continued to play at being a Texas Ranger. It is as if I knew then that Texas was in my future. When I returned from Florida in better health, the doctors prescribed a permanent climate change as my best prognosis. The move to Texas worked in that regard.

My mom and I traveled by train from Pittsburgh to San Antonio, via St. Louis, in the spring of 1944 to meet up with my dad who was already living in San Antonio. We traveled on the Missouri-Pacific "Sunshine Special" from St. Louis to the M-K-T "Katy" depot in San Antonio. Soldiers in uniform were everywhere on the train and in San Antonio which had five military bases. As we stepped out of the train into sunny San Antonio, I was struck by two images: orange trees full of fruit in the yard surrounding the train depot (which exemplified "Mission design" architecture), and people of a brown complexion I had not seen before.

Since San Antonio in those days was residentially segregated, I had few opportunities to socialize with Mexicans in school but did have several opportunities over the years to travel to Mexican border towns with my dad and, on one occasion, to associate with several Mexican vaqueros who were ranch hands on a South Texas ranch near Laredo owned by a family friend. The sights and sounds of Mexican life pervaded San Antonio, and I found them to be alluring. For me, it would not be the "Enormous Vogue of Things Mexican" (Delpar 1992) that would later draw me to Mexico but its enticing sensuality and "foreign-ness."

There was no housing available in San Antonio when we arrived there in 1943–1944 due to a wartime construction curfew. My dad had a room in the Bluebonnet Hotel, and when mom and I arrived we lived for at least two months or so in the Plaza Hotel across the street from the Transit Tower and near the River Walk and La Villita. The two main movie theaters in San Antonio, the Aztec and the Majestic, were not far from the hotel and we went to both regularly. I was puzzled by the fact that Mexicans were lined up at side entrances at both theaters rather than at the main entrance. I did not understand why but, of course, Jim Crow in Texas was applied to both Mexican-descent and African-American citizens equally, even in a city founded by Spanish-Mexicans in a state that was a Spanish colony and then a Mexican territory. Very curious indeed, and solely attributable to the invasive "White Scourge" documented so well by historians like Neil Foley (1997) and David Montejano (1987).

In San Antonio daily we walked along the river, through La Villita, and the downtown streets, sometimes stopping to get delicious fresh fruit drinks at a stand on Houston Street. We also ate ice cold slices of watermelon served outdoors in "gardens" established for that purpose. Despite wartime rationing, it was not a life of deprivation.

By the summer of 1944 my parents had managed to acquire a newly constructed house in Alamo Heights, so we moved out of the downtown hotels. For a while after moving we traveled downtown on the Broadway bus line that was only two blocks from our house. My dad still had only a company car, a two-door Ford coupe, but by the time my sister, Beverly, was born later that same year he had acquired a 1937 four-door black Packard from a Chinese restaurant owner who was a customer of his. Thus, began our weekend trips to various south and central Texas locations, often to state or roadside parks from Uvalde to González; and sometimes longer weekend trips to Corpus on the Gulf, to Harlingen in the Rio Grande valley, or to Laredo on the border with Mexico. We continued to go downtown often to make purchases at Joske's (now Dilliard's), a big department store near the Menger Hotel and the Alamo. My dad would be fitted for suits at either of two men's stores, Frank Brothers and Frost's, to the south of Alamo Plaza. He was also particularly attentive about his business-style felt hats and his shoes (later wearing hand-crafted Church's from England).

In the afternoon of April 12, 1945, I was participating in marching exercises in San Antonio's Mahncke Park on Broadway with a uniformed group known as "Junior Yanks of America" that my mom had enrolled me in. Our activities were abruptly suspended by the announcement that President Roosevelt had died. The atmosphere was solemn, and we were all very shaken by the sad news.

My dad told many stories of his experiences during his time with Armour and Company in San Antonio and Austin. Two stories standout. Once he was on a sales trip to the Rio Grande Valley from San Antonio with one of his salesmen driving the car. One morning as they were on the highway from Alice to McAllen through the middle of the King Ranch they saw a dark mass ahead on the highway and, as the car was being braked, it hit and skidded through the mass which turned out to be a large cluster of rattlesnakes apparently driven out of the surrounding mesquite and prickly pear thickets (*chaparral*), their natural habitat, by land clearing. During the skid, rattlesnakes were flying up onto the hood and roof of the car; and windows were quickly rolled up. My dad never forgot that incident. Who would?

The Armour and Company branch in Austin was located on 3rd and Lavaca (appropriately named "the cow") streets in the so-called "warehouse district" along a railroad siding. A short walk up the street to the next block at 4th and Lavaca was the Miller Produce warehouse, better known as the

"Hidehouse." It was a foul-smelling tannery supplied with raw hides from livestock slaughtered in the city-owned abattoir on Waller Creek. Tanned hides were sold as one of many income-generating businesses owned by the portly Miller brothers (Clark-Madison 2003). I visited the place only once with my dad and saw nothing but piles of still-bloody hides everywhere, and still remember the unbearable stench.

Jim Miller managed the Hidehouse. Tom, the elder brother, was mayor of Austin at the time (an elected office he had held since 1933) and was also chairman of the Texas Democratic Party. Dad was friendly with Jim, and a regular visitor to his office at the Hidehouse. On one such visit, dad noticed that Tom's chauffeur-driven black Cadillac was parked in front of the business and, as he walked into the office, he noticed that Tom was on the telephone. Tom nodded to him and then said something like "Hi Howard, I have someone on the phone who wants to say hello to you." My dad took the phone and a recognizable voice said, "Hi Howard, this is Harry Truman, pleased to talk to you." Dad, flabbergasted, mumbled something like "Thank you, Mr. President" and handed the phone back to Tom. Of course, Tom as mayor and chairman of the Texas Democratic Party was on the phone with US President Harry Truman quite regularly, so it was no big deal for him to talk to the President, but he knew that it would be for my dad, and it certainly was!

Dad left Armour and Company and went to work for Oscar Mayer and Company at the end of my first year of high school. This resulted in several family relocations affecting my schooling. My second year of high school was split between Oklahoma City and Alamo Heights in San Antonio, where I reunited with some of my elementary school friends. My final year of high school was in Davenport, Iowa where my dad had been promoted to sales manager of a large Oscar Mayer plant.

Dad eventually resigned in disgust at Oscar Mayer when he had policy differences with a new generation of junior executives with MBAs – without a pension after years of productive, dedicated service. He had been hired by Oscar Mayer Jr, met Oscar Mayer Sr, and felt comfortable working for the family. But their influence had waned through death and corporate reorganization. His final corporate job was with a family-owned peanut processing company (oil and peanut butter) in Enterprise, Alabama (Sessions Company) where he was both plant and sales manager.

My parents were not particularly interested in politics but they tended to be supportive of the Democratic Party, especially FDR but also Truman. In 1948, when Lyndon Baines Johnson was voted into the US Senate, he was replaced in his congressional seat by a neighbor of ours in Tarrytown, Homer Thornberry, who my parents knew and supported. They were disturbed by LBJ's razor-thin victory over Coke Stevenson, however, and were sympathetic to Stevenson's post-election charges of "ballot stuffing." In later years, my mom and I used to argue a lot about politics, but my Dad remained mostly silent. In retirement he regularly read newspapers, listened to cable news, and became more outspoken about politics, usually to the detriment of Republicans.

Mom was a sort of "Maude-like" (reference to the character played by Beatrice Arthur in the television series "Maude") opponent of racial discrimination regarding "blacks and whites" but had a somewhat harder time dealing with Latinos. She always insisted that our cleaning ladies, whether white or black, sit down at the kitchen table to have lunch with us. I felt uncomfortable with this in my junior high school days and my mom reprimanded me for my discomfort with the exclamation, "They are no different than we are." I think language was a main barrier in her relations with Latinos.

When I was growing up in San Antonio and Austin, my parents (and grandma McKelvey who lived with us) were regular church-goers and choir-members in mainstream Methodism. My mom, reflecting her own dad's fervent religiosity (I read a letter he wrote to her on one occasion), was always more of a Methodist than my dad was. When I announced to the family early in my freshman year at UT that I would no longer attend services in the University Methodist Church with them on Sundays, my mom (and maternal grandma) were quite upset, but my dad never uttered a word. My decision, among other things, reflected my discomfort at having to ritually recite the Apostles' Creed, not a word of which I believed. I did find some of the presiding reverend's (Dr Edmund Heinsohn) sermons to be thoughtful and well presented but simply could not relate to biblical stories, to the God postulate, nor to the idea of personal salvation. All of this struck me then, and still does, as implausible.

Before my dad retired, I was visiting my parents in Alabama on Thanksgiving break from Pitt on the day JFK was assassinated (November 22, 63). My mom and I had been playing golf on the local country club course next to their home (incidentally I had my second lifetime "hole-in-one" on a 160-yard hole that morning), and we learned about the tragic event when we got home. Later that afternoon, we were visited by the pastor of the Methodist church my parents were attending. He expressed his delight regarding JFK's demise. My mom was appalled by the good pastor's remark and essentially ushered him out the front door. The pastor's delight, I think, reflected his dissatisfaction with JFK's Catholicism and of his support for civil rights, whereas my dislike for JFK at the time was due to his foreign policy blunders in Vietnam and Cuba. I do not think my parents ever attended that pastor's church again.

My parents got along well with my wife Hilda's family in rural Puerto Rico where she and my Dad lived on our small farm in Yabucoa's Barrio Guayabota alone for two months one winter in the early 1990s. They drove around Puerto Rico's narrow and winding mountain roads when they were in their 80s. They also traveled to Mexico when Hilda and I resided there and, after retirement, drove a mobile home to south Texas and to California, and spent one or two winters in the Costa del Sol in Spain.

After retirement, dad developed a business relationship with my brother-in-law, David Newell, that took him to Asheville, North Carolina where he operated a craft business in a large interior decore emporium owned by my brother-in-law (Interiors Marketplace). Among the items sold in my dad's Mexican crafts shop, El Gallo del Sol, were many supplied by me during the years I was researching the border brick industry. He had clearly developed a fondness for Mexican crafts during his several visits to the Mexican interior during the years that I worked there. Among his best-selling items were attractive ironwood (*palo fierro*) figurines of land and sea animals, originally handmade by nomadic Seri Indians of the Sonoran Desert but later being machine-carved in urban mestizo workshops in Sonora and distributed by Nogales-based intermediaries. During my period of research on the border brick industry, I was able to acquire these craft commodities from street vendors in Nuevo Progreso, Tamaulipas and ship them to North Carolina. My dad passed away on June 19, 2011 at the age of 100+ years in Hendersonville, NC, having outlived my mom by some four years.

Early Education and Mis-Education

I do not remember learning much in elementary, junior high, and high school beyond the rudiments of reading, writing, and arithmetic. To learn about Texas history in junior high school, I remember reading a comic book printed by Magnolia Petroleum Company which sold Mobiloil and Mobilgas in a chain of gas stations under the iconic sign of the Flying Red Horse (Crisp 2005:7–9). In San Antonio one such station was located in Alamo Heights on the corner of Broadway and the Austin Highway. The people and incidents depicted in the comic book history went from 1821 when Anglo settlers started arriving in Mexican Texas until 1846 when the Texas Republic became an American State.

Many of the depictions were clever representations of stereotypes most of us had already absorbed through popular culture. The Mexican soldiers in the nineteenth century were portrayed much like the Japanese soldiers fighting in World War II: as vicious weapons-wielding cutthroats and torturers (Crisp 2005:9). Other images were less strident and more accurate in acknowledging ignorance of Mexican history and language on the part of Anglo settlers, and the prevalence of ethnic prejudice – Mexicans calling Anglos "Gringos" and Anglos calling Mexicans "Greasers" (Crisp 2005:23). We did learn that Texas had been a slave State in the Civil War but, earlier under Mexico, had prohibited slavery (Crisp 2005:17). The implications of that correct information were not discussed.

Most striking, in retrospect, was that Mexican-descent Texans (*Tejanos*), even heroic and politically-involved figures like Juan Seguin, were absent from the narrative. Caricatured sombrero-and-sarape-clad Mexicans were juxtaposed with white Anglo-Texans portrayed as freedom-fighters against Mexican tyranny including heroes like the knife-fighting, land-grabbing (by marrying into the Mexican elite), Louisiana slave trader, James Bowie. The Alamo was, of course, viewed as a shrine of freedom and much was made of how the Anglo dead were burned and desecrated by order of the victorious but ruthless and bloodthirsty Mexican general Santa Ana. Again, the Tejanos that suffered the same fate were ignored. This was all part of the reproduction of Anglo-Texan identity and the embellishment of the creation myths of the Anglo-Texas Republic through a series of visible, if chaotic and hardly epic but bloody, military skirmishes which distracted from the real story: the realization of Manifest destiny and the establishment of Anglo-American hegemony in territory that had belonged to New Spain and then to independent Mexico after the early 1820s (Hamnett 2006:141–142; De la Teja 1995).

The history of Anglos and Mexicans in south Texas during the nineteenth century is complex. Minimally, its proper understanding requires a careful reading and evaluation of three key studies: Carey McWilliams (1948), David Montejano (1987), and Armando Alonso (1998). Although McWilliams study was more comprehensive in scope and less dependent on the archival record or primary sources than those by Montejano and Alonso, it established the canon and the paradigm for examining and interpreting Anglo and Mexican relations in the region as an asymmetrically conflictive process. The newly arrived Anglo-Americans were interloping actors, longer-established Mexicans were defensive actors. The Mexican population was divided by class and national loyalty – during and after the establishment of the Republic of Texas in 1836 as independent of Mexico, a process in which Texanized Mexicans or Tejanos played a supporting role (McWilliams 1948/1968:101–102). This contradictory scenario continued in the subsequent decade culminating in the 1846 annexation of Texas by the United States, and during and after the US-Mexico War it precipitated.

Violent episodes of the Texas Rebellion like the battle of the Alamo were certainly sufficient as subject matter for myth-making in popular and political culture in the Hollywood film industry. In this semi-mythical history, which has been a high-yield debunking ground for historians (e.g., Crisp 2005), there were only hints of the later nineteenth-century expropriation and despoliation of the Mexican-descent population by intruding Anglos in vast areas of south Texas. The nineteenth-century Anglo-American settlers arrived first from the slave-plantation-ridden Deep South or from its Appalachia. In the early twentieth century they were recruited from Midwest farming country by land developers.

Starting after the Treaty of Guadalupe-Hidalgo which ended the war in 1848 and continuing into the early decades of the twentieth century, deep south Texas was reorganized administratively into a tiered series of originally seven and then thirteen sprawling counties (Montejano 1987:133–135). On the eastern or Gulf side – Nueces, Wells, Kleberg, Kennedy, Willacy, and Cameron; in the central zone – Duval, Brooks, Hogg, and Hidalgo; on the western side – Webb, Zapata, and Starr. Seven of the thirteen counties, including the largest Webb with Laredo as the county seat, were predominantly ranching, two (Duval and Starr) were mixed, and four including the southernmost group of Willacy, Cameron, and Hidalgo (the heart of the Rio Grande Valley) were predominantly dedicated to farming.

The story of Anglo-Mexican relations in these counties from can be inferred from their names but verified only through records of land and livestock (cattle and horses) sales. The surnames of the counties reflect Anglo dominance politically which often, but not uniformly, was matched by records of land and livestock transfers. Those records from 1850 to 1900 present a mixed picture: For example, livestock transactions in Hidalgo County show about a 60–40 split between Mexican-descent and Anglo sellers whereas those from Webb county show a preponderance of sellers of Mexican-descent (Alonso 1998:291–300). However, even Armando Alonso, who interprets nineteenth-century Anglo-Mexican relations in south Texas less harshly than either Carey McWilliams or David Montejano, concluded his study with the following generalization: "Land loss proceeded haphazardly until the 1880s, when Tejanos lost control of their lands in a rapid fashion…it is the period between 1885 and 1900 in which most Tejanos became minority landholders in their own land" (1998:283). By 1920 in Cameron and Hidalgo counties, Mexican ranching had been displaced by Anglo farming and Mexicans became landless laborers who cleared Anglo-owned land of brush and tended the crops (Montejano 1987:114; cf. Rubel 1966:35–36).

The second half of the nineteenth century witnessed the establishment of vast agricultural and ranching enterprises in south Texas, mostly under Anglo proprietorship. The "Magic Valley" irrigation project and the urbanization of the Rio Grande Valley in the early twentieth century involved the replacement of many Mexican-owned cattle ranches by Anglo-owned farm enterprises, and led to the formation of a Mexican agrarian proletariat seasonally split between local and migratory field labor (Montejano 1987:Ch.5; Richardson 1999:8–10).[5]

In my school days, there was also a humorous current of thought regarding Texas's pre-Alaska statehood boastful status as the "biggest state" in the form of a map of the United States (available as a post card, placemat or wall hanging) with a hugely oversized Texas juxtaposed with an undersized north and northeast " Damn Yankee Land." There was definitely an undercurrent of loyalty to the Confederacy in this anti-Yankee sentiment, although my recollection is that the Texas state flag was much more prominently displayed in neighborhoods and public places than was the confederate one. Aside from not being allowed to date a girl that I liked in junior high school because of her dad's prejudice against Yankees, I did not have any difficulty in assuming a Texan identity – and, ironically, I was identified as "Tex" by some acquaintances during my senior year at the Davenport, Iowa high school.

Round-Up on the Ranch and Early Job Experiences

In 1952, when I was in junior high school, I spent a few days during "round-up" time on a south Texas ranch outside of Laredo owned by an Austin neighbor and friend of my parents, Earnest Roberts Armstrong. A friend of mine and I stayed at one of the Armstrong family's houses in Hebbronville and traveled out to the ranch each morning to return to town in the early evening. The ranch was large, had lots of cattle grazing throughout the vast and almost impenetrable chaparral consisting of endless thickets of thorny mesquite bushes and trees interspersed with clusters of spiked nopal cactus and rattlesnakes everywhere – especially lying in the shade provided by the mesquite and nopal. Not a hospitable environment. There were endless numbers of jackrabbits (liebres) which we shot with our .22 rifles and gave to the vaqueros to be skinned, roasted and eaten that way, or in stew.

Round-up consisted of mounted vaqueros going out into the chaparral to herd cattle into corrals or holding pens (and shoots) where they could be branded, castrated, and vaccinated and otherwise treated medicinally. We mostly observed, but were given saddled horses and a few times accompanied the vaqueros on the round-up. On one such day my horse was frightened by a bunch of rattlesnakes in a mesquite thicket and proceeded to bolt through the chaparral until one of the vaqueros helped to get the beast under control (which I could not). As a result of that experience I learned why the vaqueros – despite brutally hot conditions – wore heavy canvas jackets over their long-sleeved shirts, leather chaps over their jeans, and heavy gloves covering their hands. It was to protect their face, arms, hands, and legs from being mangled by the thorny, spiked chaparral. I was not so protected and was pretty scratched up during the above incident – but it could have been worse.

The vaqueros also humored us by allowing us to go into the corral for the purpose of bull-dogging (throwing them down on the ground) calves and holding them in position for branding. They laughed raucously as we were unable to bring down or hold the smallest calf! We were treated to "mountain oysters" as a reward for our mostly-failed effort – namely, calves testicles removed by castration, hung up to dry on the fencing enclosing the corral, and then roasted by hanging from a branding iron in the fire used to turn heat-up the branding irons.

At the end of our visit to the ranch we drove into Laredo where Mr Armstrong met-up with some of his rancher buddies in a local café. My friend and I were seated at an adjacent table but I was intrigued by some raunchy conversation I overheard about *queridas* (girlfriends) on the other side of the border.

The name of the ranch was "El Sordo" and Mr Armstrong's share was only about 693 acres, a small portion of the 23,400 acres of his original family ranch. It was located 12 miles southwest of Hebbronville off Highway 16 (Alicia Garza, Handbook of Texas Online) in Jim Hogg county.

Every summer after that ranch visit, starting in my last year of junior high school my dad arranged jobs for me – either linked to his own place of employment or to acquaintance's businesses. I worked at a supermarket in Austin as a stock-boy and bagger and also as a "rod-and-chainman" on a survey crew, and later in Davenport, Iowa for two summers (1955 and 1956), as a vacation replacement meter reader for the Iowa-Illinois Gas and Electric Company.

In Davenport, I read gas and electric meters on routes of vacationing regulars, following instructions annotated on each sheet of the route book for each residence or business establishment visited. This was especially useful regarding "dangerous" dogs (the meter reader's number one enemy) – but, unfortunately, did not prevent me from being bitten on the arm by a German shepherd protecting her newborn litter hidden on the floor underneath several electric meters in the basement of an apartment building. I also read meters for the company across the Mississippi River in Rock Island, Moline, and East Moline, Illinois.

Aside from the "dog bite" incident the other most memorable incident as a meter reader was in downtown Davenport when I read meters located down an alley inside a ground floor "apartment." It turns out that the apartment was a well-known local brothel and the regular meter reader had an arrangement to record a "favorable" reading in exchange for a "freebie." I saw no reason to interrupt that established practice.

Although I graduated from high school in Iowa, I never seriously considered attending college anywhere but the University of Texas, especially when I learned that my dad's new job at Oscar Mayer put him in charge of opening up new markets and distribution centers for their products starting first in central Texas. After my graduation from Davenport High, and at the end of my first summer working as a meter reader, we moved back to Austin temporarily. That was convenient since I had already enrolled at the University of Texas for the fall semester. I had no set plans regarding an undergraduate major, and naively considered everything from engineering to pre-law but ended up with economics. I had no counseling information or aptitude test data to guide me but knew that I had more difficulty getting good grades in math and science courses than I had with everything else.

Undergraduate Education in Texas and Washington DC: Hell Week and Hell Month

Two episodes stick in my mind from the period from 1955 to 1957: "Hell Week" and "Hell Month." Prior to or just after graduation from Davenport High School, one of my friends and I capriciously decided to join the US Marine Corps on the "buddy plan." We went to the local recruiting office and signed up to enter boot camp during the summer of 1955 for a four-year hitch. My parents were appalled, since they wanted me to be the first family member to attend college. Dad immediately went to the recruiting office and negotiated a deal that waived my active duty commitment and re-enlisted me in the Marine Corps Reserve. Consequently, during my two years at the University of Texas I attended weekly drills at the Marine Corps Reserve facility. When I transferred from the University of Texas to American University in 1957, I was notified by the USMCR that I would have to report to the Marine Corps Recruit Depot at Parris Island, South Carolina for one month of training prior to my discharge in order to be released from two additional years of service.

My "month of hell" was served in that mosquito-infested, sweltering Parris Island swampland in the summer of 1958. I remember seeing two signs posted in the recruit reception room at Parris Island Depot: "Profanity Will Not be Tolerated in This Command" and "Profanity Is the Crutch of the Intellectual Cripple." As we filed out of the reception area to get our gear, including an M-1 rifle, the kindest epithets I heard shouted by the drill instructors was "fucking maggots," "numbnuts," and "tearing of new assholes." These insults and many others were shouted at us with regularity during our drills, exercises, and marches led by our drill instructor who was proud of the fact that the Corps gave him his first pair of shoes.

We endured much verbal abuse and punishing activities such as holding our rifles over our heads at swamp side and forced to allow mosquitos suck our blood without moving an eyelash or muttering a word. The drill instructor kindly reminded us of the rationale for not trying to defend ourselves from the aggressive mosquitos by shouting "Them skeeters got to

eat too." There were also endless marches on the parade grounds usually in
the glaring afternoon sun. I actually enjoyed time spent on the rifle range.

Violation of commands or inability to follow routines meant being
verbally abused and possibly removed to a "Psychological Observation
Unit" (POU) for special mess hall or janitorial duty until discharge.
A good number of the hundred or so "college boys" in my entering group
at the PI Depot ended up in POUs, and we never saw them again. They
simply would not obey the rules, tolerate the discipline, and keep their
mouths shut.

On my last day at Parris Island. I was ushered into a small room with
some smooth-talking officers who were recruiting for immediate entry
into Marine Corps Officer's Candidate School at Quantico, Virginia.
I thanked them for their interest in me but rejected their offer, turned in
my military gear, picked up my civilian clothes, and headed for the long-
term parking lot for my car. On the way back to Atlanta where my dad
was then heading-up a new plant for Oscar Mayer, I thanked him in my
mind a hundred times over for saving me from four years of active duty in
the United States Marine Corps. Admittedly, I have never been in better
physical condition in my life than I was after experiencing that "month of
hell" at Parris Island.

That hellish month at Parris Island had been preceded by "Hell Week"
at the University of Texas in the spring of 1956. That was the term used to
describe the ritual initiation period suffered by new members (pledges) to
fraternities. Two of my boyhood friends who lived on the same street in
Tarrytown (McCulloch) were upperclassmen and members ("brothers") of
Sigma Nu – indeed, one of them was president of the UT chapter. During
my first semester I had proudly become a "GDI" (God Damn Independent)
which was how the non-fraternity majority of the student population was
referred to in those days. Apparently, the designation "Independents" for
non-fraternity and sorority students at UT, always a large majority, started
with John Connally in 1936 (later as Texas governor shot while accompanying JFK on his fatal trip to Dallas) to counter the influence of Greek
culture at UT (Hollandsworth 1991). But the pressure from two boyhood
friends from Tarrytown who had joined Sigma Nu, and from the mom of
one of them directly to my mom, was persistent.

Toward the end of the fall semester and over the winter break, I was once again subjected to pressure from my Sigma Nu friends to become a pledge. The pledge captain, an especially charismatic, friendly, smooth-talking, and savvy member of a well-to-do Austin family, was assigned the mission of recruiting me. My friends knew that I had a high fidelity system mainly for classical music listening and, by coincidence, he was a hi-fi aficionado who had the newest state-of-the art amplifier, turntable, and powerful high-quality speakers. They knew that I would be impressed. He offered advice and helped me upgrade my own system, and later drove me to his own separate quarters on his family's property in the exclusive Austin riverside neighborhood near Barton Springs in his MG sports car to listen to his system. Afterwards, we went on a scenic, winding drive on Mount Bonnell road above the dammed Colorado River known as "Lake Austin" during which he expounded upon the advantages of fraternity life. I finally relented, became a pledge, and Sigma Nu "Hell Week" began during the early weeks of the spring semester. Ironically, two years later I was informed that the pledge captain did not survive a crash in his MG on that same road.

Only those who have experienced them can truly appreciate the bizarre and dehumanizing nature of fraternity initiation rites at the University of Texas in the 1950s. These were conducted in unsupervised, unmonitored secrecy presumably with a wink and nod from university and public authorities. Pledges were forced to attend class during the entire week with little sleep and wearing a combination of prickly burlap and female panties under our regular clothing. Our temporary "home" was in the unfinished portion of the basement of the large, two-story fraternity house. That unfinished part of the basement apparently later became known as the "pit."

One hazing incident occurred in the finished part of the basement, a rec room, where pledges had to lie face-up on the floor as upperclassmen screamed "open the mouth pledge" and dumped bottles of Louisiana hot sauce into our open mouths. Two other hazing events stand-out in my memory: (1) the "late night city storm-sewer crawl": a man-hole cover on a city street was opened, pledges bound to a rope line went down into the storm sewers and crawled through to resurface through another open manhole a block away (one claustrophobic pledge barely survived); (2) the "hill country night-time hands-and-knees race": a tree-cleared rocky space about 50 yards long in the cedar-forested hill country a few miles outside of Austin was chosen as the race site. A galvanized tub with a mixture of alum and gasoline was placed at one end of the clearing and a bonfire burned at the other. The race consisted in pledges having to suck up mouthfuls of the volatile mixture, crawl on hands and knees to spit the fuel into the bonfire which would flame-up as a result. The alum caused the mouth to pucker up to make spitting difficult. After the "race" was finished, pledges were lined up, chained together – chain-gang style – and told to walk several miles back to a designated pick-up spot. We barely made it back by dawn (cf. Morris 2000/1967:156–158).

I survived all of the above hazing incidents and became a bonafide "pinned" brother of Sigma Nu, along with about fifteen or so of my fellow pledges. Two cars full of newly installed "brothers" celebrated with a trip to "boystown" (red-light district) in Nuevo Laredo. My dad had agreed to loan me his brand-new two-tone Chevrolet Bel Air sport sedan overnight (he was unaware of our itinerary), so I drove three or four of my "brothers" to Laredo (about a three-plus-hour drive). Among those accompanying me were a frat brother from Corpus whose dad was a refinery executive, another who was the son of a Ralston-Purina executive from St. Louis, Missouri, and, if my memory serves me, a non-frat friend of mine from Crystal City. On the return trip, in the early hours of the morning. I was driving (perfectly sober) on a deserted highway at a high speed and had the misfortune of hitting a speed trap somewhere around Cotulla or Dilley (south of San Antonio) and was issued a ticket for about $100; fortunately, a collection from my frat brothers helped to pay the fine.

This had not been my first experience in border boystowns. I had a few such trips during my high school days in San Antonio (Alamo Heights), accompanied by my friend who was a San Antonio obstetrician's son who lived in the exclusive Olmos Park neighborhood, and a few additional trips during my two years at UT. Only someone from my generation can truly appreciate the lyrics from a Ry Cooder song "The Old Skin Game" for the soundtrack of the movie entitled "The Border" which says repeatedly "A boy becomes a man in Mexico." Incidentally, aside from Jack Nicholson's acting, the music soundtrack was the best thing about that rather sappy movie.

In those days, when few of us had steady girlfriends due to our resistance to the restrictive customs of dating culture and also faced legal restrictions regarding alcoholic beverage consumption, respectable Mexican restaurants and bars (e.g., the Cadillac Bar in Nuevo Laredo) welcomed us and treated us as adults. Within the boundaries of the red-light districts and their many striptease parlors and cabarets, we were free to play the field regarding female companionship.[6]

Aside from racism, there was an unquestionable element of class snobbery and social climbing plus status confirmation at the heart of Greek culture at UT. Once I became a "brother" I was immediately encouraged to enter an arranged dating system with sorority girls; I went only once or twice to get-togethers at sorority houses but never paired-up with one of the girls. Prior to my resignation from the fraternity, I insisted on finding my own date to invite to a formal dance at Sigma Nu house. I had made the acquaintance of a petite, pretty unpretentious girl from a working-class family in Pasadena (Houston) in one of my classes, and invited her to be my date. She resisted owing to misgivings about mixing with the fraternity-sorority crowd – she lacked appropriate formal clothing and clearly was aware of the snobbery factor.

Nevertheless, I insisted, convinced her to be my date for the occasion, and actually drove to her home in Pasadena where she had go to pick-up a proper party dress. She was clearly uncomfortable and felt out of place at the event, and I received some criticism for bucking the system and not dating a proper "sorority" girl. As it turns out, I shared Willie Morris' revulsion over the class control and snobbery element in fraternity-sorority culture. He neatly described "hell week" at UT as "a four-day ordeal of petty torture and sadism which preceded 'initiation' as a full-fledged brother," and also observed: "Led by the organized structure of the fraternities and sororities, the great hotbed of philistinism in the 1950s, this campus … reached unprecedented heights of carefully planned frivolity…" (Morris 2000/1967:156, 170).

Before the 1956–1957 fall semester began, I had decided that frat life was not for me because it was phony, frivolous, time-wasting, and would interfere with, rather than assist, my studies. I was better off as a "GDI," living in private student housing, and hanging out with fellow classmates.

I submitted a letter of resignation to the fraternity, and ceased all contacts with the "brothers." After all, when I first entered UT in the fall of 1955, I had no intention of joining any campus organizations.

In retrospect, with regard to fraternities, two key questions are: (1) Why would any young man in his right mind continue to participate in an organization requiring such barbaric initiation rituals under the pretext of lifelong male bonding? and (2) why would he wish to maintain bonds with men who failed to quit the offending organization after experiencing Hell Week?

My self-identification as a "GDI" at UT was not an indication of my conscious participation in a political movement, a precursor to the 1960s civil rights movement, that was associated with well-known campus personalities, Ronnie Dugger and Willie Morris, and reflected in their journalism at the Daily Texan and the Texas Observer – both of which I regularly read. The term "GDI" may have originated in frat lingo as disparaging of the non-frat majority but was proudly embraced as a self-identity by independent students.

In those years my political views were in flux and contradictory. I was naïve but in the process of developing a cynical posture regarding partisan causes and movements, and was developing more as an independent critical observer rather than as a supporter of or believer in anything smacking of religious or political faith. I did, however, believe in selective fact-gathering and knowledge acquisition, personal experience and judgment, and a sense of rightness and wrongness in human affairs; and in the practice of straightforward discourse, telling it like it was. The last thing I was interested in those years was the happenings in the Texas Legislature regarding higher education or any other matter. My main focus was on pursuing opportunities to further my own higher education and intellectual development.

It is not at all surprising that the UT chapter of Sigma Nu was finally shutdown in 1990 in the aftermath of a notorious hazing incident which was later revealed to have involved the television actor Jon Hamm of Mad Men television series fame. Hamm, then twenty and a sophomore, participated in beating a pledge brother with paddles and brooms, lighting his pants on fire, forcing him to do strenuous exercise, and leading him around the rec room by the claw of a hammer hooked under his genitals. The pledge ended up in the hospital. Arrests were made, court proceedings initiated, three Sigma Nu brothers served thirty-day jail sentences. Hamm negotiated a plea deal, completed probation under the terms of a deferred adjudication, and charges were dismissed in 1995 (Argetsinger 2015; Hollandsworth 1991; Wikipedia "Jon Hamm, Early Life").

Thus ended the history at the University of Texas of the Sigma Nu house, founded in 1886 and one of the university's oldest and, allegedly, "most distinguished" fraternities, claiming among its alumni dignitaries men like Senator Lloyd Bentsen. Although Jon Hamm left UT and completed his undergraduate education at the University of Missouri, I propose that he be invited back to UT and presented with a Distinguished Service Award for his role in ridding the campus of at least one noxious fraternity.

Economics and Russian History at the University of Texas

As a freshman, I think I took only one or two courses in introductory economics but took several more advanced economics courses during my sophomore year. I had several excellent teachers of economics – marginalists, Keynesians, and institutionalists – as an undergraduate at the University of Texas. Until the early 1960s the department was located in Garrison Hall with history and other social sciences and apart from the School of Business.

Ironically, one of my teachers, Murray Polakoff, I found out later, had been a graduate student of Polanyi's at Columbia (Polanyi et al., eds, 1957:vi). Still, I do not recall him ever mentioning Polanyi in his course on money and banking. Nor was Polanyi's name mentioned in lectures I attended by institutionalists at that university – including Clarence Ayres who was a Veblen enthusiast and long retired. Surely, if I had remained at UT to complete my undergraduate degree and taken a course with Walter Neale (1957), I would have been introduced to Polanyi's thought. I later met Neale, after he had relocated from Texas to Tennessee and got along well with him. We corresponded and I learned a lot from reading his publications.

My formal introduction to socialist economics was in a course on labor taught by W. Campbell Balfour (a visiting professor from the London School of Economics) at the University of Texas in 1957. I distinctly remember his first lecture when in his thick British accent, the professor told us, somewhat condescendingly (he knew the limitations of our educational backgrounds), that every American student should read the autobiographical novel by one of our country's greatest author's, namely, Jack London's *Martin Eden*. Reading it, he assured us, would be our best introduction to the topic of labor economics, not assigned economics textbooks. I do not remember Balfour specifically lecturing about Marx but I came away from his course with a good overview of the trials and tribulations of the working classes in Euro American capitalist societies and, of course, with a copy of Jack London's book which I acquired and read immediately following his recommendation.

Other memorable economics teachers at the University of Texas were Herbert Liebhafsky who taught a course on the social control of business which focused heavily on relevant policies and institutions of the New Deal, and Wendell Gordon who taught several courses on international economics. Gordon was also an institutionalist but eclectic in his overall approach to economics, and also a well-prepared and lucid lecturer (see Adams 1996).

During my sophomore year I took a course on the history of the Russian revolution from Oliver Henry Radkey, Harvard-educated and a polished lecturer, who presented compelling first-hand material on major Bolshevik and Menshevik protagonists and on the politics of the revolutionary period. Professor Radkey was always immaculately dressed in a suit and tie in Ivy-League style, and was always followed into the lecture hall by a graduate student assistant carrying maps. He had the habit of regularly inviting students to lunch at the El Matamoros Mexican restaurant on Red River Street just off the campus. I went one time and remember telling him during lunch that I was interested in Latin American studies. He frowned upon hearing my statement and commented rather disparagingly that, in his opinion, "Latin American Studies is an intellectual desert." I was puzzled by his comment since I knew that his own department had a few well-known professors of Latin American history. In retrospect, I can only say that Radkey was born and raised as an Anglo-Texan in the coastal bend of southeast Texas, and clearly was more respectful of Europe and Russia than he was of our neighbors south of the border.

If I had remained at UT as an economics major, I would probably have entered the graduate program with a concentration in Keynesian and institutionalist economics and a minor in Latin American Studies. I found Clarence Ayres' particular brand of institutionalist economic anthropology to be rather nebulous, eccentric, and difficult to understand, much like some of Veblen's work – although it was intellectually challenging. Professor Bob Montgomery, who was a colorful, much-admired lecturer on institutionalist economics (cf. Morris 2000:175) would have been much more to my liking. Still, at that early stage of my study of economics, I was much impressed by the logic, precision, and coherence of Keynesianism and Neoclassical marginalism.

Liberal Arts and Economics at American University

American University, which I knew to be where one of my favorite economics professors at the University of Texas, Wendell Gordon, had studied for his MA (PhD from NYU), and considering its location in the heart of Washington DC, seemed like an attractive new environment and a good place to pursue my education in international economics and diplomacy. I discussed with Professor Gordon my plan to transfer and he seemed to be supportive. My course work at Texas was accepted for credit at American University, so I decided, somewhat rashly, that it was time for me to get the hell out of Texas. My parents were skeptical but agreed to support (and finance) my move.

Although majoring in economics, I was able to cobble together a liberal arts education of sorts at American University – including courses in intensive conversational Spanish, philosophy, comparative literature, art history, international relations, and Latin American politics. The main campus was in the elite NW suburbs of Washington DC (Ward Circle on Massachusetts Avenue) but there was a downtown campus on F Street right in the heart of the federal government complex of buildings where I also took a few courses. There were libraries on both campuses but several of my research papers were based mostly on consulting materials at the Library of Congress and the library of the Pan American Union. My art history class was often conducted in the National Gallery of Art. In short, the resources available to any serious student at any university in DC are truly impressive.

One of the concrete benefits for students contemplating a career in government service is that many faculty members at American University were adjunct, had full-time jobs in the federal bureaucracy, and taught evening classes at the downtown campus. On at least two occasions, I visited adjunct economics professors in their federal government offices to get a sense of what they were doing – one in the Commerce Department, Prof. Virgil Salera, and the other, a public finance expert whose name I have forgotten, in the Treasury Department.

Since American University was known for its "Washington Semester" program which was established to accommodate students from other universities, I explored the possibility of entering that program during the second semester of my junior year and to transfer back to UT to complete my senior year. Everything was approved to do so, but I decided to remain at American.

At American University I had made friends with two graduate students who were in the School of International Service, and we decided to find an apartment to share for the 1958–1959 academic year. We found one near DuPont Circle on Connecticut Avenue, and it worked out well for all of us. Since I had been seriously considering applying to the graduate program in the School of International Service, I questioned my apartment-mates constantly about their experience and prospects; nothing I learned from them inclined me towards pursuing that route. For me, then, time spent at American University was valuable in terms of education but did not present me with concrete opportunities to employment in the federal civil service as I thought it might.

One of the most stimulating course experiences in my senior year was in comparative literature taught by Rudolph Von Abele, who ranks among the most intellectually stimulating and eclectic professors I ever had. The course covered novels by Dostoyevsky, Turgenev, Proust, Mann, Kafka, and Melville. I did a term paper on Melville's short novel "Billy Budd, Foretopman" which fascinated me as a morality tale. My framework for approaching Melville came from my reading of Northrup Frye's *Anatomy of Criticism* which I had acquired at the remarkable Saville bookstore in Georgetown. Von Abele was ecstatic about my paper, gave me an A+, and wrote a note to me below the grade on the title page saying something like "Why don't you consider graduate study in comparative literature?" I was flattered, but realized that if I followed up on his suggestion, I would have to learn several foreign languages aside from Spanish to pursue a degree in comparative literature at the graduate level. That was too intimidating a path for me to follow.

A topic of interest to me at that time was addressed in another term paper I wrote as a senior focused on the inter-American economic system and especially the role of Adolph A. Berle in shaping it. I had learned about Berle in my coursework at UT and read his famous book, *The Modern Corporation and Private Property*, but I wanted to further explore his role as an economic diplomat in Latin America. Marx was simply one of several classical economists covered in a course on the history of economic thought with Melville Ulmer that I took during my senior year at American University – but I remember spending most of my time reading and re-reading excerpts from Adam Smith on value, markets, and the division of labor; from Marx on commodities, value, and capital; from David Ricardo on theories of value, differential rent, and international trade/comparative advantage; and from Carl Menger on marginalism and Alfred Marshall's *Principles of Economics*. Polanyi was never mentioned, but Schumpeter was spoken of often. I took several other economics courses there including intermediate price theory, fiscal policy, comparative economic systems, and international trade.

The undergraduate student body at American University was more ethnically and regionally diverse than that at the University of Texas with, perhaps, the largest percentage coming from New York and New Jersey, but many also from the DC suburbs and DC itself – except no blacks. There was also a contingent of offspring of international diplomats – including many Latin Americans.

One morning during the fall semester of my senior year I went to the cafeteria on the main campus and noticed several attractive Spanish-speaking young ladies of what I identified to be of either Latin American or Mexican descent seated together at a table. I managed to engage in conversation with them and learned that they were a group of teachers from Puerto Rico on leave to study English for a year at the university's language institute. I had absolutely no knowledge about Puerto Rico at the time – except a vague memory of a US congressional shoot-out involving political terrorists from that island. Little did I realize then that my future wife, Hilda Almenas, was among that group, and that my entire career would be shaped by that breakfast encounter. In the spring of 1959, Hilda and I were married without family knowledge or participation by a Unitarian minister in Rockville, Maryland.

Meanwhile, my dad had been promoted yet again at Oscar Mayer, and now had the titles of sales manager of the main Madison, Wisconsin plant and "general distributive manager" of all regional operations across the country. It was during his tenure, I now realize, that Oscar Mayer became a major player in the national market for processed meat products. So, I explored graduate school offerings at the University of Wisconsin as a possibility for continuing my graduate education. I knew that the Wisconsin economics department had a strong institutionalist tradition (Veblen and Commons) and might present similar opportunities to the University of Texas for graduate study.

Graduation day at American University was a happy occasion for all concerned and attended by my parents and sister, my two surviving grandmas, and Hilda. Immediately following graduation at American University, we drove to Oil City, Pennsylvania to the home of my paternal grandma and, after visiting paternal relatives there, we drove to my parents' home in Madison, Wisconsin. That summer Hilda and I enrolled in the University of Wisconsin where she took a course in Spanish literature, and I took a course in economics and another in Spanish grammar.

From Wisconsin to Borínquen via the "Big Apple"

During the summer of 1959, I applied for a teaching assistantship in the Department of Economics at the University of Wisconsin and was fortunate to receive one for the 1959–1960 academic year as an MA candidate. I was making a sort of trial-run with graduate study in the field of economics but was really in search of interdisciplinary program oriented toward a career involvement in Latin America, perhaps as a specialist involved in economic diplomacy or business. I was not then committed to the prospect of doctoral studies, nor specifically to an academic career. I had learned during the summer that the University of Wisconsin had a graduate program in Latin American Studies, and decided to attempt to pursue an advanced degree in that program with a concentration in economics. Hilda was contractually obligated to return to Puerto Rico in the fall of 1959 to resume her job as an English teacher, and we had agreed to have a formal re-marriage ceremony there during the 1959–1960 winter break.

Although my winter break trip to Puerto Rico and the re-marriage ceremony did occur, I had found out that the Latin American Studies program at Wisconsin was in disarray due to faculty turnover and was in search of a new director. Consequently, I was discouraged from following an interdisciplinary course of study. However, in view of the disarray in the Latin American Studies Program at the time, and of my lack of enthusiasm about an Atlantic history course I took with Philip Curtin discouraged me from pursuing that option. Curtin was a specialist in African history, the slave trade, and Brazil, and was one of the few Wisconsin faculty members then, outside of the Spanish department, with Latin American studies credentials. His Afro-Brazilian material and focus was completely new to me at the time, and I would surely have responded to them more intelligently a few years later after my training in Puerto Rico. I was simply unprepared to do so as an economics student in 1960.

My experience in the Wisconsin economics department also confirmed that, like UT, program emphasis was trending away from Institutionalism and toward Keynesianism and Neoclassical marginalism. I was disappointed to learn that the trend was more pronounced at Wisconsin than at UT where there remained a strong contingent of faculty inclined toward Institutionalism.

As a teaching assistant at Wisconsin, I was charged with leading undergraduate discussion sections for students who were enrolled in introductory

economics taught by Professor H. Edwin Young, the department chair
(later president). I also was assigned to tutor a freshman football player
who was taking introductory economics taught by Young. The student's
name was Pat Richter who would become a two-time All American tight
end, Rose Bowl hero and, subsequently, athletic director. I was able to
handle the semester's teaching assistant duties with a two-course load but
did not look forward to doing so with a heavier load.

In any case, my graduate course work had left me with contradictory
feelings regarding my intellectual commitment to the discipline of economics. I was stimulated by the lectures and readings on economic development and underdevelopment in a course taught by Paul Ellsworth.
Especially enlightening was the textbook by Benjamin Higgins (1956,
1959) that included material on Indonesia and summaries of Furnivall's
"plural society" and Boeke's "dual economy" theories. A course on micro-
economics, ably taught by the author of the assigned textbook, Professor
Joseph Coppock, was simply a more advanced version of a course I had
taken at American University. Its abstract, logic-driven, and graphical
approach to economics was less challenging to me than the more interdisciplinary approach of development economics. I remember sitting in
the University of Wisconsin library poring over page after page of graphs
depicting relationships between supply, demand, cost-price, marginal productivity, marginal utility, indifference curves and a seemingly endless array
of economic variables, and asking myself, why was I doing this?

My most memorable experience at Wisconsin occurred one morning
on the first day of the summer session (1959) as we were awaiting the arrival
of Professor Coppock in the designated classroom. In walked a scraggly-
bearded man, with greying hair and wearing glasses, very casually dressed,
and struggling to carry a tall stack of books. He proceeded to the lectern
and, without any introductory remarks, began talking in a thick German
accent about historical sociology, seemingly oblivious to his surroundings or
his audience. Clearly, I surmised, that this was not our economics professor.

We listened politely, yet were spellbound by the words of this charismatic lecturer for a few moments – until someone (presumably a sociology
department representative) entered the scene to inform Professor Hans
Gerth that he was in the wrong classroom. Gerth, who I subsequently

learned was an exile from Nazi Germany, an expert on Max Weber, and a prize student of Karl Mannheim, had been a distinguished member of the sociology faculty at Wisconsin since 1940 where he formed a lasting collaborative relationship with C. Wright Mills. He was only in his early 50s when the above incident occurred, but seemed to fit the classic stereotype of the aging, absent-minded professor. On the basis of books I subsequently read by professor Gerth, my graduate education at Wisconsin would probably have been better served if I had followed him as he left our classroom and enrolled in his course.

The combination of transitional disarray in the Latin American Studies program and my ambivalence regarding graduate coursework in economics, led me to decide to give up my teaching assistantship in the University of Wisconsin economics department at the end of the 1959–1960 fall semester. Because I was now tied by marriage to Puerto Rico, my planning for the future no longer included returning to the University of Texas but toward either graduate study or employment on the east coast, especially New York City, or in Puerto Rico.

Statistical Quality Control Inspector at Oscar Mayer

Withdrawal from the University of Wisconsin in January 1960 meant that I had to find a job. Thanks to my dad's connections, I quickly got a job at the huge Oscar Mayer plant in Madison. At the time, it was the world's largest facility for hog slaughter and processing – several hundred hogs, hooked onto overhead conveyors, moved through the horrific assembly line per hour as men wielding long knives punctured their throats until they bled out and moved on to be fully eviscerated and butchered. I had been exposed to a hog kill floor in a small locker plant my dad operated for a time in Georgetown, Texas between jobs at Armour and Oscar Mayer; a small number of hogs were killed and processed either as fresh-frozen meat in familiar cuts or smoked as hams and bacon. But my job there, one summer, was simply to operate an ice cream machine and fill pint, quart and gallon containers for freezing and sale. The kill floor at any meat processing facility will quickly make any outside observer seriously consider vegetarianism.

Fortunately, my job at Oscar Mayer and Company did not involve the kill floor or the unpleasant-smelling cook room where sausage products (i.e., all processed meat products) were mixed and cooked, but the packaging room where different products including everything from sliced bologna to hot dogs were packaged. My job consisted in grabbing different products randomly off the conveyors, weighing, and inspecting them. Any serious variations in specified weights or sealing problems in packaging could lead to shutdowns in the assembly lines – especially if detected by federal Department of Agriculture inspectors who roamed throughout the plant. My job was to avoid USDA shutdowns by finding problems before their inspectors did. Even though I was working in the company's interest, and was an executive's son, I would still get shouted complaints from the foreman if I spotted a problem causing a brief shutdown of a production line – which I did on occasion. He was caught between the union representative and the USDA inspectors and did not want to shut down the line on the basis of my findings.

Any outside observer who sees and smells the boiling vats of meat parts and spices in the cook room of any meat processing company will be hesitant ever again to consume hot dogs or luncheon meat. Oscar Mayer meat processing was a nasty business but it provided an executive's salary for my dad and, of course, funded my undergraduate education. One morning, as I was entering the main gate of the plant which had several thousand employees, I remember being greeted by smiling Hubert Humphrey who was shaking hands on his US presidential campaign (unsuccessful) that year (1960).

During the Christmas-New Year's break at the University of Wisconsin in 1959, I traveled for the first time to Puerto Rico to visit Hilda's family in urban (Caguas) and rural (Yabucoa) parts of the island, and to get officially re-married in a religious ceremony. Aside from occasional visits to Mexican border towns during the years I was growing up in Texas, this was my first experience in a Latin American environment. Puerto Rico at the time was still in the throes of transformation from agrarian to urban life and the contrast between life in the two sectors was stunning. Since

Hilda's family was involved in both sectors, I was exposed to Puerto Rican middle-class urban life and to that of the *jíbaros*, the subsistence and cash-cropping (tobacco, plantains, citrus, mangos, papaya and a variety of root crops) peasants of the mountainous interior. I had never seen anything like the life of the *jíbaros* and found it to be fascinating. We traveled from Caguas to San Juan and Yabucoa on *públicos*, an inter-city public taxi network – a very convenient and efficient way to travel – if sometimes a little scary due to high speeds and/or curving roads.

It was on that trip that I experienced my first earthquake. In the middle of the night I was suddenly awakened by a rumbling noise and the bed shaking, and I found myself on the floor looking up at the ceiling. Scary – but, fortunately, there were no noticeable aftershocks as there would be later in Oaxaca.

The job at Oscar Mayer during the spring of 1960 was only temporary until I could either continue graduate study or find another job that would suit my rather ill-defined, but Latin America/Puerto Rico-oriented, career aspirations. With that intention in mind, I responded to an announcement in the New York Times regarding a newly established Graduate Institute of Book Publishing at New York University. Interviews were being scheduled for applicants at the Palmer House hotel in Chicago.

I submitted an application and supporting materials, was interviewed by the institute's designated director, John Tebbel, who confirmed that the new program would include apprenticeships in a New York City-based publishing houses, and an MA degree upon of completion of coursework and the apprenticeship. All accepted applicants were to receive tuition waivers and a stipend to be determined in conjunction with the apprenticing publisher. Tebbel's recruitment presentation convinced me that publishing held promise as a long-term, if offbeat, career option. Shortly after my Chicago interview, I was informed that I had been accepted with a fellowship into the NYU program. Hilda had satisfied her teaching obligation in Puerto Rico, and in the summer of 1960 had returned to Madison. In late August, we left Madison for New York city. Our first child, Dana Lyn, was born in NYC on February 20, 1961.

To make a long story short, after moving into a furnished efficiency apartment in a building on 14 Washington Place near the Washington

Square NYU campus, and making daily visits to the fledgling Institute, I was unable to get reliable, concrete information regarding stipend, apprenticeship, and related program details. It became clear that the Institute's start-up process was slow-moving, and I became impatient with the situation. I cannot recall the exact specifics of the matter but the end result was that, after several days of unsuccessful efforts to formally register in the program, get my stipend, and find placement as an apprentice with a publisher, I decided to withdraw from the Institute before it was officially up and running.

Obviously, I had no immediate alternative job prospects but, thanks to my earnings at Oscar Mayer and to Hilda's savings, we had enough money to tide us over until I found a job. I began looking for a job that had the potential of relocation to Puerto Rico. It was a trying time.

Curacao Trading Company, Inc. on Wall Street

After a few days of job interviews (Hertz International and W. R. Grace), I found employment as assistant to an export-import manager at a Dutch trading company, the Curacao Trading Company, Inc. at 120 Wall Street. The unique art deco building in which the office was located was built in 1930 with its original anchor tenant as American Sugar Refining Company, a dominant player in the US occupation of Puerto Rico in 1898 and afterwards. In the 1960s the building was the only major high rise (thirty-four floors) on the East River downtown waterfront and was near Pier 11, the Wall Street Terminal.

My job at CTC involved activities such as typing endless bills of lading and other documents, researching suppliers for a whole host of general merchandise products by paging through the Thomas Register, and calling new suppliers I had identified, or repeat suppliers, to get current price quotations for general merchandise that included most manufacture products ranging from fire trucks to tallow and various chemical products for soap-making. Sometimes interesting but not very challenging or creative work – but you had to start somewhere.

The export manager for the general merchandise section was Alejandro Avilés, a friendly, unpretentious and serious Mexican married to the daughter of a Venezuelan general. He never really got angry with me for my mistakes or slowness in meeting deadlines, and was patient in teaching me the details of the business. Mr De Jong, the general manager of the entire office sat behind a big desk encased in a glass-walled office with a view of all of his nearly 50 or so employees. He was a rather dour man who would now and then bellow out orders but he mostly allowed his separate managers run their own departments. His main interest seemed to be in following raw commodity prices for cacao and coffee which the company was heavily involved in trading.

I became friends with the export manager for textiles, Vincent Accardi, who was a long-term employee and had spent time in Guayaquil, Ecuador where he had met and married his wife, Leonora. He lived in Brooklyn, where he was born and raised in a Sicilian family, with Leonora and his son. I visited him at home for dinner on one occasion.

Vince and I would lunch together every day, usually in a Chock-Full-Of-Nuts shop not far from our building, and then stroll along the nearby wharves or through Battery Park talking a lot about the export industry, current events, world problems, or the vicissitudes of life in general. My conversations with him led me to believe that there was little likelihood of a job in the New York office would lead to permanent posting in the Caribbean or Latin America with Curacao Trading Company. Vince never had the opportunity to go to college and urged me to continue my graduate studies wherever they led. I corresponded with him for several years after that year we walked and talked together in Battery Park in Lower Manhattan.

Graduate Study in Anthropology at the Universities of Puerto Rico and Pittsburgh

To the Island of Borinquen

One evening in our Greenwich Village apartment Hilda called my attention to an announcement posted in a Spanish-language newspaper *El Mundo* (San Juan, Puerto Rico) regarding the availability of fellowships for a graduate program in the social sciences, under the auspices of the Department of Social Affairs of the Pan American Union/Organization of American States, at the University of Puerto Rico. I immediately applied and was accepted to enter that interdisciplinary program with a tuition-waiver and fellowship. That acceptance shifted my career trajectory onto a new and different path. I had already determined by then that the export-import business was not for me, and was exploring ways to further my graduate education including at The New School for Social Research which was only a few blocks from my apartment.

In the early 1960s, Puerto Rico was in the midst of its Operation Bootstrap/Showcase of Democracy phase under the leadership of Luís Muñoz Marín and his Popular Democratic Party. It was a staging area for US government, OAS, and UN developmental and foreign technical assistance programs. The University of Puerto Rico under the leadership of its dynamic chancellor Jaime Benítez, a protégé of Robert Hutchins of the University of Chicago, was hosting academic involvement in Third World-focused development projects.

One manifestation of this role was a collaboration with the OAS/ PAU through the newly established Institute of Caribbean Studies and its founding director, the historian Richard Morse. The OAS/PAU program, officially designated as the Inter-American Program in Advanced Social

Sciences (Programa Interamericano de Estudios Superiores en Ciencias Sociales en la Región del Caribe), was essentially the brainchild of Angel Palerm, the Spanish-Mexican anthropologist, who administered it from Washington DC as Director of Social Affairs for the Organization of American States/Pan American Union; and it also operated in Mexico (I think at UNAM). Palerm was involved in the recruitment of participating faculty like James Blaut, Hugo Nutini and Gabriel Ospina, and also in curriculum design for the program. Fellows in the program took courses offered by both program and UPR faculty. Later in Mexico, I got to know Palerm and benefitted from his counsel and writings.

As a program fellow at UPR, I studied social anthropology and Mesoamerica with Hugo Nutini, cultural anthropology and Caribbean religions with Donald Hogg (who became my graduate thesis advisor), cultural geography with James Blaut (program director), Puerto Rican and Caribbean history and politics with Thomas Mathews and Gordon Lewis, Latin American community studies with Gabriel Ospina (who had received his doctorate at UCal-Berkeley through participation in George Foster's original Tzintzuntzán project), and sociology with Howard Stanton (expertise in social theory and Robert Merton) and Harmanus (Harry) Hoetink (1967) from whom I learned about pluriethnic societies in the region.

I also took a course in social psychology with Abigaíl Concepción de Gracia (who had studied under Abraham Kardiner at Columbia and was married to a prominent *independentista* politician). I attended lectures by several anthropologists including Carlos Buitrago Ortíz, Eduardo Seda Bonilla, Rafael Ramírez, Anthony Lauria, and Ricardo Alegría. Sidney Mintz visited the program as a lecturer/advisor and talked about his recently completed *Worker in the Cane* (1960) project, and Oscar Lewis (1966) also gave a talk about his forthcoming project in a San Juan slum.

There were about fifteen or so students in the program. Only two of us were from the continental United States and a few from Puerto Rico. There were three from the Dominican Republic, one each from Peru, Colombia, Haiti, Trinidad, Guyana, El Salvador, and Panama. Roy Simon-Bryce (Panama), Anselme Remy (Haiti), and Anthony Maingot (Trinidad) were among those who, like me, received doctorates at other universities after graduating from the UPR program.

My graduate thesis directed by Donald Hogg, who had done his doctoral dissertation on Jamaican folk religion at Yale under the direction of Sidney Mintz, involved fieldwork among revivalistic religious groups in Caguas with a special focus on a prophecy-based cult (Cook 1963; 1965a). Aside from Hogg's doctoral dissertation (1964), I was influenced by reading Mintz's *Worker in the Cane*, and Bryan Wilson's *Sects and Society*. An article derived from my UPR graduate thesis, together with a review article of a monograph by E. Seda Bonilla, resulted in my first publications (Cook 1965a reprinted in Horowitz, ed. 1971:560–580; Cook 1965b).

I remember Tony Lauria wincing when I told him that I had decided to do my graduate thesis fieldwork on a religious cult. But he realized that I had been influenced by Hogg's fieldwork in Jamaica directed by Mintz, and by Mintz's own focus on the religious conversion of his Puerto Rican sugarcane worker, Don Taso. What he did not realize was my own curiosity, as a non-believer, regarding people's motivations in believing implausible narratives and practicing strange behaviors to honor them. This presented an immediate challenge to me regarding "participant observation" – what it actually entailed and how to justify it to "true believers" with a minimum of deception. In other words, would I allow the devout cult members to believe that I was potentially a convert to their particular spiritualist brand of revivalistic, fundamentalist Christianity; or would I simply convince them of my interest to respectfully observe their most intimate forms of worship as an objective observer for the purpose of reporting about their beliefs and activities to interested readers? I chose the latter path without, of course, disclosing my own apostasy. I simply allowed them to think, as most of them assumed, that I was nothing other than a typical American mainstream Protestant.

This was the same strategy I used with the more moderate Pentecostal group also included in my study for comparative purposes. The Pentecostals expressed confidence that I would be more impressed with their less emotionally demonstrative approach to worship than that of the extremist "Prophets." The "Prophets" by contrast were convinced that I would see through the hypocrisy of the more uptight, restrained forms of worship of the Pentecostals, and realize that their prophetic forms were closer to the true spirit of the original relationship between the Messiah, his disciples, and their converts – the primitive Christians. So, I was able to observe spirit possession, prophesying, and spiritual dancing by the "*Profetas*" without participating in (or mimicking) their actual behaviors or sharing their beliefs.

It was at UPR, then, that I took my first courses in sociology, anthropology, social psychology, descriptive statistics and cultural geography, and conducted my first fieldwork. It was also there that an adjunct faculty member and sometimes lecturer in the program, Hazel DuBois (wife of Howard Stanton), who was a doctoral student with the anthropologist Margaret Mead at Columbia University, in a casual conversation planted the idea of economic anthropology in my head as a possible area of specialization for doctoral study. At the time, I had not known of the existence of that specialized field, much less about its subject matter.

Apart from formal coursework and reading, a key element in my intellectual formation in Puerto Rico was regular exposure to radical, anticolonial thought from conversations with faculty, students, co-workers, family, and friends. During 2–1/2 years in Puerto Rico, which included a 1962 week-long field trip to the Dominican Republic, I learned first-hand the differences between cultural nationalist and class-based responses to colonialism and imperialism. I also experienced daily life in a tolerant, multicultural, multiethnic, easy-going, sub-tropical environment. It was exhilarating and would contrast markedly with the more regimented and staid academic environment that lay ahead of me in Pittsburgh.

After receiving my graduate diploma, I worked for a few months as a research associate in the Social Science Program in the Commonwealth's health department. There, among other things, I was involved in a field study of a working-class barrio in Rio Piedras, socio-geographic surveys of shantytowns (*arrabales*) in the San Juan metropolitan area, including the infamous El Fanguito in the Martín Peña canal (*caño*) area. I also served as a "power and support score observer" (Straus 1968:417) in an experimental social psychology project, directed by Murray Straus from the University of Minnesota, dealing with communication and power relations in Puerto Rican middle- and working-class families.

One of my colleagues in that health department program was Manuel "Pito" Colón, a bearded, charismatic man who had been expelled from the University of Puerto Rico several years earlier for participating in a rally in support of independence for the island – even though he was scheduled to be valedictorian of his graduating class. He had entered the university on the G. I. Bill having served in the US Army Special Forces in the Philippines. After his expulsion from the university, he got a job, somewhat paradoxically, in the public relations department, the San Juan-based Corona brewery. At the time I met him, Pito had clearly abandoned his efforts to make up for the rebelliousness of his student days, had quit his job at the Corona brewery, and renounced bourgeois life. He was once again a radical *independentista* whose collection of Marxist books and pamphlets had recently been confiscated during a FBI raid on his Rio Piedras apartment.

I told Pito that before leaving New York City, while browsing the shelves of a leftist bookstore near the BMT entrance on Broadway, I had found (and purchased) a mint copy of the out-of-print and much-coveted *Handbook of Marxism* (published by Random House in the late 1930s); it contained an excellent collection of selected writings of Marx, Engels, Lenin, and others. He wanted it badly and made me an offer I could not refuse at the time, namely, to trade it for a copy of *The People of Puerto Rico* by Steward et al., which he knew I wanted but could not find at the time in Puerto Rico.

As we were on our way to do fieldwork in the San Juan *arrabales* one morning, Pito told me to stop in front of a commercial building not far from the Corona brewery where he had previously worked. He jumped out of my VW beetle, went into the building and came out a few moments later holding a near-mint copy of *The People of Puerto Rico*. We were parked in front of the Texaco office building and Pito had remembered on a past public relations visit there that he had paged through a copy of that book he saw lying on a table in the reception area. The inside cover of the book was clearly stamped "Property of Texaco de Puerto Rico." Several years later when I was teaching Puerto Rican Studies at the University of Connecticut, I placed that same copy on reserve in the library of the Puerto Rican Cultural Center and never saw it again. I have often regretted that loss but, more often, have regretted my trade of the *Handbook*.

Pito accompanied a small group of representatives of the UPR-PAU program on our trip to the Dominican Republic in the Spring of 1963, organized for the purpose of meeting up with other members of the program who were completing their graduate thesis fieldwork. Pito's principal purpose for making the trip was to meet with Manuel Tavares Justo a leader of a Dominican left-wing opposition on behalf of the Puerto Rican independence movement. He did not reveal much to us about the substance of his meeting at the time.

If the political climate in Puerto Rico at the time was charged by a reinvigorated independence movement and debates spurred by the Cuban Revolution, we encountered a supercharged political culture in the Dominican Republic driven also by the post-Trujillo democratic reform process. Unlike Puerto Rico, there was a notable military presence on the streets of Santo Domingo. Everyone, from taxi drivers to waiters, university faculty and staff, had politics on their minds. This proved to be the case also on our visits north to San Francisco de Macorís, Santiago de los Caballeros and, finally, Mao – a town in the northeast not far from the Haitian border where Anselme Remy had conducted fieldwork for his UPR program thesis. Overall, this visit to Santo Domingo and to the interior of the Dominican Republic left me with an impression of a vibrant, more "traditional," less ostensibly "Americanized" sociocultural milieu than I was experiencing in Puerto Rico.

Upon our return to Puerto Rico, my colleagues, especially Pito, were given a hard time by US immigration officials at the airport. I passed through the process without even having my bag inspected, whereas my Puerto Rican colleagues (including Delia Pabón, a University of Chicago-trained sociologist) not only had their luggage inspected but were body-searched. We all, of course, had US passports. That incident provided a powerful example to me of what it meant to be colonial subjects treated as foreigners in their own country.

Manuel Tavares was killed a few months later in an armed revolutionary uprising to restore democratically elected President Juan Bosch to power after he had been deposed through a military coup led by former

Trujillo generals in late September 1963. Shortly after that, US president Lyndon B. Johnson sent troops to intervene in the Dominican civil war. I lost touch with Pito after I left Puerto Rico for Pittsburgh before those regrettable events occurred.

By August, 1963 my stint as an employee of the commonwealth government was winding down, and I was invited by Oscar Lewis to have lunch with him at the faculty club of the University of Puerto Rico. During lunch he discussed with me in some detail the research plan for his project in La Perla, one of San Juan's most notorious *arrabales* (slums) which he knew was among the areas I had recently surveyed with the Department of Health. I was flattered to learn that he also was informed about reports I had written on social surveys of two working-class barrios in Rio Piedras, and about my study of the "prophets" cult in the urban slums of Caguas, even though it had not yet been published.

In our conversation, he disclosed that he had just negotiated a lucrative contract to do a movie version of *The Children of Sánchez*, his famous study of a Mexico City family that had migrated from the village of Tepoztlán. The film would have Anthony Quinn playing the role of the family patriarch. He further explained that his reading of the writings of the French author, Emile Zola, had inspired his anthropological vision of urban poverty. He emphasized that he was inventing a new genre with his focus on family case studies and life histories – a more humanistic and personal type of narrative writing. I was impressed.

Lewis also discussed his plans to expand the study of poverty in Puerto Rico to Cuba for the purpose of comparing socialist and capitalist policy approaches to economic development. He said that his forthcoming life history of *Pedro Martínez* (1964), a key informant from Tepoztlán (state of Morelos, Mexico), would surpass Mintz's *Worker in the Cane* (1960) in terms of historical and cultural content and as a model of anthropological method.[7]

At that point in his career, Lewis was definitely more of a project entrepreneur than a fieldworker; he had just received his largest research grant ever from the US Social Security Administration, and had extra income from his book sales and movie contract (Rigdon 1988:44, 73). At the end of our lunch, he offered me a job on his project and the opportunity to subsequently pursue doctoral studies at the University of Illinois. I accepted, and for a week or so assisted him and his wife, Ruth, in moving into an apartment and setting up an office in the upscale Condado neighborhood before the research project was officially launched.

Shortly before my meeting with Oscar Lewis, I learned from Hugo Nutini that he had been hired for a tenure-track position at the University of Pittsburgh, and that he would support me for a predoctoral fellowship to begin study there in September. So, I was confronted with another career-changing decision: to work as a research assistant on Oscar Lewis' Puerto Rico project in a yet-to-be-clarified arrangement to complete doctoral studies at the University of Illinois; or to enroll at Pitt fully-funded starting in the fall trimester of 1963, where Nutini would be my principal advisor.

It was not a difficult decision since working on Lewis' project would have effectively postponed satisfying residency and course requirements in the doctoral program at Illinois, where I had not yet applied or been officially accepted. I decided to immediately accept Nutini's offer, quickly initiated the formal application process at the University of Pittsburgh, was accepted and awarded a Mellon Predoctoral Fellowship for the 1963–1964 academic year.

In retrospect, considering the less than ideal execution and out-come of Lewis' Puerto Rico project, I do not regret that decision (Rigdon 1988:Ch.4). I would later criticize Lewis for making an invidious comparison between Mexicans and Puerto Ricans regarding the issue of personal and national identity in his book resulting from that project, *La Vida* (Cook 1973a:xiii–xiv; Lewis 1966; cf. Lewis exchange of letters with Muna Muñoz Lee in Rigdon 1988:245–247).

By the late 1950s, the University of Pittsburgh was upgrading its academic programs under the leadership of an entrepreneurial chancellor, Edward Litchfield, who hired established senior scholars as program developers. John Gillin, a well-known anthropologist, was hired from the University of North Carolina in 1959 to serve as Dean of Social Sciences. Donald Hogg my thesis advisor in the UPR program, prior to going to Yale for his doctorate, had studied under Gillin at North Carolina, and held him in high regard as a teacher. Gillin promptly established a separate department of anthropology, hired George Peter Murdock from Yale as a distinguished professor, and David Landy, who had done research in Puerto Rico, from Harvard as department head. Hugo Nutini was one of several new junior faculty members in anthropology hired in 1963.

The Imagined Cockfighting' Project

One thing I regret about my period in Puerto Rico is not pursuing a research project that circumstances had placed before me, namely, cockfighting. During our first year of residence on the island, Hilda, our daughter, Dana, and I lived in Hilda's hometown of Caguas. The porch of our second-story apartment in the Caguas Lumber Yard building on the road to Gurabo gave us a bird's eye view of a large, ramshackle, and noisy *gallera* or cockfighting arena directly across the road.

The *gallera* was located on the western edge of a large *arrabal* named "Checo" which, in turn, was on the periphery of cane fields (*cañaverales*) dependent upon the *Central* (grinding mill) *Santa Juana*. At least weekly, if not more often, cockfights were held that generated high decibels of raucous crowd noise. Occasionally, I observed these activities up-close and was surprised to see mixed audiences (both by gender and social class) as well as open betting since cockfighting and gambling were both legal in Puerto Rico. My father-in-law, Arcadio Almenas Quiñones, a local government official, had some experience with fighting cocks, as did members of Hilda's maternal family in rural Yabucoa. Indeed, cockfighting, after baseball, was arguably the island's second national pastime. To this day there is an air-conditioned *gallera* in Isla Verde in the San Juan metropolitan area, and cockfighting events are televised island-wide. As a first-year graduate student at Pitt, I considered Puerto Rican cockfighting as a potential dissertation topic.

Ironically, by the late 1980s and 1990s when Hilda and I owned a small citrus and plantain farm (*finca*) in Barrio Guayabota in the municipality of Yabucoa, the old Caguas *gallera*, as well as the nearby *arrabal*, the *central*, and the *cañaveral*, had long been removed by urbanization. Also, her family's involvement in cockfighting had diminished due to death and changing recreational patterns. The imagined project was never realized.

As it turned out, the prospect of undertaking doctoral dissertation fieldwork in Puerto Rico changed owing to my participation in an ethnographic field school in the Oaxaca Valley, Mexico in the summer of 1965 (Cook 1965c). From that year until 1990, my career revolved around ethnographic fieldwork in Oaxaca.

Pursuing a Doctorate in Anthropology in the Cathedral of Learning

In September 1963 Hilda (who was pregnant with our second child, a son, Scott Allen) and my daughter, Dana, remained in Puerto Rico, and I caught a flight to Pittsburgh where I moved into a new graduate student residence tower not far from the Cathedral of Learning. It was also close to Schenley Park and to Forbes Field where I had seen the Pirates play. I had revisited Pittsburgh briefly only once or twice with my parents after leaving there in 1944, so it was not completely alien to me. But, if it had not been a question of completing my graduate education at Pitt, I would not have chosen to return. The Puerto Rican climate and lifestyle was much more to my liking.

Hilda finished out a half-year as a teacher in Caguas, and then left Puerto Rico with Dana to live with my parents in Enterprise, Alabama where my dad was managing a peanut processing plant (Sessions Company). My son, Scott Allen, was born there on February 26, 1964. Dad arranged for me to rendezvous with a Sessions Company 18-wheeler making deliveries in Pennsylvania to travel to Alabama over spring break that year to see Hilda and my newborn son. Before the start of my second year at Pitt I, Hilda, the two kids moved into an upstairs duplex in the Shadyside neighborhood near Squirrel Hill where many of the faculty lived.

Nutini had warned me that my first year in the graduate program at Pitt would require a deviation from my research interests in contemporary populations of Latin America and the Caribbean because I would have to meet core requirements in archaeology, physical anthropology, linguistics, and Old World ethnography. I somehow managed to get through those courses with only one retake in Old World Ethnography, George Peter Murdock's hellish brainchild. Success on the exam for that course required encyclopedic knowledge a la Murdock's "Our Primitive Contemporaries" and his world ethnology project (the Ethnographic Atlas) based on the Human Relations Area Files which were conveniently housed in a separate room in the Pitt library. Luck was required to have prepared for the right questions on the exam for that course. I had good luck the second time around.

The Pitt department was essentially a white male patrician gerontocracy, headed by Gillin and Murdock, with Landy as a middle manager, and a varied assortment of new junior faculty members comprising the lower ranks – but all competitive and in hopes of tenure or promotion. Due to Gillin's weakened condition, George Peter Murdock (GPM) was the de facto patriarch whose approval was essential to the success of every underling – faculty and graduate students. His Ivy-league bearing, dress (always a suit and tie), and businesslike demeanor were somewhat intimidating – yet he was pleasant enough to talk to if you knew what to say. Pitt was in essence a one-building campus – the massive neo-gothic Cathedral of Learning housed the anthropology department on one of the highest of its forty-two stories. Elevators, each with a uniformed attendant, were usually well-occupied and, invariably, it seemed that when I got on one I was standing next to either Gillin or GPM himself – very awkward!

The two-trimester core course on world ethnography (Peoples and Cultures of the World I and II) required every junior faculty member to lecture under the intimidating watchful eye of GPM who regularly attended every session. There was little interaction between students and faculty in the lecture hall but all of the faculty were very accessible in their offices for discussion and follow-up questioning.

The purpose of this course sequence, aside from exposing students to the entire faculty, was also to familiarize us as comprehensively as possible with the ethnographic records of the Old and New Worlds, and to force us to consult the Human Relations Area Files for our comparative research papers. It was, in fact, a very successful format since it enabled students to profit from the best work of faculty without necessarily enrolling in one of their specialized seminars. This enabled me, for example, to learn quite a bit about India and its peasantries from a stimulating lecturer like Harold Gould without taking his seminar on the subject. He also agreed to serve on my dissertation committee.

All of us felt obliged to take at least one seminar with Murdock. I opted to take his seminar on the history of anthropology rather than another he offered on kinship and social structure. I remember on at least one occasion during a winter trimester seminar, scheduled in a room in the upper reaches of the Cathedral, I watched as the elements – clouds, rain, sleet, and snow – swirled around the windows as I listened to Murdock drone on about some topic.

The seminar was essentially built around student presentations on the work of prominent anthropologists chosen in consultation with Murdock. He would comment on each presentation and provide relevant anecdotes. I wanted to do a presentation on the sociologist, Max Weber, which GPM agreed to let me do if I would also do another on his favorite anthropologist, Julius Lippert, an Austrian cultural evolutionist.

I presented a strongly methodology-slanted paper on Weber that GPM seemed to like but he was rather piqued when in my paper on Lippert I mentioned his concern with what he termed the "bread-and-butter question" which to me demonstrated a degree of class consciousness on Lippert's part. There was only one work by Lippert available in English – a massive, complex 700-page tome that had been translated with a long and quite thorough introduction by none other than George Peter Murdock himself as his doctoral dissertation (Lippert 1930). Its scope was all-encompassing, based as it was on Lippert's reliance on a comparative ethnographic method combined with a pioneering multilineal evolutionary approach. I do not think my presentation did the work justice.

Aside from this, the most memorable moments in that seminar, apart from those when Murdock nodded off in the middle of someone's presentation (a bad sign!), was his obvious delight in mimicking Bronislaw Malinowski's demonstration of Trobriand coital positions during cocktail parties at Yale when Murdock was chair. There was also Eileen Kane's sparkling presentation on Ibn Khaldun (Kane 2010).

My most disappointing seminar was taught by John Gillin on Latin American ethnology. Gillin had undergone surgery for lung cancer and was no longer the inspiring teacher remembered by my UPR thesis advisor, Donald Hogg, who had taken courses with him at the University of North Carolina when Gillin was in his prime. Moreover, Gillin's views about Latin America were outdated and, in fact, quite elitist, psychologistic, and reactionary – at odds with everything I had learned in Puerto Rico. Not only was Gillin a member of the US Latin American policy establishment, he was supportive of US counterinsurgency involvement in countries like Guatemala and, as I surmised from things he said, was sympathetic to the interests of the United Fruit Company (where, I think, he may have served as a consultant and shareholder). In essence, our views clashed, and I escaped his seminar with a grade of B and unhappy with mainstream Latin Americanist sociocultural anthropology.

To make a long story short, my discontent with Pitt during 1963–1964 led me to consider transferring to the doctoral program in anthropology at the University of Illinois where I formally applied. I was accepted on the basis of Oscar Lewis's recommendation, so again had to decide between the Lewis-Illinois option and continuing at Pitt in the fall of 1964. I decided to remain at Pitt thanks to Nutini's assurance that I would get through the Old World ethnography exam retake, and could then proceed toward preparation for my doctoral dissertation project full speed ahead. If I had accepted the Illinois offer, I would have had to start by working on Lewis's project in Puerto Rico.

The "Anti-Market" Mentality Paper

All the rage in anthropological discourse at the time was the theme of models and model-building which was the organizing theme of Leonard Kasdan's theory seminar. In the same time period, Nutini (1965), who had doctorates in both anthropology and the philosophy of science from

UCLA, was also engaged in work on that topic with a particular focus on Levi-Strauss and French structuralism. I had assumed the role in the models seminar as a discussant of deductive model-building in economics, so I was especially focused on that theme as I started reading Polanyi and related materials in the economic anthropology literature.

I brought to that reading another interest, namely, Max Weber's work on the Protestant ethic, sects, and sectarianism, and the role of charismatic leaders in religious cults – the topic of my first fieldwork project and graduate thesis in Puerto Rico (Cook 1965a). When examining their arguments in the debate regarding the applicability of neoclassical economics in anthropology, I viewed the relationship between Polanyi and his followers as sort of a secular version of that between Messiah and disciples. This led me to examine the source of interest in Polanyi's contribution among anthropologists, not so much for its "scientific" content, but as a phenomenon requiring explanation from a sociology-of-knowledge perspective. My reading in the field, and my association with anthropologists, had led me to believe, correctly or not, that most of them had little formal training in economics, and were susceptible to a biased "quick fix" by latching onto Polanyi's anti-economics doctrines. I hoped to raise questions in anthropologists' minds about the deficiencies of a non-economic approach to economics.

In reading Polanyi's writings I was struck by his very selective consultation of the ethnographic literature, and by his heavy emphasis on either ancient economic history or European/English economic history. I found some of his ideas to be provocative regarding non-market, socially-integrative institutions like reciprocity and redistribution but rather skimpy regarding market exchange in non-European economies, and emotionally-charged regarding markets as integrative and disintegrative institutions in the British economy. Also, I thought his interpretation of Weber on formal vs. substantive rationality was too narrow, and that he had drawn wrong conclusions from it. Cost-accounting rationality had an exceptional evolutionary trajectory in Western European capitalism but that did not mean that other world economies were, ipso facto, irrational in the sense of calculations regarding commodity value. I think my article was the first to use the Weber-Polanyi formal vs. substantive rationality distinction as a basis for describing the divide in economic anthropological discourse as one between the "formalist" and the "substantivist" schools of thought (Cook 1966).

George Dalton's 1961 article in the *American Anthropologist* "Economic Theory and Primitive Society," along with *Trade and Market in the Early Empires* (Polanyi et al. 1957), brought substantivism and Polanyi's work to the attention of mainstream sociocultural anthropology. Dalton, studied under Polanyi at Columbia for an MA degree in economics (1951) and wrote his doctoral dissertation on Robert Owen and Polanyi at the University of Oregon (1959). He embraced Polanyi's thesis of limiting the applicability of classical-neoclassical economics to its capitalist economies of origin and, hence, calling into question the validity of most of the best work done by anthropologists in studying so-called "tribal" or "primitive" economies since the 1930s (e.g., those trained by Malinowski at the London School of Economics like Raymond Firth and Firth's own students like Richard Salisbury, Cyril Belshaw and many others; as well as by Herskovits and his students in the US). Firth had completed an MA degree in economics before beginning doctoral studies in anthropology, and had set the standard for the use of neoclassical economics in the study of non-capitalist economies such as the Maori and the Tikopia of Polynesia.

Dalton was very selective in his criticism of anthropologists like Firth, Salisbury, and Belshaw whose careful application of neoclassical economic concepts and quantitative tools was balanced by solid anthropological treatment of the sociocultural context of economic behavior. He focused on the issue of money and markets, asserting that "Where all-purpose money is absent in primitive economy, it is because market exchange as the economy-wide principle of integration is absent" (Dalton 1961/1968:159).

This statement was simply a roundabout way of asserting the obvious: Capitalist economy and pre-capitalist economy are different. This was never in dispute. The issue in dispute was how to approach or understand exchange activities in economies without money or with special purpose money. Ever since Malinowski wrote about *gimwali* (barter) in the Trobriand economy, it had been documented that market exchange was present in situations where general purpose money circulation was either limited or absent. It appears that the presence or absence of general purpose money or integrative markets did not disprove the validity of specific explanations of economic behavior in the work of Firth in Tikopia, of Salisbury in New Guinea, or of Belshaw in Melanesia using concepts or principles developed deductively to explain economic behavior in capitalist economies. There was never any consideration by Dalton in his 1961 article of the fact that pre-capitalist, "primitive," or "tribal" economies were not market-integrated but did, in fact, have subjects/agents who made calculations about costs and exchange rates in barter and reciprocity transactions as a normal part of daily economic life. It was precisely regarding those performances and their results that selective neoclassical analysis was employed despite its European capitalist origins. My main complaint against Dalton and the substantivists was their lack of empirical demonstration of their assertions about the inappropriate or misleading nature of doing so. My assessment was that their critiques were ideologically, not scientifically, grounded.

From today's perspective, the primary benefit to me from participating in the formalist-substantivist controversy between 1966 and 1974 was to enable me to clarify the meaning of "economic" and to better understand the articulation and interpenetration of that field of activity with other fields in given sociocultural formations, that is, how it simultaneously functioned inside and outside non-economic fields. Its "inside functioning" demanded hard, systematic, quantitative economic analysis to justify assertions like "It's the economy, stupid." But, its outside functioning in its enveloping matrix of sociocultural relations was also constitutive of its inside functioning. Marx's dialectical method, and Godelier's skillful use of it, provided the theoretical and conceptual elements of an approach that resolved the dead-end standoff represented by the formalist-substantivist controversy (Godelier 1967; cf. Cook 1969:399–401).

Another benefit to me was to focus my attention on household decision-making regarding participation in reciprocal and redistributive activities in addition to market activities. The more that I looked at this mix of activities in Oaxaca the more convinced I became that decision-making was the same. Allocations of labor within the household, dispositions of products, expenditures on goods and services, savings and investment, and consumption involved the same deliberative and prudently rational decision-making. This cross-cut the division between in-kind and cash-mediated transactions and activities.

Nutini and the "Camelot" Fiasco

One of the worst moments in my years at Pitt occurred in 1965 at the Denver meeting of the American Anthropological Association. I was seated next to Nutini during the main convocation when Marvin Harris from the podium launched into a tirade against the infamous "Camelot" project and Nutini's role in it. Nutini must have known what was about to take place but I did not have a clue; it was disconcerting.

Nutini, a person of calm, serious demeanor, was visibly shaken probably because he knew (as I learned later) that he had been set-up to take a hit from a spurned ex-lover who was the daughter of the president of the University of Chile and, a graduate student of Harris' at Columbia. Nutini, who aristocratically always thought himself to be above politics and was intellectually apolitical, was presented with an opportunity to get a free trip to his home country of Chile by political science professor at Pitt, Rex Hopper, who was deeply involved in the notorious US Army counterinsurgency project known as Camelot.

Apparently all Nutini had to do in return was spread the word among Chilean academics about the availability of social science research funds from the US government. He did so without specifying the actual source of the funding which he knew would be the kiss of death. He was reportedly intentionally deceptive in specifying the National Science Foundation as one funding source. Only a highbrow, apolitical type like Nutini – who saw himself above the fray – could get into such a mess for purely selfish reasons. Ximena Bunster years later, when she was a visiting faculty member at UConn, confirmed to me her complicity with Harris in exposing Nutini's *faux pas*.

After that traumatic day in Denver my relationship with Nutini changed. We still carried on normally as advisor and advisee but when the time came to choose between sites in the 1965 summer field school in Mexico earlier that year, I had already opted to go with the Stanford group to Oaxaca rather than with the Pitt group, under Nutini, to Puebla. Nutini accepted this as reasonable given my interest in Malinowski's work on Oaxaca markets. Also, he was helpful and did everything possible to expedite my dissertation defense and approval process in 1967 – and successfully so. For my part, I was fortunate to get a one year extension on my research in Oaxaca through my affiliation with Ralph Beals' project and, by so doing, avoided having to attend 1968 graduation ceremonies at Pitt, so my degree was awarded in absentia. I never went back.

In the early summer of 1965 before the field schools were to begin in Puebla and Oaxaca, I met Nutini in Mexico City where he introduced me to some fine restaurants and, most importantly, to key members of the anthropology establishment and key archival depositories. He personally introduced me to Angel Palerm, Gonzalo Aguirre Beltran, Wigberto Jimenez Moreno, Ignacio Bernal, Fernando Cámara, Mercedes Olivera, Andrés Medina, and to his close friend, Pedro Carrasco with whom I developed a lasting relationship. He also introduced me to the archives at *Asuntos Agrarios* and the *Archivo General de la Nación* which he knew intimately.

Nutini took me to lunch at the *Restaurant Prendes* (located on Calle 16 de septiembre about two blocks south of the Alameda on the way to the Zócalo) which was especially interesting, not only for its superior menu (best *coctél de camarón* and *huachinango al mojo de ajo* anywhere) and décor (murals and photos on the walls) but because it was a meeting place during siesta time for high government functionaries, members of the intelligentsia, and their "secretaries." He also invited me to a *cena* at the home (in Polanco I think) of his first wife's French-Mexican family in which *chiles rellenos* stuffed with *queso de Chihuahua* were served. Delicious, but still not as good as *chiles en nogada* I would later enjoy in Oaxaca and at the *Hostería de Santo Domingo* in Mexico City. Nutini also introduced me to two of Mexico City's best bookstores: *Hermanos Porrua* and *Antigua Librería Robredo*. Later on my favorites also included *Librería El Sotano* and *Librería Gandhi*. In sum, I owe a big debt of gratitude to Nutini as a teacher and counselor.

UCLA or Michigan State?

As my two-year period of dissertation and postdoctoral fieldwork in Oaxaca was approaching its end in 1968, the issue of my future employment became pressing. Hilda had given birth to our third child, a daughter Lisa, in June so family considerations weighed heavily on my job choice. The obvious choice, since I was already on the UCLA payroll, was to seek a tenure-track appointment there. In the meantime, Leonard Kasdan, my professor at Pittsburgh, had taken a new job in the Anthropology Department at Michigan State University in East Lansing. He contacted me about a job opening at Michigan State. I traveled there for to give a talk on my research in Oaxaca and, shortly thereafter, was offered a tenure-track assistant professorship.

The UCLA possibility was still open at that time and, if an offer had been made without a site visit, I probably would have accepted it. However, it became clear that there was no way to transition from Research Associate to Assistant Professor on the UCLA payroll without the usual delivery of a paper and evaluation from future possible colleagues. This was made clear to me in correspondence with Walter Goldschmidt who was the department head. I was short on money and did not want to borrow from Beals (which he offered) to pay for my flight to LA – which I would have had to do since the UCLA bureaucracy could not function quickly enough to get a travel advance processed for me. At the time, I had never been to California and moving there would have meant that both Hilda and I would have been as equally distant from family and familiar places as we had been for almost three years in Mexico. So, I accepted the job at Michigan State.

We left Oaxaca in August of 1968 in a VW microbus loaded to the brim and headed to the border via a route that took us through the mountains of the Huasteca through Veracruz and then to Ciudad Victoria, Tamaulipas and, finally to Matamoros-Brownsville on highway 101 through the forsaken and isolated highway stop of San Fernando. We were lucky to arrive at a hotel in Ciudad Victoria that evening because on a slick road between Ciudad Valles and Ciudad Mante the overloaded VW bus spun out and smashed into a large boulder precisely on the side where the doors opened.

Fortunately, we were all only bruised and shaken, and not seriously injured. The boulder had prevented the vehicle from turning over and rolling down a steep ravine. The VW had not sustained any additional damage so we were able to continue our journey to the day's destination – Ciudad Victoria. After a night in a quite nice hotel, we left the following morning for the US border through San Fernando and into Matamoros by late afternoon.

Then came the necessary border crossing which I knew would be no picnic – especially after two years of residence in Oaxaca and with a damaged, fully-loaded vehicle. I had carefully loaded the bus in Oaxaca so that various artifacts of Pre-Hispanic origin were wrapped and buried deep in boxes at the bottom of the load. I was counting on Mexican customs being lenient once realizing my family situation, including a two-month old baby, and the damage to the vehicle – and allowing me to pass to the other side of the bridge without full inspection. They did a cursory check of luggage and a few boxes but, as I expected, they waved us through without much delay.

Then came the US Immigration checkpoint and an especially excruciating experience with US Immigration officers. First, they gave Hilda a hard time viewing her as a possible Mexican citizen feigning Puerto Rican identity and US citizenship. One officer who considered himself an expert in Latino identities, and had been posted in Puerto Rico, went through a checklist of questions which would demonstrate to his satisfaction that she was, indeed, a Puerto Rican – questions that would elicit answers like *público* (a Puerto Rican term for inter-city taxi), *guagua* (PR term for bus), and *habichuelas* (PR term for frijoles). She passed the exam.

Next came the property search. The INS officers agreed that my loaded VW minibus, a favorite among Hippie drug smugglers, had to be thoroughly unloaded and searched – especially since we had spent two years in Oaxaca, the land of hallucinogenic mushrooms and world-class marijuana. Remember: the side doors if the minibus had been smashed in the accident and could not be opened. Whereas the Mexican officials had been compassionate, their US counterparts insisted on going by the book. All of our possessions, including many boxes full of research files, had to be pulled out by me for inspection through the back lift-window – in 100 degree plus deep south Texas humid heat. At the bottom of the load, I had carefully packed several prize pieces of pre-Hispanic Zapotec ceramics; an inspector opened the box and pulled out every piece and asked me what they were. I said they were just examples of old Mexican pottery that had only sentimental value. He could have cared less because he was looking for plastic bags of pot that might have been stashed inside them.

When the minibus was completely unloaded, its contents strewn everywhere on the unloading tables, the INS officers finally released us into the welcoming city of Brownsville – but not before I had to repack everything without their assistance. Finally, by seven in the evening we had managed to check into an air conditioned motel where we all enjoyed the swimming pool. The next morning Hilda and the kids boarded a plane in Brownvsille for Alabama to stay with my parents for a few days until I arrived in the damaged VW bus and prepared for the long drive to Michigan.

CHAPTER 3

Appointment to the Professoriate: Negotiating the Labyrinth at a Midwestern Megaversity

In late August 1968 I, Hilda and our children (Dana, Scott, and Lisa) moved into a rental house on MAC Avenue in East Lansing which was only two blocks from the central business district and the campus. Many graduate students were living nearby in rental houses and were constant visitors – especially attracted by our youngest Oaxaca-born daughter, Lisa Veronica, who was quite the charmer. The campus was immense with many impressive modern and older buildings and very well land-scaped with an impressive mix of flower beds, shrubbery and trees. It had a student population of 42,000, and the physical plant and bureaucratic management was state of the art. MSU functioned like a large multinational corporate enterprise – which, in fact, is what it was. It had, among other things, a hotel management school with an operating hotel, an eighteen-hole golf course, and an impressive international program and foreign student constituency heavily involved with the schools of agriculture, education, communication, and the large department of agricultural economics; and a typical range of departments in the sciences, humanities, and social sciences. The president at the time was Clifton Wharton, a well-known agricultural development economist from the Rockefeller Foundation, who happened to have been an associate of Raymond Firth in development circles in southeast Asia.

During my second year there, the anthropology department invited Raymond Firth to campus as a guest speaker. President Wharton was delighted to support this initiative, and Firth was a guest on campus for a few days. He was a likable man, if rather guarded in conversations. I accompanied him during his official visit with President Wharton and was most impressed by Wharton's articulate discussion of development economics and subsistence agriculture. I was able to talk with Firth about the problem with the original English version of the Malinowski Oaxaca markets manuscript and field notes, and the formalist-substantivist controversy. I learned that he had conferred with Ralph Beals regarding the disposition of Malinowski's Oaxaca papers but that they had left the matter in the hands of Yale and Malinowski's heirs. Regarding the formalist-substantivist controversy my impression from our conversation was that, at the time, he considered it to be a minor squabble among American cultural anthropologists. Indeed, he made no direct reference to it in his essay on "Themes in Economic Anthropology" published just two years before our conversation took place (Firth 1967). The issues raised in the controversy, and relevant early publications by American cultural anthropologists, were a major concern of Frankenberg's and Cohen's essays in the edited volume that Firth's essay introduced (Firth, ed. 1967). Unfortunately, my 1966 article was published too late to be referenced in the British discussion, and was written before Firth's book was published, so I had written it uninformed by that discussion. My follow-up article on the controversy, however, did include references to discussions in Firth's book (Cook 1969).

My appointment at MSU was to fill a position previously occupied by Louis Faron who moved on to a position in the Pittsburgh department and then to SUNY-Stony Brook. Since Faron was a specialist in the Indians of South America, I was responsible for teaching the course he had developed, using a textbook he had co-authored (Steward and Faron 1959). I had an interest in the topic, but limited knowledge, although I had acquired a complete set of the *Handbook of South American Indians* while at Pitt. Between consulting Steward and Faron's textbook and the *Handbook* I managed to cobble together a course which had a fairly large enrollment of thirty-five to forty undergraduates and graduate students.

I devoted a lot of time to lecturing about the only two ethnic groups I knew anything about, the Nambicuara and the Sirionó, thanks to research papers I had done at Pitt. I remember having among my students a man in his 40s who, it turns out, had spent years in Amazonia as a missionary. He had first-hand knowledge of many indigenous peoples, so I was quite happy to allow him to ask and answer his own questions – to the edification of all of us. That is one of the few courses I ever taught where I felt somewhat like the proverbial "fish out of water." There is always a point when you cannot fully answer questions posed to you by students when you are dealing with materials outside the range of your own ethnographic experience and expertise.

I had several graduate students at Michigan State, two of whom, Yván Bretón from Quebec and Alice Littlefield, completed their doctoral dissertations under my direction. A third, Sonia Ruíz was my doctoral student but, when I left MSU for UConn, she completed her unique dissertation on street beggars (limosneros) in San Cristóbal de las Casas in the Mexican state of Chiapas, under the direction of Horacio Fabrega. Sonia, a talented artist and photographer, afterwards became a member of the faculty at the University of Puerto Rico-Mayagüez, where she has remained to this day. Bretón conducted fieldwork on the artisan fishing industry on the Yucatan coast in the community of Chabihau in summer field school, and then did his dissertation research in fishing communities near Cumaná in the Paria peninsula of Sucre state in Venezuela. Littlefield worked in Yucatan on the putting-out system in the hammock industry based in the community of Cacalchén. Her dissertation, a pioneering study of the topic, was translated into Spanish and published in Mexico by the *Instituto Nacional Indigenista* (Littlefield 1976). She would later work as a research associate on my NSF project (OVSIP) in Oaxaca.

During the fall semester of 1970, the Mexican anthropologist, Fernando Cámara Barbachano, was invited to East Lansing as a visiting professor. At the time, Cámara was heading the Social Anthropology Department at the School of Anthropology at the National Institute of Anthropology and History in Mexico City, and was curating an indigenous Mexican cultural exhibition which was set-up for public display at the Michigan State University museum.To his dismay and ours, Don Fernando was poorly received by immigration officers at the Detroit airport; his luggage was examined and he was apparently strip-searched for narcotics in an obvious case of ethnic profiling. The overzealous treatment of Cámara by US Immigration officers did not sit well with his prickly, dramatic personality but we were finally able to pacify him and soothe his bruised ego.

Cámara, Joe Spielberg, and I organized and taught a well-attended joint graduate seminar on Mexican social anthropology that fall. Among our graduate students was Luís Berruecos who had been a *licenciatura* student of Cámara's at the School of Anthropology in Mexico City. Cámara knew his subject well and was a very articulate lecturer but, as we found out, was mercilessly sarcastic in his treatment of his students. He interrupted Berrueco's presentation of his term paper several times to correct him in the most disparaging way possible. Berruecos, the son of a prominent audiologist, had a privileged upbringing in a luxurious home in Lomas de Chapultepec – adorned with original works by Diego Rivera and tiered gardens with a spectacular night-time view of Mexico City (which Spielberg and I later enjoyed as guests at a sumptuous late-evening *cena* with the Berruecos family) – so he was flustered but not threatened by Camara's withering criticism.

During the summer of 1970 we conducted a Summer Field School in Yucatán, where Cámara was born and had many relatives. Before arriving in Yucatan, Spielberg and I visited Cámara in his offices at INAH in Mexico City, and from there we accompanied him to a *cena* in his well-appointed home in the San Gerónimo suburb. It was obvious from the exterior and interior décor of his home that many prize pre-Hispanic and colonial artifacts had never made it into the inventory of the INAH museum. As we got out of the car, Cámara proudly pointed to the house of his next door neighbor, Luís Echeverría, who was still Interior Minister but as of December 1 would be President of Mexico. Cámara was Echeverria's compadre, and fully expected to be upgraded to a higher position in INAH of the cultural sub-secretariat after the inauguration. Unfortunately, it did not work out that way; as fallout from the Tlatelolco massacre the INAH-ENAH system was reorganized and Cámara was demoted to a lesser position in the bureaucracy. Not even his special relationship to the Presidente could save him from the popular backlash in Mexico against the abuse of executive power (Cook 2017c).

In the fall of 1970, I was invited to the University of British Columbia by Cyril Belshaw who was then chair of the anthropology department. Belshaw was a very gracious host, and I was accommodated in the Faculty Club which had a room-and-board set-up – and a nice bar. The purpose of the trip was to give a public lecture and to be screened for a faculty appointment. I had met Cyril previously at a professional conference and used his well-written 1965 introductory textbook *Traditional Exchange and Modern Markets* (1965) in my courses on economic anthropology. The paper I presented at UBC on the "Productionist Approach" was essentially a version of my 1969 article proposing a theoretical emphasis on production (as opposed to exchange, consumption, and distribution) as the central economic process. This approach, I argued, would help us to discern the essential aspects of what Belshaw (1965) defined as the "market principle," to isolate "traditional" from "modern" aspects of that principle, and to analyze their respective roles in economies of the contemporary Third World (Cook 1969:398–399)

A member of the department took me on a tour across the Burrard Inlet to the mountainside roads in residential West Vancouver where I felt that the vehicle I was riding in was surely going to flip-over and roll back down the steeply sloped streets. The members of the department all loved the outdoor life style and mountainous ambience of the campus, located on an elevated peninsula, with a spectacular view of sea and mountains. Vancouver's Chinatown was extensive and had many excellent restaurants. Belshaw was probably interested in hiring me because he knew that I was not totally hostile to the neoclassical tradition in economics practiced by his dad and by his mentor, Raymond Firth, and sensed that my emphasis on production was, in fact, compatible with that tradition. Being an astute observer of international trends, I think he also surmised that my turn toward Marxist discourse, that was underway in the social sciences across the world in those years, would have provided the UBC department with some needed participation in that increasingly popular current of thought. More importantly, the department faculty at the time lacked a specialist in Latin American Studies, Mexican Studies, or Latino Studies, so I would have met their needs in that sense as well. However, I felt uncomfortable in that spectacular environment, so far from Puerto Rico and Mexico, and decided not to consider a position there.

In 1979, everyone in the world of anthropology was either shocked or titillated by Belshaw's imprisonment and trial for allegedly murdering his wife at a Swiss ski resort (Gee 2019; Godfrey 1981). After all, at the time, he was one of the world's most accomplished anthropologists with a substantial bibliography. After receiving his doctorate at the London School of Economics in 1949 under the direction of Raymond Firth, he conducted extensive field work in New Guinea, Fiji and Northern British Columbia and, among other positions, served with UNESCO, the UN Bureau of Social Affairs, the International Social Science Council, as President of the International Union of Anthropological and Ethnological Sciences, as editor of *Current Anthropology*, as an Honorary Life Member of the Royal Anthropological Institute, an Honorary Fellow of the Association for Social Anthropology in Oceania (ASAO) and as a Fellow of the Royal Society of Canada. So, quite a scandal, indeed, for the staid world of academic anthropology involving one of its best-known practitioners.

Back East to New England: Anthropology, Puerto Rican, and Latin American Studies at the University of Connecticut

A major factor in my move from Michigan to Connecticut was that it took us much closer to Puerto Rico's two island homelands – the Caribbean island itself and the diaspora island of Manhattan. Moreover, I had never been to New England, was flattered by the University of Connecticut anthropology department's interest in recruiting me, and in its program potential. Also, I was attracted by the relatively small size and somewhat rustic, archaic, provincial nature of the UConn campus – in sharp contrast with the huge, bureaucratically efficient, highly corporate, heavily internationalized, megaversity that was MSU.

So, we moved to Connecticut which Hilda found to be suited to furthering her career in bilingual education. She was able to combine teaching in the Migratory Children's Program and the public school system with study for an MA degree at Eastern Connecticut State University and, later, for an additional graduate degree at the University of Connecticut School of Education. I, of course, was able to resume my interest in Puerto Rican studies without lessening my involvement in Mexican studies and economic anthropology. We also benefitted from the fact that Puerto Rico was only three-hours away on non-stop flights from Hartford. In the 1980s we decided to acquire a small farm property in Yabucoa (Barrio Guayabota) not far from the properties of Hilda's mother and maternal relatives; we went there regularly over a twelve-year period during the Christmas-New Year's break and, when possible, during the summer. Maintenance was rather costly, if tax deductible thanks to our cultivation of minor citrus and root crops (yautia and malanga), as well as bananas and plantains. It was a nice retreat over a period of twelve years but we finally decided that it was not ideal for retirement purposes. I still remember with fondness the daiquiris I fashioned with brown sugar and the unique *limón chivo*, an especially juicy, large wrinkled variety of lemon-lime citrus that grew on our farm.

The existential contrast between East Lansing and Storrs was stunning across the board. The flatness and long, straight roads of the Michigan landscape were replaced by the hills and narrow, winding roads of Connecticut. In terms of the rural-urban continuum, they seemed to represent polar opposites. Dairy cows grazed in pastures on the fringes of the UConn campus and the nearest urban area was the town of Willimantic 7 miles distant. But only 15 miles or so distant from Storrs there was direct access to a complex network of high-speed turnpikes and parkways that connected to a maze of populated places in many directions, and of all sizes and levels of affluence.

Faculty in East Lansing lived dispersed in neighborhoods near the campus or in outlying subdivisions, whereas the faculty in Storrs lived mostly in housing dispersed in woodlands and colonial-origin villages in every direction, and typically miles away, from the campus. Department head, Norm Chance, for example, lived several miles from campus in a modern wood and glass-wrapped home located on a heavily wooded lot on a winding paved road accessible only by a long gravel driveway. Jim Faris lived in a rambling old farmhouse with a long gravel driveway off a paved country road on property with outbuildings, one of which had housed the folk singer Joan Collins; it was located a few miles south of campus toward the Mountain Dairy farm and Willimantic. Seth Leacock lived in a relatively new two-story Cape Cod style home down a narrow road in the deep forest of Chaplin, a dispersed rural community about 12 miles or so from Storrs. Denny Nash lived in a slightly remodeled colonial-style carriage house on the property of a larger two-story main house in the village of Mansfield Center located 3 or 4 miles down the road from Storrs to Willimantic. By contrast, the historian, Hugh Hamill, lived in one of the larger colonial-style farm "mansions" not far from Denny Nash's carriage house.

Most of these hearty UConn academics chopped and stacked wood to burn in their fireplaces or stoves during the winter. A bucolic academic utopia, indeed, except in the winter months when ice, snow, and wind made negotiating the roads and walkways on the campus itself dangerous and intimidating – not to speak of getting to campus from remote residences on hilly, icy, winding roads with stone walls or thick-trunked trees along the roadsides awaiting vehicles that lose control. Night-time travel was especially risky due to plentiful deer liable to leap in front of your car seemingly out of nowhere. And then there are the thick fogs that roll in without warning to drastically decrease visibility.

As it turned out, my appointment at the University of Connecticut in the Department of Anthropology might well have been joint with Latin American Studies and Puerto Rican Studies. I spent nearly a decade in directing those two programs and the rest of my years involved in them from my base as a member of the anthropology faculty. In retrospect, however, I think I was recruited by the UConn department as much for my specialization in economic anthropology as for my culture area involvement. Ellen Antler, a graduate student member of the departmental search committee, had supported my recruitment on the basis of her own specialization in the field of economic anthropology for her doctoral dissertation (Antler 1982).

Also, a factor that surely supported my hire was the materialist orientation of the sociocultural program at the time under the headship of Norman Chance. He, a neophyte Chinese specialist, together with Jim Faris and Ben Magubane, both Africanists, were promoting the development of a program attuned to radical perspectives emerging from the Third World and drawing upon radical thought from the United States and Europe. My background and areas of specialization complemented theirs.

Outstanding Graduate Students

Our graduate students came from diverse backgrounds. A few stand out in my memory bank, and will be discussed below in alphabetical order. I maintained ties with several of them after their dissertations were completed, and collaborated with a few like Leigh Binford and Jorge Hernández-Díaz in my Mexican research. I have benefitted over the years from reading the publications by these two and, also, those by Jim Wessman and Bill Roseberry. Roseberry's 1996 essay "The Unbearable

Lightness of Anthropology" has proved especially helpful in thinking about my career in anthropology, and his 1989 book *Anthropologies and Histories* greatly influenced my thinking about the economy/culture interface.

Leigh Binford was a workaholic as a student and has recently retired as a tenured professor in the CUNY system. He has an unusual combination of skills, both qualitative and quantitative, and an independent streak to follow his own set course. His work on my Oaxaca project in 1979–1980 resulted in a meticulous time and motion study of brickmaking in a periurban village and gave him the opportunity to learn Spanish which was essential for the conduct of his dissertation fieldwork on the sugar industry in Oaxaca's Isthmus of Tehuantepec – a punishingly hot and windy place that I tried to persuade him to avoid. But he persisted and produced a rigorous and long overdue study of land tenure and sugar cane production in that inhospitable setting.

I passed through the Isthmus on several trips to the Guatemalan border in the 1970s for document-renewal purposes since academic researchers in Mexico were best advised to get tourist permits, rather than longer work permits which involved more bureaucratic hassles. Tourist permits had to be renewed at either border every six months. I had encountered many female metate traders or regatonas-*viajeras* (Cook 1968:257–258; Chiñas 1976) from the Isthmus in the Oaxaca valley marketplaces where they regularly traveled to buy metates for resale in the Isthmus where metates were not produced. They were striking in appearance, playfully aggressive, tough-minded hagglers, and identifiable either as *Juchitecas* (from Juchitán) or *Tejuanas* (from Tehuantepec) according to their different styles of native apparel. I was able to observe their sales activities in Isthmus markets a few times (they referred to me as a güero or white guy) and on, at least, one occasion in jest I was invited to "mezclar las sangre" (i.e., "mix blood" via mating).

On one of our family trips to the Guatemalan border there was an obligatory credentials checkpoint in the Isthmus at the properly named La Ventosa ("Windy place"). I rolled down the windows of my vehicle, had all of my documents in my hand to present to the officer in charge, and in the attempted hand-over they were all blown away in a sudden wind gust. I was simultaneously shocked and concerned – knowing full well that new documents would require time and a hefty *mordida* (bribe), even if I could have them processed locally. Standing off to one side was a peasant carrying a sack who ambled over and told me that he had spied the ultimate destination of our blown-away documents, among literally hundreds of pieces of paper stuck to the undergrowth surrounding the windy station. He said he would retrieve them in exchange for a lift to a destination further south along the highway. I was pleased to oblige him and the documents were retrieved.

There were only two places in the Isthmus that attracted me: an excellent seafood restaurant in Salina Cruz and the Huave peninsula – a totally unique, sand-duned homeland of the Huave-speaking fishers and artisans. I went to that unique place on two occasions – once in the hope that Pierre Bernier, Bretón's MA student from Laval who had entered our doctoral program, would choose it as a site for his doctoral dissertation fieldwork; and, on another occasion, with a delegation from FONART to explore craft production there. They are excellent weavers and mask makers. I still have several ceremonial masks acquired from Huave artisans that are strikingly fashioned from hand-carved wood in unique combination with tortoise shells and animal hair. Disappointingly, Bernier opted for Puerto Escondido instead of the Huave peninsula as a fieldwork site but returned to Quebec before he finished his dissertation research.

The UConn Anthropology Department in Manchester Hall had a library room with a long couch and there, as well as in the nearby men's room, there were often signs (e.g., toothpaste droppings, toothbrushes, shaving cream) in the 1970s that we had an overnight camper. It was clearly one of our graduate students and Leigh Binford recently confided to me that, as I had always suspected, it was him. He came to us via Memphis State and Long Beach State from a background in Memphis where his dad was a successful dentist. Leigh, like me, learned to play golf when he was growing up, and we played together once or twice in Connecticut during our period of collaboration on the *Obliging Need* project. He regularly hit his drives farther and straighter than I did.

A few years earlier, however, Leigh did not display many visible signs of an upper-middle-class upbringing – he was a little rough around the edges.

At some point, his widowed mom came to visit, a very nice, soft-spoken lady concerned for her wayward son's welfare. I lied and assured her that there was no need for her concern about Leigh. If I recall properly, he earned an MA degree at Long Beach State where he had specialized in Melanesia.

At some point, Leigh asked me to accompany him to buy his first car – perhaps as a co-signer. I remember the salesman in a Hartford dealership asking Leigh for his credit card to start the process – and, of course, Leigh did not have one (possibly not atypical of unmarried students in those years). He led life very simply. Truly Spartan- or, actually, California Hippie-like. In 1979–1980 when Leigh started working for my project, I had arranged room and board for him in a large multi-room house of a widow, with a very attractive teenage daughter, in Santa Lucia del Camino. It was certainly a more comfortable lodging for Leigh than the department library in Manchester hall.

During that period, Leigh accompanied me on a trip in my manual four-wheel drive Jeep Cherokee into the mountains north of Oaxaca to the Zapotec community of Yalalag where we spent the night. We saw a lot of sights along the way, including a few exotic-looking *trapiches* (sugar cane mills) in the deep valleys (which I hoped would tweak Leigh's interest) and were listening to a new Donna Summers' cassette full-blast as we traveled. Truly surrealistic. We completed a full circle on the compass (N – E – S – W) on that trip, passing through Ayutla in Mixe territory and then back through San Lorenzo Albarradas and down to the Valley through Mitla. Quite a trip!

In the early period of the 1980s when I was engaged in the analysis of the large qualitative and quantitative household survey data set collected during my Oaxaca Valley project between 1977 and 1980, I needed to hire someone to do the computer analysis of the already coded and digitized data set. Ron Rohner, a colleague in the department, recommended Leigh Binford as one who could do the job since he had worked on one of his projects requiring quantitative analysis. I was quite surprised since I had no inkling of Leigh's abilities with computer programming and data analysis. I immediately put him back on the project payroll, and the result was a full and stimulating collaboration and two publications (Cook and Binford 1990, 1991).

Later on Leigh followed his own instincts, and against my advice once again, pursued his interest in the violent politics of El Salvador. Later, on the faculty of the University of Puebla in Mexico, he became a specialist in the understudied and policy-relevant problem of migrant remittances and temporary foreign worker programs with special reference to Mexico's relationship with Canada. On the flyleaf of a complimentary copy of his very well received book on this topic Leigh wrote: "For good and/or bad this definitely has the mark you left on me" (Binford 2013). Well expressed ambivalence.

When I recently viewed the acclaimed Mexican movie *Roma* I immediately thought about another of my graduate students, Mary Goldsmith. She had done her undergraduate degree at American University so we had something in common. She actually had taken courses with the same professors I had years before she studied there. She also had an interest in Mexico. I do not remember how she acquired it but I think she never considered doing her doctoral dissertation research anywhere else. She developed an interest in researching the status of women with a focus on domestic servants and left for Mexico to begin her research. I do not think she needed to worry especially about being dependent on grants to fund her research but she may have successfully applied for funding of some sort. I do not recall. Her widowed mom lived in Fort Lauderdale, Florida and, I think, was able to help Mary out financially. In any case Mary rented an apartment in or near Colonia Roma in Mexico City and began her dissertation research on domestic servants. Hence the double connection to the movie.

Among other accomplishments, Mary became a friend and colleague of Marta Lamas, one of Mexico City's prominent feminists and collaborated in various projects related to that movement as she conducted her research in the city and surrounding countryside. Her project expanded from a contemporary ethnographic study to encompass the topic of female domestic servants throughout Mexican history. It took her years to finish and it was a huge tome when completed. Meanwhile, she had married, Manuel Rimada, a native of Torreón, Coahuila who was a free-lance commercial artist and sometimes *guionista* (scriptwriter) with whom she had two sons. She had academic jobs before she completed her dissertation entitled *Female Household Workers in the Mexico City Metropolitan Area* in 1990.

Afterwards, she secured a permanent position on the faculty of the *Universidad Aútonoma Metropolitana* (UAM) at its Xochimilco campus, where she was (and is) a colleague of Eli Bartra in the Department of Politics and Culture in the program *"Mujer, Identidad y Poder"* (Women, Identity and Power). She is very close to the domestic workers from the *Sindicato Nacional de Trabajadoras y Trabajadores del Hogar* who have used the Roma film as a pedagogical tool. She was involved with the *Sindicato* in securing a ruling by the Mexican Supreme Court that recognizes the constitutional right of domestic workers to social security (IMSS) and to reforms in labor legislation.

Before she and Manuel had children, I visited them a few times in their Mexico City apartment. On one occasion, I gave a talk on my Oaxaca research at UAM-Xochimilco at Mary's (and Eli's) invitation. That was one of the occasions that I used a version of my commodity economy flow schematic as the basis for a sort of rambling, extemporaneous presentation which, I think, was successful. On another occasion we attended a *Vela*, an Isthmus Zapotec patron saint's celebration, with food, drink (*mezcal* and *aguardiente*) and music, sponsored by a *mayordomo* and including a flower-crowned queen (*"reina"*) who was the fiancé of Mary Goldsmith's nephew. In attendance were a few hundred guests in full traditional regalia (women with *huipiles,* men with *guayaberas*). It was held in a ballroom of the María Isabel Sheraton hotel and was quite an affair.

Mary has done very well in the labyrinth of Mexican academia, learning how to negotiate her way through all the bureaucratic hurdles including credential exams and peer-panel interviews to obtain permanent employment. She did it the best way you can – by self-Mexicanization and marrying-in. She is also known as María Rosaria Goldsmith.

I first met Jorge Hernández-Díaz in the 1970s when he was a *licenciatura* candidate in a program initiated and operated by the *Instituto de Investigaciones Sociales* in UNAM (in Mexico City) at UABJO in Oaxaca City. The program known as the *Programa único para la Formación de Investigadores y Profesores en Ciencias Sociales* transitioned into the new *Instituto de Investigaciones Sociológicas* at UABJO in 1980. Jorge was one of fifteen students who participated in this very selective program and received their *licenciaturas* (Benítez Zenteno, ed. 1980). I had served as advisor (*asesor*) for the thesis of Fausto Díaz Móntes on the mezcal industry. He worked for a time on my NSF-funded project but opted for a career in political science rather than anthropology. He graduated with a doctorate from Notre Dame and, in the early 1990s, when I directed the Latin American Studies Center, I invited him to come to UConn as a visiting Tinker Fellow. Later he returned to Oaxaca and the *Instituto,* became an elected member of the state legislature, and then served as *Presidente Municipal* of his native municipio of Tlacolula.

Many of Fausto's and Jorge's colleagues, as new *licenciados,* comprised the teaching and research staff of the *Instituto* established in 1980. The genius of their training program was its intent to decentralize and regionalize social science research in Mexico, and to promote the training of indigenous people as university-based academic social scientists. It was unattached to the *indigenista* bureaucracy and was free to set and pursue its own programmatic agenda. I wholeheartedly supported this enlightened effort and still do, and give credit to the Mexico City-based social science establishment for that effort. Both Fausto, who was born and raised in the Zapotec town of Tlacolula and Jorge, who was born and raised in a Zapotec village in the district of Etla, fit the bill perfectly.

When I taught at the *Instituto* as a Fulbright Academic Specialist in 1987 Jorge was director and had already several publications including an excellent book on the Chatino coffee industry (1987). I got to know him very well at that time and we began to discuss the possibility of his coming to UConn for his doctorate. He was able to arrange a leave of absence from his faculty position at UABJO and had secured funding from the Fulbright-Laspau program, the *Universidad Autónoma Benito Júarez de Oaxaca,* and the University of Connecticut for his doctoral studies.

After completing his coursework in 1990, and since he already had conducted ethnographic fieldwork in Oaxaca and had a substantial corpus of ethnographic data, Jorge decided, with my encouragement, to write a library dissertation that did not require additional fieldwork. Before Jorge completed his dissertation in 1991 we drove together to visit Yván Bretón at Laval University in Quebec City and on his farm outside the city. Jorge and I stayed, for a night, in the historic hotel, the Chateau Frontenac, overlooking the St. Lawrence River. It was Jorge's first visit to Canada.

I remember that we had a delay at the border on our return trip due to US Customs-Immigration officers doing "background checks" related to his student visa. Jorge's dissertation deceptively entitled "Ethnic and Class Relations in Oaxaca, Mexico" encompassed, in fact, much more. It was a comprehensive history and critical rethinking of the entire ideological superstructure of *indigenismo* which had dominated policy-making and academic approaches to mestizo nation-building and ethno-class relations in late nineteenth-century and post-revolutionary Mexico down to the present (Hernández-Díaz 1991).

Through many subsequent publications on this theme, many embodying new ethnographic research, Jorge has become Oaxaca's leading social anthropologists. He is also recognized as one of Mexico's most productive and influential voices on constitutional issues of citizenship status and rights for indigenous people in the Mexico or what he refers to as "differential citizenships in a multicultural state" (Hernández-Díaz, ed. 2007). Most recently his research and writing have focused on the topic of crafts and craftspeople, and has brought to light facts and nuances missed by other specialists who have explored the same terrain. In the first paragraph of the acknowledgments section of his latest book for which I wrote a prologue (Hernández-Díaz 2016) Jorge wrote: "To my friend and teacher Scott Cook I owe my interest in the small-scale production of commodities. While I have not followed all of his footsteps, and I doubt that he agrees with my ideas, I will always be grateful for his critical observations, for his moral support and the friendship that he has provided to me." ("A mi amigo y maestro Scott Cook le debo el interés por lo que sucede con la producción de mercancías en pequeña escala. Aunque no he seguido del todo sus pasos, y dudo que él coincida con mis ideas, le estoy siempre agradecido por sus observaciones críticas, por su apoyo moral y la amistad que me ha brindado.") I have been educated about ethno-political movements in Oaxaca and their national repercussions by reading Jorge's work, and he has served as my major source of information about these and other issues since I last visited him in Oaxaca in 2004.

William (Bill) Roseberry, who came to UConn from Southern Methodist University via Little Rock, Arkansas, is memorable for his quiet, soft-spoken demeanor and ferocious intellect. He was a naturally critical thinker who took a while to find his bearings but, once he did, it was full-steam ahead. In my correspondence with him during his dissertation fieldwork period in Venezuela it became clear to me that he preferred archival work to fieldwork; he did both but excelled at the former. I had no problem with that. He was never keen to do my kind of economy-focused, analytical ethnography but few of my students were. In my estimation, Bill was going to thrive as an interpreter/critic of archival material and publications, and as an original researcher of areas of human activity which were best approached through the combined methods of social history and anthropological political economy.

One memorable episode I experienced with Bill occurred on a Saturday in a late spring of his second year at UConn. I told him that I was attempting to build a fence on the back of my property in Willimantic and, in characteristic southwestern-friendly fashion, he volunteered to help out. He showed up at my house early and we set to work digging holes for the fence posts and nailing sections of an interleaved cedar fence to them. It was hot and we stopped occasionally to drink beer. At one point, I noticed two of my male neighbors approaching our work site from different directions – both were retired gentlemen; one lived next door and was walking from his yard into mine, and the other lived two houses up the street and was approaching down an alleyway running behind all of our lots. I knew that there was a longtime feud between the two of them dating from their careers together in the Connecticut Light and Power Company – one as supervisor of the other (my next door neighbor). Both were fairly cantankerous types, and had been involved in disputes regarding a "right of way" that allegedly paralleled the alleyway through the back of our properties. My next door neighbor had previously owned and lived in my house, which I had bought from his son-in-law, and had built a new corner house on his subdivided original lot.

I warned Bill to be on guard and that something might happen given the bad blood between these two approaching gentlemen. Well, it did. They immediately got into a curse-laden and very heated argument about the "right of way" and whether or not a fence could be built on or through it. Then, suddenly, my pugnacious next-door neighbor, who was standing next to me, lunged at his ex-boss and tried to throw a punch; I partially

1983) demonstrated the sharpening of his thinking about issues of peasantries and capitalist development, a process that was more fully realized, broadened, and deepened in his provocative book *Anthropologies and Histories* (Roseberry 1989). An inscription on the flyleaf of a copy of that book he sent me reads: "For Scott, mentor and friend." Reading that book caused me to rethink my position on the economy–society-culture relationship. Up to that time, I had an un-nuanced, mechanistic view – although I had convinced myself it was "dialectical." I was particularly struck by his critique of dichotomous thinking about the "mental" vs. "material" question, and his insertion of agency to compel a truly dialectical alternative to oppositional thinking (Roseberry 1989:esp. Ch.2).

His well-expressed emphasis was upon "meaningful action that … is shaped by the meanings people take to their action even as meanings are shaped by people's activities" (1989:33). The relationship was mutually constitutive. The impact of those lines caused me to rethink my previous views through a protracted process that finally resulted in my own book (Cook 2004). I am sure that Bill Roseberry appreciated my effort to absorb his contribution, but I regretted that by the time I acknowledged this in print he was no longer alive to give me his opinion in that regard. I think the last time I saw him was when I invited him to present a talk at UConn in the early 1990s several years before his untimely death from cancer in 2000. He was destined, I think, to become the "Eric Wolf" of a new century – but possibly even a more profound critical thinker than the original.

Jim Wessman was already in the graduate program when I arrived at UConn in 1971. During the first semester Jim asked me to be his graduate advisor and I agreed. He was the son of a Calvinist academic and sometimes minister in Minnesota, tightly wound, intense, rapid in his speech, and unusually bright and articulate. He thrived in our emerging materialist studies program and, at some point, possibly after taking my spring 1973 seminar on Latin American Rural Economy and Society which included Puerto Rican material, he began drafting a dissertation proposal for research in Puerto Rico. He did so, secured funding, and went to Puerto Rico around 1975. He may have completed the write-up of his dissertation while teaching at Inter-American University in San German where he married one of his students. While still at Inter-American University, he organized a symposium on Puerto Rico in which Bill Roseberry (1978) presented his paper on *The People of Puerto Rico* which had also been an important reference in Wessman's study of a sugarcane plantation in southwestern Puerto Rico.

Jim's book *Anthropology and Marxism* published in 1981, after his departure from Puerto Rico to a new faculty position at the University of North Carolina, emerged somewhat unexpectedly like a bolt of lightning. It was a clearly written, lucid anthropological interpretation of Marxist thought with a final chapter drawing on his Puerto Rican experience. In many ways, with a different slant, it was a precursor to Roseberry's 1989 book but with a more pedagogic or introductory approach to the subject matter. It also displayed a unique talent for distilling key concepts and principles of Marxism for ethnographic application. I liked the book then and still do.

A good example of Wessman's unique talent is illustrated in the early pages of his book when he describes the dialectical method (1981:8–9): "Using the dialectical method, a person begins with a relatively abstract conceptualization – abstract but unrefined – which is the result of previous cognitive acts. Simplifying assumptions define a priori the field of analysis and make it possible to define the necessary concepts (or categories) and to link them together. Deductions reproduce the logical relations among the categories, which are elaborated to form a complex model of the essential structures of the system…One analyzes the situation to see how close this idea comes to what appears to exist. The next step is to revise the original idea and attempt a new synthesis of the revised conceptualization with one's other knowledge. This latter step is essentially what is meant by induction or an a posteriori mode of reasoning. These steps are repeated several times, not performed simply once. In subsequent steps of the dialectical method, the conceptual model is analyzed in motion, making it possible to study basic relationships and processes, as well as contradictions." This is a much clearer and more operationally-attuned statement of the "method of successive abstractions and successive approximations" that I wrote about in my 1974 article (Cook 1974a:806–808). Jim had a unique gift for expressing complex thoughts and cognitive processes in simple, straightforward language.

Jim moved from North Carolina to the Department of Latin American and Latino Studies at SUNY-Albany, after a brief stint at Saint Olaf College in Minnesota. He knew of my study of handmade brick production in Oaxaca (Cook 1984a), and sent me a clipping of an ethnographically provocative newspaper article in the Albany newspaper (via the Dallas Morning News) by a reporter named Patrick McDonnell (1985) which first drew my attention to the thriving handmade brick industry on the Mexican side of the lower Rio Grande/Rio Bravo border (Cook 1998:xix). That information prompted me to visit the area mentioned in the article and to launch a research project that resulted in two books (Cook 1998; Cook 2011). I gratefully acknowledged his thoughtfulness for calling my attention to that border industry, unknown to me at the time I received his correspondence, and also for reviewing a draft of my book manuscript on the topic (Cook 1998:xxvii).

A few years later, Jim communicated with me about a new project he had undertaken which represented his long-standing interest in the literary genre represented by Peter Matthiesen's novel *At Play in the Fields of the Lord*. I immediately expected the worst. He explained to me at the time that he had re-discovered his long-repressed faith and had become a deacon in the Presbyterian church. So, when I received his manuscript, I was not completely surprised when I discovered it to be a sort of biographical history of a Presbyterian missionary in Central America. Although it was well-written, I did not like it and told him that it would surely not be publishable as a contribution to the anthropological literature without substantial re-working. His career-shifting epiphany had led him backwards from being the author of *Anthropology and Marxism* to being the biographer of an American Calvinist missionary involved in proselytizing Central Americans. There has been no communication between us since.

Economic Anthropology Seminars and Commodity Production

A review of syllabi from three seminars in economic anthropology that I taught in 1974, 1975, and 1993 shows that my approach to the subject matter evolved during this period from an initial point of a sort of scatter-gun approach (1974, 1975) to a point of a more problem-focused approach deeply influenced by my Mexican research. The juxtaposition of the two syllabi from the 1970s with the 1993 syllabus shows a decided tendency to organize the seminar around my ethnographic research in Oaxaca especially around the theme of petty commodity production in capitalism and the distinction between intrusive foreign capitalism and indigenous capitalist development.

The formalist vs. substantivist theme was still present but Marxist discourse was singled-out as a source of rescue from the dualistic discourse of substantivism as represented in Marshall Sahlins' notion of one economics for the West, and another for the Rest (Sahlins 1976:165; cf. 1972:xiii–xiv). The resolution of this opposition in my thinking lay in commodity economics since I was convinced on the basis of fieldwork in Oaxaca that gifts were commodities but that commodities were mostly not gifts. I did not develop this thesis fully until much later in my book on *Commodity Culture(s)* (Cook 2004b) but was also presented in a public lecture delivered in Oaxaca (Cook 2004) and then in articles in Spanish and English (Cook 2005, 2006).

It is clear from the nature of the problems and questions posed in these seminars that I was looking for feedback from student participants that might influence my own thinking about many thorny issues. During those years I did correspond with academic peers about theoretical issues in the field but these were mostly occasional rather than regular conversations. Interaction with graduate students was an essential stimulant to critical thinking and rethinking of fundamental sources and problems.

"Don Mauricio" Godelier and the Quebec Connection

The economic anthropology I have practiced since 1969 was based in part on my reading of the path-breaking study by Maurice Godelier in its 1967 Spanish translation five years prior to its availability in English. My 1970 article on price and output variability was exemplified by Hal Schneider to illustrate "how a market can be discussed in terms of general equilib-rium analysis (1974:80–83)." Ironically, in that same article, I inserted a long footnote note on Godelier's notion of the interior/exterior aspect of economy/society articulation as a major breakthrough that neatly re-solved the "maximizationalist" fallacy of equating economics with econo-mizing with all behavior, as well as the substantivist fallacy of substituting the study of social phenomena for the study of economic phenomena (Cook 1970:794–795 n2; cf. Cook 1974:813–814). That footnote was a better indicator of where my work was headed than the time series ana-lysis itself.

Thanks to Yván Bretón, I had the opportunity to know Godelier per-sonally in the 1970s. During 1975 when Yván chaired the anthropology department at Laval University, Godelier was invited to spend a semester there as visiting professor. There was a meeting of the Northeastern Anthropological Association Conference in April which had a session on "Modes of Production: Marxist Studies in Anthropology" in which Godelier was invited to participate at the SUNY-Potsdam campus in up-state New York. In consultation with Bretón, I arranged with the UConn anthropology department to invite Godelier for a colloquium. Bretón agreed to drive Godelier to Connecticut and then we would all travel to-gether to the SEA meeting at SUNY-Potsdam, and then back to Quebec City. Godelier's topic for both presentations was "The Mental and the Material" which he handled with his characteristically brilliant flair for exposition. This was soon to be published as a book (Godelier 1986) which I have thought ever since was one of his most accessible and important publications.

The arrangements worked out well. I had an informal dinner party at my house in the evening after Godelier gave his talk at UConn in which the main dish was a tasty rabbit stew (*fricasé de conejo*), accompanied by the standard *arroz y habichuelas* (rice and beans) prepared by a Puerto Rican chef, Doris Rodríguez, a friend of Hilda's who had owned a restaurant in Puerto Rico. Hilda remembers that Don Mauricio dined alone at our kit-chen table as she and Doris served him. They had difficulty keeping his plate full. Fortunately, for the rest of us, drinking and talking in the living room, enough of that *fiscasé de conejo* was left for us to enjoy.

Godelier, a very friendly, gregarious, and unpretentious man, in contrast to his highly intellectual writings, told me later that it was one of the best meals he had eaten in a long time. Incidentally, this leads me to register my vote on behalf of Puerto Rican cuisine which, over the years, I have found to match Mexican as the best in Latin America. Also, travel has taught me that a Puerto Rican *asopao de camarón y langosta* (shrimp and lobster soup) is tastier than a Spanish *paella*.

The next day we drove to Potsdam meeting and afterwards to Quebec City. Among other things, I remember going out for an evening to eat and party in Quebec City. The evening began at a French restaurant where Godelier displayed his intimate knowledge of French viniculture; we had several bottles of wine at various courses of the meal all selected by him. Afterwards, at the party I saw evidence of Godelier's reputation as a charming ladies' man since there was a bevy of attractive Laval University graduate students and female faculty surrounding him most of the evening. I was envious.

I got along well with Godelier especially since he was fluent in Spanish which is the language we sometimes used to communicate. His fluency in Spanish may have reflected the fact that his wife in the 1970s was a professor specializing in that language (Bretón, personal communication). I always addressed him as "Don Mauricio" as he was probably addressed in Mexico City where he also had visited to give lectures. He presented his talks at UConn and at the SEA meeting in fluent English. We conversed mostly about the labor theory of value, his use of it in his study of the Baruya (1971), and about some thought-provoking ideas he presented in his "mental and material" project. Yvan Bretón who knew Godelier well both professionally and personally over years of association in Quebec and in France emphasizes two points that Godelier made in discussions with him regarding understanding Marx's *Capital*. First, there was a constant need to refer back to the original German text to avoid errors of interpretation derived from texts translated to French (or English). Second, dialectical or oppositional thinking was necessary to understand the meaning of fundamental concepts. For example, the meaning of a concept like "abstract labor" as a creator of value must be analyzed through its opposite "concrete labor," the source of satisfaction. The former cannot be actualized without the latter. Consequently, satisfaction has a variable content, ranging from direct profit to a symbolic value. Likewise, the meaning of "commodity" cannot be fathomed without analyzing its posited opposite, the "gift" (Bretón, personal communication, August 20, 2020).

On that occasion and others I visited Laval University and Bretón's farm outside of Quebec City which had a sugar shack (*cabane á sucre*) to process sap from groves of sugar maples; he was an expert in collecting, cooking, and bottling the syrup. It is always festival time in Quebec but the Winter Ice Carnival is very special; streets are lined with gigantic figures carved of ice, people staggering around everywhere drinking alcohol of all types from hollowed-out walking canes or other containers. Local lore has it that you cannot survive for long if you stumble, fall, and pass-out on a snow bank during the Ice Festival since the temperature is always well below zero.

Harmony and Discord in the Department

After Norman Chance stepped down from the position of Chairperson around 1973, the department was never the same. The materialist group of four never again had a department chair who was supportive of our program orientation. Our main problem was maintaining workable relationships with other members of the sociocultural faculty who were uncomfortable with Marxist studies, and were mostly involved in undergraduate teaching. All that we shared with them, aside from our departmental identity, were strained relations with the archaeologists, medical anthropologists, and bio-behaviorists most of whom occupied separate offices in Beach Hall. Consequently, every issue of faculty hiring, graduate student admissions, promotion and tenure, and so on was contested. Most of the time the group of four was either out-voted, out-maneuvered, or double-crossed. It was not a particularly collegial departmental environment.

The tie that united Norman Chance, Jim Faris, Ben Magubane, and I was our common interest in the Marxist literature although we each had different interests and interpretations of it. Also uniting us was our commitment to diversity in faculty hiring and student recruitment, and our collaboration on graduate student advisory committees. Most of the graduate students we advised had entered our department with a specific interest in the Marxist studies program.

Our program was built around two required core seminars which were taught on a rotating basis by me, Chance, Faris, and Magubane. Also, three of us four, in different combinations, served on individual student advisory committees which one of us chaired. Aside from our ideological orientation, we were bonded through our collaboration on graduate student advisory committees, our cooperation in designing and teaching graduate seminars, and in inviting and hosting guest speakers.

I was never much involved in the squabble with the Beach Hall-based bio-behaviorists and medical anthropologists led by William Laughlin and Bert and Gretel Pelto. Thankfully, that was mostly the province of Jim Faris and the Committee Against Racism group. Ironically, during my last four years at UConn, as director of the Puerto Rican and Latino Studies Institute, I left my office in Manchester Hall and was housed in an office in Beach Hall around the corner and down the hall from the archaeologists, bio-behaviorists, and medical anthropologists. I had little reason to visit them. I never set foot in Manchester Hall again after I vacated my office there in 1996.

Puerto Rican Studies and Latin American Studies at the University of Connecticut

The main campus of the University of Connecticut is about 27 miles east of Hartford, a few miles off of the interstate highway system that connects to Boston and destinations north and to New York City and destinations south. It is located in the village of Storrs in the town of Mansfield within eastern Tolland County. Confusing? Welcome to Connecticut.

From the UConn campus, give or take a half hour, Boston or New York City are only a two-hour drive away. So, UConn is deceptively isolated smack in the middle of the NYC-Boston corridor. It is in a rural area with dairy farms dotting the landscape. On the outskirts of the campus on all sides the campus is surrounded by suburban-like neighborhoods where many of the faculty and upper echelon administrators live. When I got there in 1971, Storrs had a minimal downtown area with a few buildings including a post office, town offices, a bank and a credit union, a movie theater, a gas station, and a few stores. There were no hotels or motels. Visitors were accommodated in a few university-owned guest rooms and apartments scattered around the campus, or in a few quaint inns scattered around the countryside. The campus had a faculty club for those who wished to pay the country club fees, an out of date and rather austere art deco Student Union building with few amenities, a small bookstore in the basement of a far end of the Student Union building, and a somewhat anti-quated library. Probably the most impressive building on campus was the Jorgensen Auditorium which had suitable capacity to host an impressive array of cultural events owing to its strategic booking location in the NYC-Boston corridor. All together a strange, almost surrealistic mish-mash of rural and suburban, colonial and low-grade contemporary, sophisticated and pedestrian elements.

The most suitable housing I could find for my family with three school kids was in the nearby town of Eastford where a large rural two-story house across the road from a state forest and the Natchuag River stocked with trout was available to rent. It was about 14 miles from campus and about a twenty-five minute drive, depending on road conditions; black ice and snow in the winter months made for treacherous driving. My kids were bused to school in the village center and I learned how to fly-fish as a wader in the Natchaug River. This was quite a contrast with East Lansing.

The nearest urban area to the Storrs campus was Willimantic 8 miles south, with a population of 14,000 in 1970, and a fifteen-minute drive away by back road or a state highway. Willimantic had a storied history revolving around its designation as "Thread City" as a center of the nineteenth-century textile industry. This name derived from the formidable rows of American Thread Company's mills along both sides of the Willimantic River until they shut down when the company moved to South Carolina in 1985. The strange name of the place comes from its original Algonquian

inhabitants and means "place near the evergreen swamp" – a quite appropriate designation since it still had in nearby rural areas residents known
as "Swamp Yankees," a New England variety of rednecks some of whom
were reported to have burned crosses early in the twentieth century on top
of Storrs hill. The town's population was comprised of waves of European,
French Canadian, and Puerto Rican immigrants. The arrival of Puerto
Ricans dated from the mid-1950s and continued thereafter so that by the
end of the century about one-quarter of the population was of Puerto Rican
descent. Hence the nickname "Willi-Rico." The majority "white" population was heavily multiethnic including people of Irish, Italian, Polish,
German, Estonian, Ukrainian, Latvian, and Lithuanian descent.

When I arrived at UConn in 1971 there was no faculty member of
Puerto Rican descent and only one social scientist with any interest in
Latino studies – Rosalío Wences, a Mexican sociologist who for a year
taught a course on the subject for a handful of Latino students. Wences
returned to Mexico in 1972 where he became president of the university
in his native state of Guerrero, so it fell upon me to teach a Puerto Rican
studies course during my second year. There was a slowly increasing number
of Puerto Rican students entering the university especially from the greater
New York City area and the urban areas of southern Connecticut, the
so-called "Niuyoricans." Several of them participated in protest organizations like the Young Lords, were quite street savvy, politically-oriented,
and tended to view the island homeland of their parents very idealistically
(and naively) as a possible host for a reverse "diaspora."

At the time, I was a decade removed from my period of residence in
Puerto Rico and from Puerto Rican Studies, so I had some catching up to
do. I had some personal experience with the Puerto Rican diaspora when
my wife and I were in NYC in 1960–1961 but not from an academic perspective and had visited the island a few times after departing in 1963.
During my second year at UConn, through the course I had begun to teach
dealing with Puerto Rican society and culture, I familiarized myself with
the literature on the diaspora and with the experiences of my students in it.

Until I invited Carlos Buitrago, an anthropologist at the University of
Puerto Rico, to give a talk and meet with students in 1972, I had not appreciated the extent of the divide between island-based and mainland-based

Puerto Ricans. Buitrago had studied for his doctorate in social anthropology at Cambridge University, particularly influenced by Meyer-Fortes, in the same cohort as my colleague, Jim Faris. He was very much a kinship and social organization-focused scholar who was a highly respected ethnographer of rural communities in Puerto Rico. I first met him when he lectured about his ongoing dissertation project in the PAU-UPR program in 1962–1963.

Carlos was very insular in his rigorous approach to Puerto Rican society and had little direct experience with the diaspora community. This is precisely why he accepted my invitation to visit Connecticut: to become more familiar with that community. He presented a public lecture to anthropology students and faculty, and also met and presented an informal talk to the Puerto Rican diaspora undergraduates I was teaching in my course. One evening I had a party at my house in Eastford for Carlos who was reserved in conversation but could be outspoken when riled. I invited ten or so students to the party, mostly juniors and seniors. Beer was flowing and conversations got pretty animated.

At issue was Puerto Rican identity – who is, who is not, and who is in-between, and why. Some of my ex-Young Lord students from the South Bronx and the big cities of Connecticut like Bridgeport, Hartford, and New Britain were especially vociferous in staking their claims to Puerto Rican identity and causes. Carlos was equally vociferous in arguing that they really were not Puerto Ricans at all due to their upbringing on the mainland and not on the island. For him, true Puerto Rican identity required enculturation in the insular homeland. He was not as sympathetic to the Puerto Rican identity claims of diasporans as was Eduardo Seda Bonilla who, although born and raised on the island, had done his graduate study at Columbia and then later taught Puerto Rican Studies at Hunter College. But Eduardo, like Carlos, was distraught over the disappearance of "traditional" customs and practices on the island itself, and he was one of the main contributors to the literature of "requiem" for Puerto Rican culture documenting that process (Cook 1973a; Seda 1970).

The animated discussions between Carlos Buitrago and my students that long evening finally ended in a stand-off. I do not think Carlos visited the mainland too frequently after that, and the next time I saw him was in

Puerto Rico years later when I invited him to visit our farm in Yabucoa. He was still pretty much the same in his insular focus. I, of course, had the more difficult task of walking the thin and fragile line between the Caribbean islanders and the "diasporans," and of trying to unite them through understanding the forces and conditions causing the division between them. But as Hilda's case proves, if you were born and raised in Puerto Rico before moving to the mainland, you will always be a Puerto Rican in a way that people of Puerto Rican descent born and raised on the mainland are not. They do not share the "mancha de plátano" of the Boricua. Traditions and customs that are no longer practiced will not be restored but those who retain the Spanish language, and residence on the island, should be the major players in determining the island's future status.

I had designed and taught a course attempting to address these issues but soon realized that there was a much greater need, namely to establish an interdisciplinary program in Puerto Rican Studies of the kind organized and operating in New York City and New Jersey. To achieve that goal, I organized and headed a faculty-student lobbying group called the Puerto Rican Studies and Affairs Committee which began to meet with deans and higher administration officials to promote recruitment of Puerto Rican students and hiring of Puerto Rican faculty. Meanwhile, our effort was to staff the course with available faculty and qualified graduate students from Puerto Rico and the diaspora.

Ricardo Pérez was the last of my graduate students to participate. He was an undergraduate student of Buitrago's at the University of Puerto Rico, born and raised on the island's south coast, and became quite active in Puerto Rican programs on campus and in Willimantic. He completed his dissertation on fishing communities in the Guánica area of southwestern coastal Puerto Rico in 2000 and then became a tenured member of the sociology-anthropology faculty at Eastern Connecticut State University in Willimantic. His dissertation research resulted in a book, *The State and Small-Scale Fisheries in Puerto Rico*, one of the few ever published on that topic (Pérez 2005). Ricardo has most recently been researching sustainable tourism development in Cuba and is coordinator of the Latin American and Caribbean Studies Program at ECSU.

By 1971 there was already a small contingent of UConn undergraduate students who had organized a Puerto Rican Student Movement to promote their campus agenda. It had been founded by Isnoel "Ino" Ríos, a native of the *municipio* of San Sebastián in northwest Puerto Rico who had been raised in Willimantic. Ino was one of the first Puerto Rican graduates from the local high school, and among the first to graduate from UConn a few years prior to my arrival. When I first met him, he was a Puerto Rican community leader in Willimantic and was also a doctoral student in anthropology at Stanford University where he had gone on a Ford Foundation scholarship. He was a founding member in Willimantic of the Puerto Rican Organization Program (PROP) to promote the welfare of the local community, together with other UConn undergraduate students.

PROP became the main vehicle for community development funding in Willimantic and surrounding Windham county. After Hilda and I moved to Willimantic from rural Eastford in 1974, I served for a time on the PROP board and Hilda taught bilingual education in local elementary schools, continued her graduate education at Eastern Connecticut State University in Willimantic where she received her MA degree in 1974 and at UConn where she completed the sixth year degree program in bilingual education in 1975. Later she would become involved in Democratic party politics and serve two terms on the Willimantic City Council.

One of the most successful outreach projects between UConn and PROP resulted in a publication entitled *The Puerto Rican Experience in Willimantic*. This was a joint effort directed by me and the Executive Director of the Windham Regional Community Council (WRCC), Jeff Beadle, who had taken my undergraduate course on the Latin American Minority in the United States prior to graduating and working his way up to the directorship of that agency. Funding for the project was obtained through a grant from the Connecticut Humanities Council. The research was carried out in 1983–1984 by my doctoral student Norma Boujouen and Jim Newton, who had a doctorate in anthropology from the New School for Social Research, was adept at computer programming, survey research, and statistical analysis and was available to work on the project. The purpose of the project was to conduct an ethnographic study of the Puerto Rican community in Willimantic. It was envisioned as an opportunity for

the entire community to gain a better understanding of the Puerto Rican
culture and experience in the United States. A particular aim of the proposal was to obtain information that would help produce a more effective
provision of public services to the Puerto Rican community in Willimantic
and Windham county.

Research emphasis was placed on first-hand data gathering through
interviews, case studies, and participant observation, but also employed
the household survey, statistical, and archival record analysis, including all
available government census data. It was a very complete, well-researched
and – written study, the only one of its kind for Willimantic and, perhaps,
for the entire state of Connecticut. Norma Boujouen afterwards completed
her doctoral dissertation under my direction with a pioneering, in-depth
study of Puerto Rican female migrant workers at the American Thread
Company (Boujouen 1990, 2013).

The original ink drawing on the cover of the published booklet, with a
Puerto Rican family in the foreground and the American Thread Company
in the background was drawn by Valentín Tirado, a talented artist and
school-teacher colleague of Hilda's who was born and raised in Cataño,
Puerto Rico. Hilda and I were godparents (*padrinos*) of his son. Valentín
was a good friend of mine, an admirer of Mexican mural art – Rivera,
Orozco but especially of Siquieros – and painted many murals in downtown Willimantic. On one occasion we traveled together to a Siquieros
exhibition in the Philadelphia Museum of Art. I still have hanging on the
wall of my home office a portrait of me that he painted and presented to
me in 1992. Tragically, a few years ago, before he could visit us in Texas, he
suffered a heart attack while painting a large canvas on a ladder, and died
long before his time.

Isnoel "Ino" Rios was hired at UConn in the 1970s as head of the
Puerto Rican Student Center (known as the *Casa Borinqueña*) and tran-
sitioned to director of the Puerto Rican Cultural Center when the *Casa
Borinqueña* was upgraded in the 1980s. In 1988, he completed his doctoral
dissertation under the direction of the anthropologist George Spindler at
Stanford University's School of Education (Ríos Mendez 1988).

Ino and I worked closely for more than two decades to build and secure
a Latino presence on the UConn campus. In doing so we shared some

views in common. First, Puerto Rican Studies was a field bifurcated by the diaspora. It meant one thing to Island academics and their constituencies, and quite another to migrants from the island and their offspring born and raised on the "mainland." Aside from graduate training of students from the island, our concern at UConn was to serve the needs of the diaspora population of undergraduate students. Second, Puerto Rican Studies needed to be blended with Mexican-American Studies so as to better represent the broader field of "Latino" Studies. Accordingly, I developed and taught for many years a course on the "Latin American Minority in the United States" which gave equal coverage to Puerto Rican and Mexican-American (Chicano) Studies. Third, internal politics at UConn had to be regularly stoked by external politics – that is, local-level and state-level politics. Ino was quite adept at playing the wider political card and, also, in dealing with the realities of the affirmative action regime (i.e., blacks first, Asians and Latinos fighting it out for seconds). I became fairly knowledgeable and adept in the game of administrative academic politics – that is, how to promote hiring and funding to benefit Latin American and Latino interests in a zero-sum game of academic budgeting and affirmative action. One strategy Ino and I developed and followed over the years was to coordinate as much as possible cultural programming budgets for guest speakers and other events.

The Cultural Center's budget for such purposes was always larger than the Puerto Rican Studies budget but the important element was to promote as much as possible programs with an academic or politically-relevant content. Since our leftist and pro-independence politics were compatible we were able to host an impressive array of speakers and performers like the protest singer, Roy Brown (who came twice), controversial politicians like Juan Mari Bras (also twice) and Ruben Berrios, and academics like Manuel Maldonado Denis, Eduardo Seda Bonilla, Angel Quintero Rivera, Rafael Ramírez, Pedro Cabán, Sidney Mintz, Edna Acosta Belén, and Helen Safa. I also organized a symposium on Mexican Border studies in which David Montejano, Roberto Alvarez, and Martha Menchaca participated. Our biggest and best attended event was a debate on Puerto Rico's political status with representatives from competing political parties: the Popular Democratic Party represented by ex-governor Rafael Hernández Colón, a member of the Puerto Rican Senate representing the Statehood Party, and the Puerto Rican Socialist Party represented by Juan Mari Brás who I first heard speak at a street rally in Caguas in the 1960s.

Around 1995 when Mark Emmert arrived at UConn as Chancellor and Professor of Political Science, the Institute was in the process of losing its first Director, Edgardo Meléndez. He was a political scientist from the University of Puerto Rico who was hired for a long-sought-after joint appointment with the Department of Political Science after an exhaustive search led by the Puerto Rican Studies and Affairs Committee, and approved by the Department of Political Science. No small feat in those days.

Ino and I were sorely disappointed when Edgardo decided to return to the University of Puerto Rico only two years or so following his appointment. But we knew why: Aside from some personal problems, he had been enormously frustrated in his efforts to secure additional joint appointments with mainstream departments for growing the Institute's affiliated faculty. He had underestimated the difficulties of the process at UConn. At the time of his resignation, I was heavily focused on my Mexican border project. In view of the lack of qualified faculty to step into Edgardo's shoes, however, I agreed to fill the position temporarily until such time as a search for a permanent director was launched. As it turned out, I was "interim" director from 1996 to 2000 and, owing to an early retirement incentive program, was able to retire from my faculty position and with the help of a full-time secretary and a travel budget, to divide my time between directing the institute and conducting research on the Texas-Mexico border. Those proved to be my most satisfying four years at UConn.

Mark Emmert made several overdue administrative changes in the Multicultural Affairs (i.e., affirmative action) structure: The Women's Studies Program; and the African-American, Asian-American, and Puerto Rican-Latino Studies Institutes were removed from the College of Liberal Arts and Sciences and placed directly under the Provost/Chancellor of Academic Affairs. This clearly eased the faculty hiring process by freeing us from the conservatively entrenched ways of mainstream College of Liberal Arts and Sciences departments, and allowing us to look for new and willing joint appointment partners in other schools and colleges (Tuchman 2009:166–167, and p. 229, fn. 21).

succeed in restraining him, and the punch missed. Meanwhile, Bill on the other side of the fence line was attempting to restrain the ex-boss, but unsuccessfully, and he landed a punch directly to the face of my neighbor. Both of these gentlemen were bigger and stronger than us, but Bill and I finally succeeded in restraining and calming them down, without calling the police. Finally, they went their separate ways. Bill and I regained our composure, laughed the matter off, had a few more beers, and finished the fence project.

Afterwards, I consulted my lawyer who was also the City Attorney. He researched the matter of the "right of way" and concluded that it was mentioned in an eighteenth-century statute pertaining to the area when it was a farm, and had absolutely no validity or legal standing in the twentieth century. After all, that was New England where historically "fences make good neighbors."

A few years after this incident occurred, Bill wrote an exemplary dissertation, based on fieldwork and archival research, on a regional coffee industry in Venezuela. He received his Ph.D. in 1977. The revision of his dissertation was published in 1983 as *Coffee and Capitalism in the Venezuelan Andes*, a pioneering study of that topic. His unique approach really began to emerge in a critical review of foundational works of contemporary anthropology like the *People of Puerto Rico* (Roseberry 1978).

Bill had taught a year or two at the University of Iowa but soon was recruited by Stanley Diamond at the New School for Social Research where he had his biggest impact. I remember Diamond calling me with regard to the prospect of hiring Bill and I advised him to so immediately before some other department did. It was at The New School that most of his work was done. Ironically, my former instructor and friend from our days together in Puerto Rico, Anthony Lauria (1989; Cook 2004b:12), who had completed coursework as a student of Eric Wolf at Columbia University and again at the University of Michigan, finally completed his doctoral dissertation with Bill Roseberry as his advisor at the New School.

During the late 1970s and early 1980s, Bill not only revised his dissertation for publication but developed an original interpretative framework and approach to the relationships between economy, society, and culture. The published revised version of his doctoral dissertation (Roseberry

With Emmert's funding and support, I was able to expand the Institute's joint appointment faculty in the School of Education, the School of Family Studies, in the Department of Communication Sciences, and in the History Department. Two of the faculty I hired are still at the university, Diana Ríos and Marysol Asencio, and Blanca Silvestrini became a professor emeritus in residence. As of 2019, despite a reorganization of multicultural and international studies and affairs at the university which has melded Puerto Rican/Latino Studies and Latin American Studies under the province of "El Instituto," the latter's agenda remains faithful to that of the twentieth-century Institute and to its predecessor the Puerto Rican Studies and Affairs Committee. The major difference now is that MA degree level courses and programs of study are offered. UConn is also home to the Secretariat of the Puerto Rican Studies Association (UConn El Instituto 2019).[8]

I was Director of the Title VI Center for Latin American and Caribbean Studies at UConn between 1987 and 1992. This Center operated as the main administrator of a consortium with University of Massachusetts-Amherst and Brown University in Providence, Rhode Island. The job involved dealing with the US Department of Education Title VI bureaucracy in Washington DC, maintaining good relations with our partners who shared some of the budget, administering our BA and MA programs, public relations with the wider community, programming of colloquia, and herding the diverse array of faculty who participated in the program. It is not widely recognized that UConn had a long-established involvement in Latin American studies thanks to the contribution of the sociologist and Mexico specialist Nathan Whetten who was a faculty member and administrator dating back to the 1940s when he published his monumental work entitled *Rural Mexico*. I regularly consulted Whetten's classic work, and told him so when I met him in retirement after I arrived in Storrs.

The directorship of the Title VI Center had been in the hands of the history department for several years – both Hugh Hamill and Paul Goodwin had been directors and had a very competent administrative assistant, Jo Barstow, who handled administrative details for the consortium, with UMass-Amherst and Brown University, which was administered by UConn. The Center had support from the Tinker Foundation for visiting scholars, and had a colloquium series. I established an Occasional Papers Series and turned to the matter of establishing a programmatic research theme for the Center.

I decided to address this problem by piggy-backing on an already well-established and internationally-known program at UConn, namely, the Roper Center for Public Opinion Research which, from its inception, had been directed by Everett Ladd, a prominent member of the Political Science Department. I approached Ladd about his possible interest in my idea of establishing a Latin American Survey Data Bank (LASDB) for polling and other survey research from Latin America. If he agreed, we would submit a joint proposal to the Tinker Foundation to fund the project. Ladd agreed, the proposal was written, and a grant of several tens of thousands of dollars was approved. Our consortium, which was the only Title VI-funded Latin American Studies Center in New England, already had funding from the Tinker Foundation for rotating visiting professorships, so I had floated the idea of such a proposal to the director of that foundation. She thought the idea was innovative and worthy of consideration for funding, and within a short time the proposal was funded.

Thus, the LASDB at the Roper Center was up and running and there was substantial interest in collaboration from various Latin American polling groups – especially in Mexico, Venezuela, and Brazil. We had money to bring in graduate students from those countries for training at the Roper Center, and also to invite pollsters and other survey researchers to the Center. I was able to travel as a representative of the program to all three of those countries and also to Panama and Costa Rica.

The project seemed to work out well for a few years during my tenure as director. Among other things, I was able to invite several Mexican pollsters to the Roper Center including Leonardo Valdéz who spent a semester or two in residence. Miguel Basañez, Jorge Castañeda, and others came for shorter visits. Pollsters from Brazil and Venezuela were regular visitors. Also, the establishment of the LASDB opened up travel possibilities to Latin American countries I had not visited before.

The LASDB is still up and operating although is now identified simply as the Latin American Databank (LAD), and provides a portal for Latin American datasets acquired, processed and archived by the Roper Center for Public Opinion Research. Its country coverage has been expanded, and includes data from public opinion surveys conducted by the survey research community including universities, institutes, individual scholars, private polling, and public opinion research firms.

Venezuela

The most interesting trips I made during this period were to Venezuela. In the early 1980s the University of Connecticut had established a relationship with Venezuela by contacts made with President Rafael Caldera who had visited the campus to donate a collection of books from his vast personal library to the UConn library and to be awarded an honorary doctorate. A key part of my LASDB project built upon this relationship with Caldera and the Venezuelan polling community which the political scientist Fred Turner had played a role in cultivating. The elite Universidad de Simón Bolivar in the mountains outside of Caracas had been built and inaugurated during Caldera's first presidency (1969–1974). Its excellent Department of Political Science headed by a German-trained political scientist, Federíco Welsch, was central to the LASDB project. This was owing mostly to the presence on its faculty of Arístides Torres, an MIT-trained political scientist and member of the USB faculty who also owned his own polling firm in Caracas which, together with the Gallup-affiliated firm, was dominant in that sector in Venezuela. The Tinker Foundation grant enabled us to formalize ties with USB by providing internships at the Roper Center for several graduate students. They were a well-trained, impressive group. Funding at USB also came from PDVSA (the government-owned oil company) and from a private foundation.

During the period that I visited Venezuela, there were signs of political instability to come as indicated by the "*caracazo*" riot in Caracas in 1989 during the middle of the period of rule by the Democratic Action Party of Presidents Luisinchi and Pérez. I heard people complaining about rapidly escalating prices in supermarket lines and witnessed several incidents of random street and nightclub violence during my visits. I was impressed by the bustling, modern look of the central part of the city, and by the stark contrast in living conditions of the working poor and unemployed in comparison with the middle and upper classes.

During one of my visits Fred Turner and I had a private, two-hour luncheon meeting with former (1969–1974) and future (1994–1999) President, Rafael Caldera, in the Caracas Hilton. I remember following behind Caldera as we walked through the restaurant to a small alcove in the rear, patrons at every table stood up and greeted him as "Señor Presidente" as we walked by. He was clearly a very popular, well-liked man and still a powerful politician as a tenured senator in the national congress. Following his second presidency (1994–1999) he became the longest-serving democratically elected leader to govern the country in the twentieth century. He was a strong supporter of civilian democratic rule and recognized as one of the founders of Venezuela's democratic system.

But institutional decay and social inequality had worsened to such an extent that Caldera was succeeded in office by a revolutionary socialist, Hugo Chávez, who, ironically, had been a graduate student of political science at USB as a military officer. He was pardoned by President Caldera in 1994 after spending two years in prison for leading a coup against the Democratic Action Party administration of Carlos Andrés Pérez, Caldera's predecessor in office. My experience was that compared to Mexico and Puerto Rico, Venezuelan politics was more volatile, complicated, and unpredictable. Only a lifetime specialist like Steve Ellner (2008) can begin to fathom its intricacies and nuances.

During the luncheon I talked extensively with Caldera about Puerto Rico which he had visited numerous times. I remember him telling me that if Venezuela had received as much largesse from the US as Puerto Rico had, it would be much better off. He implied that the Puerto Rican government and political class was riddled with corruption and had either wasted or appropriated much of that transferred wealth. Of course, the same could be said with regard to Venezuelan petrodollar income from its 1970s oil boom. He told me that he had given several speeches in Puerto Rico over the years and that he would provide me with copies of them before I departed Caracas.

When I returned to my hotel following the luncheon, I found several copies of reprints of his speeches laid out on the bed in my hotel room. Caldera was definitely a man of his word, and an exceptionally well-informed and scholarly politician – certainly deserving of UConn's honorary doctorate which, of course, was obscured by a plethora of honors bestowed upon him, including several from Puerto Rico, during his lifetime.

On another trip to Venezuela, after my meeting with President Caldera, I was surprised to see a sign hoisted in the air with my name on it as I walked out of the luggage area into the terminal. This is the first and only time in my travels that I had experienced this. The sign holder introduced himself to me as a driver for the US Embassy and that he was instructed to take me there for a meeting prior to being taken to my hotel. I was apprehensive but felt that I had no choice but to go with him.

Caracas is a spectacular city nestled in sort of a valley with rolling hills and surrounded by mountains on all sides – driving a car there can be challenging. The embassy, a multi-storied, modern building was located in an upscale section of the city known as Chula Vista. I was escorted into an office on an upper floor and was greeted by a pleasant, talkative, middle-aged man seated behind a big desk whose name I don't remember. I assumed at the time that he was the cultural attaché but as we talked he seemed to know an awful lot about our public opinion project, and asked questions which led me to suspect that he may have represented some other agency. He gave me his card and told me to call him if there was anything that I needed.

The realization struck me then, and has stayed with me ever since, that being Scott Cook as anthropologist and Scott Cook as representative of the Roper Center in Latin America had quite different implications. As an anthropologist, except for a handful like Oscar Lewis, access to top levels of the political-economic power structure is generally not sought nor achievable and, in fact, is best avoided. As a representative of the public opinion-political polling establishment, on the other hand, all doors are opened and more eyes are upon you. Indeed, I learned through my visits with the head of the Gallup agency in Caracas that monthly public opinion reports covering several key variables like economic well-being, job security, political party preferences, and so on were produced and delivered directly to the office of the President. This was serious business.

Not all of my time in Venezuela was devoted to the LASDB project; I also did some anthropological exploration in a rented car. I drove to Puerto La Cruz to meet with a US expatriate political scientist, Steve Ellner, married to a Venezuelan. He taught at the local Universidad de Oriente. I had read some of his articles on Venezuelan politics and wanted to meet and talk with him. We drove together to Cumaná at the tip of the Paria peninsula where Yvan Bretón, who Ellner also knew, had conducted his dissertation research. I also remember going to a local restaurant with him and his wife, who I think was a journalist, to eat pre-ordered *pescado empapelado* which was a sea bass (*mojarra*) bathed in salt, wrapped in special paper, and steamed. It was mouth-wateringly delicious. Other memorable meals I had in Venezuela were in restaurants specializing in flame-broiled beef or rabbit, the latter often served with boiled potatoes and vegetables. I later invited Ellner to give a talk at UConn. He was (and is) very knowledgeable about Venezuelan politics. His left-wing perspective was not in fashion at Simón Bolívar University but was at the Central University and in the provinces.

In Caracas, I went to an upscale Brazilian jazz club called the *Papagallo* which appropriately had a large neon parrot in front. It was a large, well-appointed establishment, with a long bar, tables, dance floor, and excellent live samba music. I was seated at the bar when in walked two gentleman in business suits escorting a beautiful young lady (as many are in Venezuela). They sat down a few stools away from me with the young lady seated between them. The music was playing, and the place was not yet full because it was still early. I was quite content sipping away at my Hemingway daiquiris on the rocks (which I had learned to appreciate in Puerto Rico and Cuba).

Suddenly, I heard shouted curses from down the bar. The two "gentlemen" had started a fist fight, and a chair-throwing free-for-all ensued. Several tables were overturned and chairs were strewn everywhere as the two of them rolled around the floor wrestling and trading punches. Finally, a combination of bouncers and waiters broke up the fight and escorted the two disheveled gentlemen out of the establishment. The attractive young lady had disappeared but I hung around a while to listen to jazz and then moved on to another club.

That was only one among several incidents of violence I witnessed in Caracas. Once I was walking along a pedestrian *paseo* lined with shops and outdoor cafes when I saw a fashionably-dressed middle-aged woman approaching with a leashed dog. Suddenly, the dog snarled and charged toward a passing male pedestrian who then aggressively defended himself against the woman and the dog, until the omnipresent police intervened.

On another occasion, I had taken the subway to *Silencio*, the colonial *casco* (center) of Caracas where the Capitol and legislature is located, and which is also the main location of gold jewelry retail businesses. I went there to shop for a piece of jewelry for Hilda. On my return subway trip back to the modern city center the train arrived at the station and, as soon as the doors opened, I saw a fist extended to smash the face of a pedestrian waiting on the platform. There had been no situational interaction possible between the fist-wielder and the victim. I hurriedly walked away toward my hotel without seeking further details about that act of random street violence which was commonplace in Caracas at the time.

In all my years in Mexico and Puerto Rico I never saw such violent incidents in public settings. Of course, it could have been much worse. Yvan Bretón was walking on a street in the center of Guatemala City carrying a shoulder bag when he was shot in the chest in an attempted robbery. He almost did not survive the assault and had to be flown by the Canadian government to a hospital back in Quebec for treatment and recuperation. I never saw such incidents in my travel through the western coastal lowlands and highlands of Guatemala in the 1970s when my family and I had to leave Oaxaca to renew our tourist visas, but I did pass nervously through many checkpoints with armed military and saw them almost everywhere I and my family went.

Brazil

My relationship with the LASDB project in Brazil was less academic and more ceremonial than the one with Venezuela. Since I was not a pollster myself and did not speak Portuguese, my trip to Brazil was very formal and impersonal. I knew Orjan Olsen whose survey research firm (IBOPE) had a relationship with the Roper Center and Fred Turner before the LASDB project was launched. He was pleasant and cooperative but I was there only to be present at a meeting of the Brazilian Manufacturers Association which funded scholarships for students in public opinion research. Olsen's firm had academic ties with the state university in Campinas. I attended the ceremonial meeting and dinner in Sao Paulo and the next morning Olsen had arranged for me to be driven to the campus of the university in Campinas to visit their survey research program.

I had planned the trip to Brazil so that I could spend a night in Rio de Janeiro before traveling by air to Sao Paulo and then by chauffeured car to Campinas. I stayed in a hotel on the beach in Copacabana and immediately headed to Ipanema to see if I could find the "girl" portrayed in one of my favorite sambas. I did not find her. Then I went back to the hotel and decided to take a nightly stroll along the walkway adjacent to Copacabana beach.

I had noticed during the walk that my shoes were getting soiled often and realized that the omnipresent shoeshine boys had a clever technique for clandestinely spraying a filthy solution on shoes of passing pedestrians. At one point I stopped to get the stuff removed from my shoes but before I had placed one shoe on the shine box I had a broken bottle stuck to my throat by one of several young thugs who surrounded me. I felt pickpockets at work and a few seconds later they had all quickly dispersed. I was left standing and unhurt but – my $200 or so in cash had been stolen from my pocket. Being a somewhat wary traveler in Latin America, I had long ago learned never to carry a wallet or billfold. My dad and I had ours stolen in the 1970s in a Oaxaca market. Whatever cash I carried was always hidden in pants or shirt pockets. But the boy thugs from Copacabana knew this, and knew where the money was. I returned to my hotel with soiled shoes and no money.

The next morning I caught the rail tram up to Corcovado, the 710 meter granite peak with the gigantic *Cristo Redentor* statue that looms over the city. I got out of the tram after a slow half-hour ascent through *favelas* up the mountain, and walked out into the promenade surrounding the statue. I was instantly overwhelmed by the spectacular view and the height, I gazed up at the gigantic statue and suffered a sudden attack of vertigo. I managed to regain my balance and composure and quickly hastened to the tram station for the descent back to the city – cursing for having exposed myself to a situation I should have realized would result in vertigo. I caught a late afternoon flight to Sao Paulo, with no regrets about leaving Rio.

After the ceremonial dinner hosted by the Manufacturers Association, I was driven the following morning to Campinas. The hosts at the state university were friendly and hospitable, showed me around their center, and then deposited me back at the downtown hotel. There was absolutely nothing to do in Campinas, and my Hispanicized effort to speak and understand Portuguese interfered with communication – even though Spanish and English were understood by some. Also, there was a nighttime curfew in place due to a plague of street violence, so I was instructed by my hosts not to leave the hotel – which was basically empty and had only a mediocre bar and restaurant with no service. All told, I did not have an enjoyable visit. I flew back to San Paulo after only one night in Campinas, went into a fairly decent hotel near a big park, visited record stores to look for Brazilian jazz CDs, found a reasonably good jazz bar in which to pass a few hours, and spent the rest of the time in my hotel room shooting at telephone books with an air pistol I had purchased in Campinas (airguns are a hobby of mine). I left Brazil the next morning and, fortunately, had no cause for a return visit.

Panama

Another of my trips during this period was to Panama where I had an appointment with a pollster regarding his possible participation in the LASDB project. But my main purpose was to tour the country and to take advantage of family connections of my UConn doctoral student, Dania Brandford-Calvo (1993), to the Canal Authority. I met her family, we drove to and toured the interesting city of Colón, and then went on a pre-arranged trip with her relative who worked for the canal authority to see the canal system. The first part of the trip involved taking a launch with an inboard motor out into Balboa Harbor to meet a huge Japanese car-transport ship that was scheduled to pass through the canal. We arrived at shipside of the ten-story high vessel, a small door opened about two stories up and a ladder dropped down which we had to ascend into the ship. It was rather scary but we climbed up and into the massive interior, climbed endless stairways and maneuvered endless passageways to finally reach the bridge where the Japanese captain greeted us. We were given a tour of the ship and its facilities, including a small cafeteria, and proceeded to slowly move into the canal, passed through the Miraflores Locks, crossed Miraflores Lake and, if my memory is correct, disembarked at the San Miguel Lock. The trip ended with a tour of the inner workings of that lock and, then, of the headquarters of the Canal Authority. It was quite an experience.

The next day I rented a car and drove to the westernmost city of Panama, David, to spend the night and returned the next day to Panama City. I passed through some interesting towns and villages, went to a local market where I bought a few craft items, and saw a few places that might merit anthropological fieldwork – but I never went back. I was favorably impressed by the country, the striking contrast between Colón on the Atlantic side and Panama City on the Pacific side, and by the contrast between colonial vs. modern sections of Panama City itself. Needless to say, the night time scene in Panama was quite lively.

I cannot imagine why President H.W. Bush invaded Panama with such excessive, force. His decision was totally reprehensible, and was an unjustifiable exercise of hegemony. Many innocent Panamanians lost their lives as a result. Besides, Manuel Noriega had been on the CIA payroll anyway, and there were surely other means available to control his allegedly delinquent behavior. But such folly has run throughout the history of US relations with the Mexico, Central America, and the Caribbean.

Cuba

In May 1977, the historian Hugh Hamill, the sociologist Josef Gugler, and I traveled together to Havana via Montreal on a Cubana airlines flight.

Each of us had agendas for possible research in Cuba and we decided it was time to see if there was any receptivity in the Castro government for our doing so. We arrived on the same day that the famous television personality Barbara Walters did for her long network interview with Castro. We essentially were under tight government monitoring throughout most of our one-week stay – although we did have freedom to move about on our own within the city of Havana without an assigned "guide." We were taken from the airport and installed in a new oceanside tourist hotel in a workers tourist complex just outside Havana to the north east off the Via Blanca called Mar Azul. It was used by the department of tourism as a training site and was quite comfortable and well-run. Upon our arrival at the Havana airport we were assigned a tourist guide who transported us to the hotel. In the group staying at the hotel, and who had arrived on our flight, was a Midwestern businessman who specialized in brokering used farm equipment. He was the only one in the group lodged in the hotel who was to have direct meetings with Fidel Castro. It appears that Castro had given priority at the time to acquiring equipment for his farming collectives.

Hamill, Gugler, and I planned ahead for each day's collective and individual activities with the assistance of our Department of Tourism guide. There were times when we split-up since each of us had to attempt to meet with specialized agencies or people who we thought might be supportive of our specific research agendas – Hamill in colonial archival research, Gugler in urban research, and me in research on the independent peasantry. If we went our separate ways, we would discuss the results of our day's experiences at the hotel bar in the evening. We usually ate together either at the hotel or at restaurants in the city – including worker's cafeterias and, of course, we went together one night to the famous El Club Tropicana to see the floor show. Another evening we went to a bar featuring a well-known group playing a new wave variety of folk music (i.e., with acoustic and electric guitars and other instruments). It was unbearably loud – almost as loud as the brassy "Dirty Dozen" ensemble I heard years later at Antone's in Austin where my son-in-law and I left the establishment temporarily stone deaf.

I went alone on a noontime Hemingway bar tour visiting *La Floridita* for daiquiris and *La Bodeguita del Medio* for mojitos just like Hemingway did on a regular basis. I remember getting out of the taxi in front of *La Floridita* and had no change to pay the driver – so I went into the bar to ask for change and several Cuban men seated at the bar took wads of dollar bills out of their pockets and asked what I needed. I was impressed because exchange controls were operative and US goods were scarce – restricted to stores for Communist Party members only. The drinks were excellent at both bars; they looked unchanged from Hemingway's days and were filled with relevant memorabilia. Both bars were full of thirsty customers at mid-day. The atmosphere was of the normal Latin American variety, no sense of "big brother watching you."

We chose one day to go to the University of Havana to walk around and see if we could make any contacts with interested like-minded faculty. We first arrived at the monument for Julio Antonio Mella an anti-Machado student activist who was exiled to Mexico and assassinated there in the 1930s while walking down the street with Tina Modotti the photographer and model for Edward Weston. Then we split-up, and I proceeded into the heart of the campus looking for an administrative office building or a social sciences building. I was finally stopped by a campus policeman, asked for my papers, and quizzed about my purpose in being there. He told me in no uncertain terms that I could not just freely wander around the campus but needed to make an appointment and know exactly where I was going. He then directed me to an administrative building where I might get some help.

I finally ended up in an agrarian studies institute headed by a young woman, whose name I do not recollect. She had studied rural sociology in East Germany. We spoke for about five minutes in a hallway, not in her office. She chose her words cautiously but I sensed that she was quite familiar with agrarian Marxist literature on peasant class differentiation in the Soviet Union. We had a friendly exchange of cards, and she left me with the impression that there might be a research possibility in the future, if I submitted a formal research proposal for review. I decided not to pursue the matter further.

Meanwhile, back at the hotel the television was on and Fidel was giving a speech on the agrarian problem that lasted more than an hour. We all listened intently. It was a virtuoso performance covering the history of agrarian problems in the post-revolutionary Soviet Union, problems with the kulaks (rich peasants), Lenin's New Economic Policy, and the debate over collectivization vs. independent farms, central planning vs. free market, and so on. Fidel dramatically emphasized his determination to avoid in Cuba the mistakes of the Soviets (i.e., Stalin) regarding forced rural collectivization and the termination of recalcitrants (usually kulaks). The one line that caught my attention was Castro's mocking exclamation *"¡Que se queden los campesinos con sus minifundios para siempre en el museo de la historia agraria!"* or something to that effect. Loosely translated, let the peasants stay on their small farms and try to make a living if that is their desire, but that is not the preferred, progressive solution which is collectivization and state farms. Castro had expounded upon precisely the problem I wanted to research. But the unfortunate reality was that, unlike the Midwestern farm machinery salesman, I would not get anywhere near to an audience with even a minor representative of the supreme *compañero* to discuss my research agenda.

Neither Hamill nor Gugler experienced better luck than me at the university so we decided after Castro's speech to try to visit a collective farm – which presumably we could do within our restricted travel area of Havana province which did have rural areas. We hired a taxi to take us to a collective farm but we never got a tour. We managed to talk to some independent cultivators in the area who clearly stated their preferences to avoid affiliation with collectivization, to be free to work their own farms, and free to sell their own produce.

That pretty much ended my involvement in the matter. I did make one last effort to find the Cuban delegation of the Puerto Rican Socialist Party which had provided me with a letter of introduction for the purpose of trying to meet with Cuban Communist Party officials to discuss my research interests. I located the Puerto Rican delegation and they said in a nutshell to forget it, such a meeting could not be arranged, and that my intentions were noble but naïve.

Meanwhile, each evening back at the hotel bar we listened enviously as the used farm machinery broker told us of his latest meeting with Castro and of his success in getting Fidel's approval to arrange for shipments of used farm equipment and payment through Panamanian channels. In essence, he had succeeded and the rest of us failed in our missions. But we were able to see and experience quite a bit, enough to form our impressions of Castro's regime.

Our last two days or so in Havana involved a visit of all three of us to the *Casa de las Americas* cultural center headed by the historian Roberto Fernández Retamar. It was a combination of a publishing house and distributor of various books and pamphlets, as well as a sort of art museum and promoter of writers, graphic artists, and painters. Fernández Retamar was very cooperative, talked with us at length, and said we could correspond with him afterwards by mail about our respective interests.

We visited the homes and workshops (*talleres*) of some talented graphic artists (*carteleros*) and painters and bought a few of their works. I still have hanging on the wall of my home office a 16 × 20″ black ink drawing of a working-class man wearing a medium-brimmed hat, and open-collared shirt, with half of his face blackened but one eye peering directly towards the viewer and standing alongside a docked fishing trawler. Only his head and neck is drawn but that image dominates three-quarters of the drawing. The title "En El Puerto" is penciled in at the bottom of the drawing as is the artist's name which appears to be "Luís Cabrano 22" or something similar. Apparently, I bought one of twenty-four lithographed copies. I purchased it directly from the artist himself in his workshop. I have been unable to find any more information about him subsequently. In any case, our visits with graphic artists proved to be one of our most enlightening and rewarding experiences.

We walked the streets, visited the photograph-laden *Museo de la Revolución*, and other places of interest. We saw a lot of armed police and military, saw many Russians and East Germans on the streets and in bars and restaurants, most notably in our evening at the Club Tropicana, and many of their ships in the port. That was not surprising considering the US blockade. We were approached a few times by Cubans in our hotel and on the streets anxious to purchase from us clothing or any other personal items that we might be willing to sell them. We noticed a scarcity of consumables in grocery stores and markets but a limited range of consumables were available – especially basic root crops and fruits. We did not encounter beggars on the streets, evidence of prostitution, or of people being ill-fed.

Granma, the communist party newspaper was available everywhere (no other newspapers were) and books available for purchase were limited mostly to *Casa de las Americas* publications or Spanish-language translations of Marxist-Leninist classics from the Soviet Union.

We visited a cigar factory run in the traditional style with a reader (*lector*) seated on an elevated sort of lectern and reading material to the workers, many women and many blacks, rolling cigars. Most of our guides, and most of the functionaries we met, were white and wore guayaberas; a majority of workers in non-supervisory positions were black. There were many female taxi drivers and their vehicles were 1940s and 1950s vintage American cars – no new vehicles, not even from Eastern Europe, seemed to be there. Locally made *guayaberas* were available for purchase and I bought a couple for later use, along with a bottle of Havana Club *añejo* rum and cigars.

Photo 1. June 16, 1940, Pittsburgh

Photo 2. Winter, 1943, Daytona Beach

Photo 3. San Antonio, Texas 1946, school play "pilgrim" with Red Ryder BB rifle

Photo 4. San Antonio, Texas, 1946, first bike

Photo 5.   Austin, Texas ca. 1953

Photo 6. June, 1959 with Hilda, American University graduation

Photo 7. Cutting cane in Magdalena, Ocotlan, Oaxaca, 1968

Photo 8. Oaxaca Shoot, Tlacolula marketplace, 1990

Photo 9. With H. A. Cook (dad) in his Asheville, NC shop, late 1990s

Photo 10.   Texas State University, talk and photo exhibit, 2013

CHAPTER 5

Malinowski and Metates in Four Oaxaca Communities, 1965–1974

My romance with metates began with my reading of Malinowki's Oaxaca market system study, first published in 1957, where in two paragraphs he identified the "grinding-stone or metate" as "the principal pre-Columbian article which appears in the modern market" and noted a "seasonal variation in sales connected with the custom that at every marriage a metate painted and decorated in gaudy colors has to be presented ritually to the bride." He also described how "When buying a metate on behalf of the donor, the woman – for grinding is women's work – would examine the surface, assess the size, and carefully look for any defects…", and that "A handful of maize is usually supplied by the vendor, so as to make a trial assessment possible. " Finally he observed regarding bridal metates, that the "godfather of the bride, who is the usual donor, will dance ritually at a certain stage of the marriage ceremony with the metate held on his back" – a ritual actually observed by Malinowski himself at a marriage ceremony in the village of Abasolo (Malinowski and de la Fuente 1982:169–170). Information was also given about metate price determination through haggling, and how the size and decorative quality of metates influenced their pricing.

Even though no information was presented in that publication about the production of metates or about their producers, the *metateros*, Malinowski's insightful comments defined these craft commodities' double role as utilitarian objects whose price was determined by haggling in the market and as gifts ritually presented in village marriage ceremonies to brides by their godparents – thus illustrating the complexity of their value as commodities. Metates had a decorative or aesthetic dimension, as well as a strictly utilitarian one for grinding corn and other spices or foodstuffs.

They were gifted to brides by godparents in wedding ceremonies (*fandangos*) where they were presented in a ritual dance by the godfather (*padrino*) – *el baile del metate* (Malinowski and de la Fuente 1982:169–170; cf. Malinowsky and de la Fuente 1957:154–155; Cook 1968:9n4).

Malinowski's only publication about his Oaxaca fieldwork was also an instruction manual in ethnographic market economics and gave the impression that his unpublished field notes from a second fieldwork session might yield even more evidence of his interest in the metate industry. Unfortunately, that evidence would not be part of the public record for many years after his death in 1942 (Cook 2017a, 2017b).

Given their status as indispensable tools for grinding corn and other foodstuffs in the Mesoamerican peasant household, it was surprising to me that metates had not been studied by anthropologists. Metates, manos, and their makers, the metateros, had been excluded from cultural anthropology's celebration of handicrafts or *artesanías* which was heavily slanted toward pottery or woven goods. Aside from the purpose of ending this record of neglect, my decision to focus on the metate industry as my summer field school project in 1965 and in my subsequent doctoral dissertation research, was motivated by my recognition of that commodity's potential for full economic anthropological treatment. This meant, in my case, applying Ed LeClair's (1959) comprehensive scheme involving production, transfer, and consumption events in my study as a guide to observation and analysis. This covered the procurement of raw stone via quarrying, the manufacture of metates (and manos) from solid blocks of stone with simple steel tools on work patios in the quarries, finishing and decorating them on household residence lots and, finally, hauling them for sale in marketplaces to buyers for own-use and/or ritual gifting (or to intermediaries who would re-sell to other buyers for own-use).

Work organization, household division of labor, and marketing in the metate industry could be observed and analyzed in detail. Total metate output could be counted and tabulated on an industry-wide basis permitting time series analysis. Unlike other higher volume craft products like pottery that required sampling techniques to study household production and estimate output, metate industry output in discrete villages involved fewer households and lower volume thus facilitating more complete observation, quantification, and monitoring of the entire production and marketing cycle.

My doctoral dissertation (Cook 1968) research plan, informed by my summer field school project in 1965, emphasized data collection through a combination of household survey, systematic observations, interviews, and archival work. It was designed as an in-depth study of village-based economic activities, especially the metate industry, not as an exercise in general ethnography (i.e., collecting data on any and every category of human behavior) but as one in economic anthropology. For me, this entailed an analysis of the production and transfer activity of the metateros as economically rational actors in a regional market system, as personnel in an artisan industry, and as citizens and members of communities. I also was motivated to establish a quantitative data base for price and output as key variables in understanding market behavior in terms of neoclassical time series and supply-and-demand analysis (Cook 1968:250–256, 259–260, 268–303; cf. Cook 1970; Schneider 1974:80–83).

This portion of my dissertation was reworked and published as an article that was my final contribution to the neoclassical current in economic anthropology. By the time I wrote that article, I was familiar with Maurice Godelier's persuasive argument that "The economy appears ... as an activity with multiple meanings and different functions, according to the specific type of relations existing among the different structures of a given society" and is "... a field at the same time interior and exterior to the other structures of social life" (Godelier 1967:263; Cook 1970:794 n.2). From that period forward, my research in Oaxaca was more in line with the approach of Godelier and the Marxist tradition than it was with the neoclassical approach.

For purposes of my dissertation, economic activities were conceived as occurring within discrete but interrelated spheres of production, exchange, distribution, and consumption. Production, not consumption, was viewed as the energizer of the economic process – following the view of Marx (Cook 1968:50 n. 10) and of Malinowski and de la Fuente (1967:181; cf. Cook 1968:8 n. 3) but also compatible with classical-neoclassical theory. I was determined to privilege a focus on a well-defined economic field of activity – emphasizing performance and quantifiable results but not overlooking social organization (e.g., household composition and residence patterns, kinship and fictive-kinship relations), the division of labor, and the role of a particular occupation/industry in these at the local community and regional levels.

The dissertation also had sections on history, cultural geography, land tenure, agriculture and animal husbandry, reciprocity, and the civil-religious hierarchy since these subjects were crucial to understanding the lives and work of the metateros and of other households in their communities (Cook 1968:52–76, 77–88, 95–120, 150–177). I collected data on the historical background of the peasant-artisan villagers from documents in local archives (governmental and private), state and national archives, and published sources, and from informant interviews (for historical periods within memory). It was not until my retirement years that I had time available to make use of the full range of data collected under these rubrics in a regional historical study (Cook 2014).

Since most communities in the districts of Tlacolula and Ocotlán were bilingual in Spanish and Zapotec, I found it most convenient to employ Spanish in my interaction with informants. I learned some simple words and phrases in the Zapotec dialect for purposes of rapport, but my use of that language in data collection was restricted to the selective elicitation of terminology in cognitive domains of special relevance to the research (e.g., taxonomies of land, the seasons, social organization, work organization) (Cook 1968:4–5). With certain elderly female informants who were monolingual in Zapotec, I conducted interviews with the help of my field assistant, Filomeno Gabriel, as an interpreter.

After writing my dissertation, I was fortunate to be able to extend my stay in Oaxaca for an additional year by accepting a position as research associate on Ralph Beals' Oaxaca Markets Study Project which was funded by the National Science Foundation and administered at UCLA. Beals agreed to allow me to continue my research on the metate industry in Magdalena Ocotlán so long as I also covered topics on his project's agenda. He was in residence for a few months during that period and we met with him regularly to discuss the ongoing research. Each fieldworker was expected to submit a type-written report and field notes weekly, and these were discussed with Beals during our meetings. When he was not in residence in Oaxaca, the reports were mailed to him and he would send his written comments back to us by mail. This was a useful experience since it forced me into a somewhat more disciplined fieldwork protocol than I had developed on my own. Also, Beals was generous in sharing his knowledge about anthropology and fieldwork with us in person and in his correspondence (Cook 2004:32–35). We all benefited from that experience.[9]

From 1966 to 1968, I accompanied the *metateros* weekly to marketplaces, using my vehicle to carry them and their metates and manos. We visited the marketplaces where they were accustomed to conduct business and explored new, smaller marketplaces where they had no prior experience. I also introduced them to *metateros* from different communities and, on occasion, brought *metateros* accustomed to selling only in the periodic marketplace of their own district (e.g., Tlacolula or Ocotlán) into a marketplace in a different district. The metateros from different districts got along surprisingly well and showed interest in inspecting their colleagues' products. There were few signs of competitiveness – but there were expressions of confidence that their brand of metates would not sell well outside of their customary market area.

That did, in fact, turn out to be the case regarding metates from San Sebastian Teitipac (whose metates had a whitish tint) in the Ocotlán market where Magdalena metates were customarily sold and where metates made of bluish-tinted stone were preferred. However, Magdalena metates sold well in the Tlacolula market simply because the stone from which they were made had the bluish tint renowned for its durability. Indeed, Inocencio Morales, Malinowski's informant and then mine, through his travels in the region became aware of this and, when he no longer was able to quarry stone from Tlacolula, where he had relocated, nor in his native community of San Juan Teitipac, he arranged to buy stone from Magdalena Ocotlán which he hauled by truck to his Tlacolula workshop. This illustrates that entrepreneurial "outsourcing" is not simply a practice of global capitalist enterprises.

This period of travel to new marketplaces was an experimental change of pace for the *metateros* and they, as well as I, were interested in observing how the buyers in particular marketplaces would react to the availability of metates where they had not been previously available. For example, buyers in the Santa Cruz Mixtepec marketplace, many of whom trekked down to this Zapotec valley community from Mixtec mountain communities a few miles to the West (e.g. San Mateo Mixtepec, San Miguel Mixtepec, San Bernardo Mixtepec, Asunción Mixtepec) had rarely seen metates available for purchase there on market day which was Sunday. Even itinerant intermediaries did not sell metates there. They were accustomed to making special trips to the Ocotlán market on Friday or to the Oaxaca City market on Saturday when they were in need of a metate or mano. On the occasions we went there, buyers immediately crowded the sales area and sales were quite brisk. These were adventurous experiments for the metateros and for me, and we all learned from them.

We shared our experiences with new and ethnically different (e.g., *indígenas de la sierra* or *serranos* many of whom were of Mixtec identity) clients. I paid the fees to local government officials for occupying space for the metate sellers and their products in the local market place; I was considered by local officials to be the *patrón* (employer) of the *metateros*. But, in fact, I was simply participating with them in new marketing experiences. Obviously, I was also collecting data but always with their help and involvement, and we constantly discussed the results of marketing data collected. On these and other occasions market information was shared openly, and we were engaged in a collective project for the interest of the *oficio* (craft). There were even occasions when I would, as a favor, keep watch over a particular seller's products when he had other business to attend to in the marketplace. My interaction with potential buyers on those occasions was simply to encourage them, if the products were to their liking, to wait for the seller's return before they made a decision to buy elsewhere.

In my fieldwork with the *metateros*, I never felt that I was engaging in a paradoxical activity, pitting me as a "distant observer" against "native peoples" in an effort to "disentangle what really goes on rather than what people say goes on" (Howell 2018:1). Much of the time we were both engaged in observing and discussing what was actually going on before our eyes. The existential fact that our places of origin, our home turfs were different, was really never much of an issue. Many of the metateros had work histories that included stints as braceros in Texas, Arizona, and California so they were by no means timid, restrained or inhibited in their interaction with me. They knew, as did I, that someday I would not be present among them – but for a span of twenty-five years I made my presence known as much as possible, and lines of communication were discontinuous but open during that period (cf. Howell 2018:4).

One research strategy that carried over from my dissertation into later work was "going into the village where production is rooted in the inter-household economy" rather than focusing exclusively on the extra-village marketplace (Cook 1968:4). I referred to this as the "production bias" and attributed it to Malinowski and de la Fuente (1957:85) but, also, recognized that it originated in the thought of Classical economists, citing the following statement by Ronald Meek: "…the Classical economists … believed that if the phenomena of the market place were to be properly understood, the investigation must begin by penetrating below the surface of those phenomena to the relations between men in their capacity as producers, which in the last analysis could be said to determine their market relations…" (1967:181; Cook 1968:4 fn. 3).

The dissertation project anticipated the practice of "multi-sited" (Marcus 1995) ethnography before this term was coined and became faddish in the 1990s and 2000s. I studied metate circulation from different intra- and inter-community production sites into marketing channels (including market-places and extra-marketplace sales) and into the possession of buyers-for-own use. Data was collected from buyers regarding their community origin and whether their purchases was for own-use or gift purposes but one shortcoming of my research was that I did not undertake a systematic study of the actual use of metates by women in food processing. Lynn Stephen, however, did collect such data especially with regard to festive preparations (1991:Ch. 8).

Based upon data from my dissertation research, the chapter in *Markets in Oaxaca* included a soliloquy in which an anthropomorphized metate engages in an imagined dialog with its producers, the metateros, as a means to depict the commodity circulation process of metates (1976a:157–158; cf. Marx 1930:58). This soliloquy expressed that the Valley of Oaxaca metatero can make metates for exchange only because, in doing so, he is satisfying a definite social demand in a system of intercommunity specialization and division of labor. As a general rule his labor power can meet the needs of his own household only to the extent that it is exchangeable for the labor power of other producers (in his own or other communities).

The market system, viewed from this perspective, served as a mechanism for the equalization of different kinds of labor (e.g., the labor of the metate maker, the potter, the weaver, the basket maker, the cultivator, and so on): It reduced these to "abstract human labor" and facilitated exchange … [so that] the metatero's metate, which has no use value to him, becomes his exchange value by enabling him to obtain, through the medium of money, another materialized form human labor power (e.g., a *sarape,* pottery, bread) whose use value he does want to actualize" (1976:157). Before the emergence of a generalized medium of exchange such exchanges still occurred as barter according to accepted standards of equivalency in which approximations of labor time played a role.

By 1976, I had adopted a version of the labor theory as my favored approach to the analysis of economic value. This was not novel in the context of the metate industry where, as I had documented in my dissertation (Cook 1968:263–264), the *metateros* themselves, uninformed by reading classical economists, held and expressed such a view regarding the value of their commodities in the market. The marketing process made the capture of surplus value minimally possible for the producer-seller (*propios*) but, more likely, for intermediaries (*regatones*). However, comparatively speaking the metate industry, like many other petty utilitarian craft-commodity industries (e.g., hard-fiber mats or petates, ceramics, wooden utensils) was not conducive to capital accumulation by direct producers.

The metateros, all of whom had experience as wage laborers either as braceros in the United States, or in agricultural or other branches of production locally and elsewhere in Mexico, knew that the cash income from their work would not make them rich. But they also were well aware that there was usually sufficient play in the market – whether directly for their labor or indirectly for the products of it – to yield cash returns sufficient to set aside as savings. This had permitted many of them as braceros to send remittances back to their families in Mexico; and permitted some of them, especially those with land and agricultural means of production, to invest small amounts in subsistence or cash crop agriculture or in metate trading.

Their occupation was physically demanding and could not be learned overnight. Indeed, if you were not born into a family where the occupation was already practiced your chances of becoming a metatero were limited. It not only required strength, stamina and hand-eye coordination but patience. Quarrying, moving, lifting, and cutting stone, even with the assistance of heavy steel tools, was not easy work. The precision-cutting, shaping, and decorating of metates and manos required a degree of finesse and an artistic touch – brute force alone would not yield a marketable product. There were also occupational health hazards related to the constant inhalation of stone dust, being hit by randomly flying pieces of stone, and from the forceful nature of the physical activity of repetitive strikes to blocks of stone with heavy steel tools. In short, it was not an ideal occupation for every man in need of one.

To realize the full value of his work, the metatero had to act as his own salesperson in the marketplace. In other words, he had to know how to calculate a minimum acceptable return for his work and how to bargain with strangers to arrive at a mutually acceptable price for it. His only advantage resided in the fact that the commodity he manufactured was essential in regional peasant households for grinding corn for tortillas – a staple food in every household. Most households, therefore, had needs at one time or another for new or replacement metates and manos – and they had to buy them in local or regional marketplaces from metateros or intermediaries. The commodities themselves, despite who sold them, were produced in only one of four communities in the entire Central Valleys region. In effect, these communities – or their industries – held natural monopolies over metate products. This gave metate sellers, collectively, a bargaining advantage which was diluted somewhat by competition between individual sellers.

I never ceased to be amazed at how well the metateros performed all of these tasks in different arenas, not to mention negotiating the sociocultural demands of citizenship and civility in their home communities. I now realize that some of the happiest times in my life were spent in the company of metateros – men whom I truly admire. The biggest regret I have about my early career is my failure to disentangle myself from the scientific and overly-intellectualized distractions of my profession to write a straightforward, humanistic account of the lives and work of those remarkable men with whom I spent a great deal of time.

Nevertheless, I did make ample use of interviews with them and fashioned capsulized life histories illustrative of patterns and processes identified as crucial. But these were economistic in focus and did not typically address non-economic matters. I was convinced of the importance of allowing the metateros to speak for themselves on questions of their livelihood. To some extent, my 2014 book was written to compensate for my earlier economism by exploring more fully connections between the metateros' market-oriented activities and those driven by other factors (religion, status) lumped together under their quest for "civility" (Cook 2014:xi–xiv, Ch. 10).

In retrospect, I should have been more inquisitive regarding the persisting demand for metates in the 1960s some twenty-five years after they had caught Malinowski's attention in Oaxaca markets. His perceptive discussion of these remarkable commodities was limited to two paragraphs buried in a late chapter of his monograph uninspiringly titled "Concrete Data on Selling and Buying" in its earliest published version translated into Spanish (1957:133–160) and in its belatedly published original English version (Malinowski and de la Fuente 1982:154–173). My fieldwork and systematic data collection focused on the manufacture and marketing of metates, but did not systematically interview women in household settings about the meaning and use of metates in their daily lives.

On several occasions I did observe and photograph the ritual gifting of metates, as well as their ceremonial use (see Stephen 1991:185–187). My impression from market transactions was that women tended to view metates pragmatically as instruments of labor and were more interested in physical features (size, height, stone texture, and color), together with those of matching manos, all of which translated into corn grinding performance and durability as a household tool. Decorative features, fit and finish were most important for gift metates which in more prosperous households were prominently displayed for status purposes, and were often not intended for daily use as opposed to use strictly on ceremonial occasions. Gift metates were larger, more skillfully finished and decorated, and more expensive, than standard, unadorned utilitarian metates. It is especially with regard to the mix of metates in the inventories of more affluent, celebration-sponsoring Zapotec households that systematic empirical data is still lacking.

CHAPTER 6

OVSIP, the Inflation Crisis Study and the Shoot, 1978–1990

My early ethnographic work in the metate industry communities stimulated me to develop a comparative concern with other peasant-artisan communities in the Oaxaca Valley with a focus on how their lives and activities were entangled with the wider regional and national capitalist market economy. It had become clear to me observationally that differences in location within the division of labor and specialization translated into differences in production organization and performance and had important implications for the level of economic rewards. The corresponding change in my theoretical orientation to one more informed by Marxist thought was implicit in comparing the sub-titles of my dissertation ("An Economic Anthropological Study of Production and Exchange in a Peasant-Artisan Economy in the Valley of Oaxaca, Mexico" – Cook 1968) with its belated revised and published version ("The Dynamics of Rural Simple Commodity Production in Modern Mexican Capitalism" – Cook 1982). The fourteen-year gap between the two publications reflected my change of research strategies which relegated my interest in the metate industry to the back burner and my new role as principal investigator in a multi-year fieldwork-based project (OVSIP) which widened the scope, theoretical orientation, and analytical focus of my earlier research.

Also, intervening in the process was the *Markets in Oaxaca* project with Martin Diskin in which we re-assessed our experience in Ralph Beals' Oaxaca Market Study Project (Beals 1975; Beals 1976; Cook and Diskin 1976a, 1976b). Two sections in *Markets in Oaxaca* best reflected the development of my thinking at the time. The first was "Oaxaca, Regional Underdevelopment, and the National Socioeconomic Structure"

(1976:17–25) in which we contrasted the mainstream *indigenista* ethno-cultural approach to the rural indigenous population with a newer economic class approach. The second was "Political Economy of Regional Development: Capitalist/Precapitalist Relations in the Valley of Oaxaca" (1976:266–275) where we argued for the relevancy of Lenin's study *The Development of Capitalism in Russia* (1964) to the study of the same theme in Mexico. There we also proposed the heuristic applicability of Marxist conceptualizations of articulation between capitalist and non-capitalist economic forms and relations in regional economies like Oaxaca (1976:266–275). In short, our discussions in these two sections posited new directions for future research and set my thinking on a different trajectory from the neoclassical economics-saturated one that predominated in my doctoral dissertation.

Sidney Mintz kindly wrote a quite incisive and provocative foreword to *Markets in Oaxaca* (Cook and Diskin, eds 1976) which praised our study as the first of its kind which "was not the study of a marketplace, nor even of a system of marketplaces ... nor a study of the class structure of a region ... It is rather a composite, synthetic overview of the ecology and economy of a region ... using distributive patterns of various sorts as a speculum for viewing a wider socioeconomic and political structure, which transcends both individual communities and particular classes" (1976:xiii).

In the penultimate paragraph of his foreword, Mintz constructively criticized us for "putting less weight upon the frequently competitive claims of different components within the capitalist sector," for implying a "calculated paternalism of an undifferentiated 'capitalism'" and glossing over the "internecine, long-term struggles among different capitalist groups, with varying but equally intense claims upon the same market or resource" (1976:xiv). I think his critique influenced my thinking about capitalist class fractions and their different relationships to direct producers as was subsequently reflected in the concluding chapter of *Zapotec Stoneworkers* (1982:353–397).

During the winter of 1976–1977, I drafted and submitted proposals to two granting agencies, the Social Science Research Council and the National Science Foundation, to support my continuing fieldwork in Oaxaca. The SSRC proposal was for a summer pilot survey of small-scale commodity production in the Central Valleys region, and the NSF proposal was for a longer-term project on the same topic.

In the late spring/early summer of 1977, thanks to a grant from the Social Science Research Council, I and a UConn graduate student/field assistant from Puerto Rico, Zoilo García, conducted a survey of craft-commodity production in each of the nine administrative districts (*distritos*) in the central valleys of Oaxaca. We conducted structured interviews with municipal authorities in each of the nine district head town (*cabeceras*) and culled data from various documentary sources and through interviews with participants in a representative sample of craft industries. We identified a total of 189 local industrial units, allocated among some twenty-four separate branches of production in eighty-seven separate municipalities (*municipios*).

The survey was neither exhaustive in its coverage of industries nor definitive as a census, but it did provide enough reliable data to serve as an empirical basis for planning future research. Three districts – Miahuatlán, Ocotlán, and Tlacolula – were shown to be the most important in terms of scale and diversity of petty industrial production, sharing between them some 56 percent of the total number of municipalities reported to have small-scale industries, 48 percent of the total number of reported local industrial units, and representation in either fourteen or fifteen of the twenty-four different branches of production identified in the survey.

Before the survey was completed, I had agreed to present a paper at a three-day conference on Oaxaca Studies sponsored by the regional center of the *Instituto Nacional de Antropología e Historia* (INAH) in late June (*Congreso de Evaluación de la Antropología en Oaxaca*). The theme in my session was "Integration of the Peasantry into the National Economic System" scheduled after a panel on urban studies and before another on ethnic minorities. My presentation had a panel of three discussants. Zoilo and I worked feverishly to piece together a coherent presentation in Spanish one or two days before the session was scheduled to begin. We minimally succeeded and barely made it to the auditorium in time for me to step up to the podium before a rather large audience. I had made a schematization of the key variables, the commodity circuits, and their social relations as a handout for the audience to follow. I think that helped but my presentation

was too long, rambling, and tedious; and the audience became somewhat glassy-eyed and restless as I droned on in minimally acceptable academic Spanish. Questions from the audience included a hostile critique
from Stefano Varese who was a presenter on the subsequent panel. As an
ethnopopulist, he objected to my Marxist analysis of rural class differentiation as dangerously overlooking indigenous identity (Esparza 2020:32,
323–328).

One of the patient listeners at the 1977 conference was Angel Palerm
(Cook 2017a:305–306) who walked with me afterwards to the bar of his
hotel (*the Calesa Real*) to quiz me about my presentation. I had met Palerm
in 1965 through Hugo Nutini, and he knew that I had been a student in
his "brainchild" graduate program at the University of Puerto Rico during
his stint in the OAS/PAU.

It turns out that Palerm liked my presentation but offered some sug-
gestions that would help me to clarify the analysis of the involvement
of peasant-artisan domestic units (PADU's) in production for auto-
consumption (PA), production for exchange (PE), and the degree of commoditization of its available labor power (CL). His view was that four mixes
were logically possible, each implying different degrees of involvement in
market processes to supplement direct subsistence production: (1) PA > PE
+ CL; (2) PA < PE + CL; (3) PA + PE > CL; and PA + PE < CL (Cook
1978:295). During his explanation, Palerm took out a ball point pen and
wrote these symbols (in Spanish) down on a napkin and then, at my urging,
gave it to me for later reference.

The first notation (1) depicts those household units in which production for auto-consumption (PA) exceeds the combination of production for
exchange (PE) and earnings from wage labor (CL). The second (2) depicts
those units in which subsistence production (PA) is less than the combined
earnings of production for exchange (PE) and wage labor (CL). The third
(3) depicts units in which subsistence production combined with market
production exceeds earnings from wage labor; and (4) depicts those units
in which it is less. A fifth logical possibility, not listed by Palerm and later to
be empirically verified in my research, pertained to landless units without
means for subsistence production which were completely dependent on
craft production or wage labor for their livelihood.

Palerm was quite a dialectician, very knowledgeable of the Marxist literature, undoubtedly quite familiar to him before he came to Mexico from Spain in 1939 at the age of 22 as an exile from the Spanish Civil War where he fought for the losing republican cause in the Catalán anarcho-syndicalist and socialist militias. His interest in peasant studies was derivative of his life, work and study in Mexico where he had a double *licenciatura* from Mexico City's *Escuela Nacional de Antropologia e Historia* (ENAH) in history and anthropology. He later became a friend and colleague of Eric Wolf. I was impressed (and surprised) by his admission in our conversation that he preferred the direct language, logical analytical thought, and empirical grounding of the English intellectual tradition, as opposed to the more literary, philosophical, roundabout, and less empirical approaches associated with Latin intellectual traditions of Spain, France, and Mexico.

Although I found Palerm's views on petty commodity production to be stimulating, I agreed with Wessman's critique that Palerm's analysis of pre-Conquest Mesoamerica in terms of Marx's Asiatic mode of production concept missed the mark by not focusing on tribute, the AMP's distinctive form of exploitation, and distinguishing it from rent in the feudal mode. This was an important issue at the time in the application of Marxist theory to Latin American social formations (Wessman 1982:329; cf. Cook 1977; Palerm 1982). I published a revision of the Oaxaca symposium paper that included a version of Palerm's notations cited as "(A. Palerm, personal communication)" (Cook 1978:295). That article also included a schematization of the production-reproduction circuits and the process of unequal exchange in the Central Valleys region that was, if my memory serves me, mimeographed and distributed to the symposium attendees (Cook 1978:306).

The summer of 1977 turned out to be an exceptionally good one: A pilot research project was completed, some of its tentative results were presented in a well-attended conference, and a private conversation was held with Angel Palerm who would tragically die of cancer only three years later at the age of 63. But, best of all, before I left Oaxaca that summer I received a phone call from the director of the National Science Foundation (NSF) Anthropology Program informing me that my research proposal for a long-term project had been approved. Not only had it been approved but, the director noted, with a total budget that was the largest awarded up to that time for a non-archaeological project in anthropology. I was ecstatic. Zoilo, his acquaintance Rosa María Salgado, who was also working on Henry Selby's and Art Murphy's urban research project in Oaxaca that summer, and I celebrated that evening at the newly opened Lagarto Bar. OVSIP was born.

Zoilo, unfortunately, decided to suspend his graduate studies at UConn to pursue a business opportunity in Puerto Rico, but Rosa María, trained as a social psychologist at UNAM, was an experienced survey research specialist, data coder, and fieldworker for INDECO, would make important contributions to the survey phase of project in 1978–1979 and to interviews conducted in 1985.

The topical headings in this 1978 article would become major areas of data collection for OVSIP: sources and nature of differentiation in production forms, the problem of economic calculation or valorization, the relationship between agriculture and non-agricultural production in the regional economy, capitalist/non-capitalist relations in the region and the circuits of production-reproduction, transfers of value between sectors, and, last but not least, class formation and relations.

The pilot project and its resulting article enabled me to refine my thinking about the interface between peasant-artisan domestic units (PADUs), subsistence, and market participation. The schematization of key variables and their relationships sharpened my focus on commodity production, circulation, and consumption resulting in household reproduction while also allowing for the possibility of capital accumulation; and always leading to value transfer to industrial capital or merchant capital, especially at regional and national levels (Cook 1978:306). This was how I now understood Mexican capitalism and the role of peasant-artisans that complex system of relations.

The process of concentrating on connections between variables helped the me to clarify how labor reproduction was achieved in a situation where various kinds of money capital were also being reproduced, and even where PADUs lose value both as sellers of labor power to capitalist employers and of commodities to merchant capitalist intermediaries. In OVSIP, the challenge would be to apply this scheme to a wider range of petty commodity producing industries.

The main variables at play in the circulatory/reproductive process as then conceptualized were: L, labor power; P, Production (or labor process) C, Commodity (product embodying use, exchange, and symbolic value); Cn, Consumption; M, Money; MP, Means of Production; and Δ indicating incremental profit. The simple reproduction circuit of the PADU can be represented as PADU $\to$ L $\to$ P $\to$ C $\to$ Cn $\to$ C_1 $\to$ M $\to$ C_2 $\to$ Cn .... $\to$ ΔP where the arrow indicates motion or circulation. The first part of the circuit represented by L $\to$ P $\to$ C $\to$ Cn indicates reproduction is achieved by the PADU's production for auto-consumption; the second part C_1 $\to$ M $\to$ C_2 $\to$ Cn indicates that reproduction is achieved through market transactions – the PADU sells commodities it produces (C_1) to acquire commodities produced by other PADUs (C_2). The symbols ... $\to$ ΔP indicate the possibility that a portion of money earned from the sale of a commodity can be invested to expand future production – the exception not the rule for PADUs.

Connections between the PADU reproduction circuit described above and capitalist circuits were assumed to be omnipresent in regional peasant-artisan economies like that of the Oaxaca Valley. They were present when PADU labor power was sold to employer enterprises for a wage. This labor power was represented as CL in the following industrial capital circuit: M $\to$ CL + Cmp $\to$ P $\to$ C $\to$ M' [Money capital (M) is invested in the acquisition of a combination of the commodities labor power and means of production (CL and CMP) to produce (P) commodities (C) to capture money profits M' or M + ΔM (selling price minus costs of production)].

Alternatively, PADU commodities were sold to intermediary capitalists who resold them at a profit as shown in the following merchant capital circuit: M $\to$ C $\to$ M' $\to$ C ....M_2. This Merchant Capital circuit initiates with the deployment of money capital (M) to purchase craft commodities (C) for a profit (M' or M + ΔM) which is deployable to either purchase more craft commodities (C) to keep growing the fund of profits (M' + ΔM) and the conduct of business. Unequal exchange operates in both of these cases to deprive the PADU of commodity value – either through low wages for its labor power or low prices for its products. Both of these variables are, of course, subject to seasonal and supply-demand fluctuations.[10]

There were many important variables not represented in these circuits like, for example, size, composition, and developmental stage of PADU's which determined their productivity. However, the circuits did show the possibility of PADU's breaking out of a cycle of simple reproduction into a petty capital accumulation process. This occurred through the deployment of wage labor and means of production acquired through investing earnings from cash sales of their craft commodities (or cash crops) into the purchase of wage labor and means of production to expand the output of the household enterprise (C' to P'). Through case studies, this process was shown to occur in the treadle-loom weaving industry and in the brickmaking industry.

The Oaxaca Small Industries Project (OVSIP)

My review of the literature in rural Mexican studies, including Oaxaca, since the completion and publication of the original OVSIP monograph, *Obliging Need* (Cook and Binford 1990; Cook and Binford 1991), suggests that it remains alone as a combined, theoretically-informed and systematic empirical survey and case study of peasant-artisan household production in a regional indigenous economy. The machine-readable data set for the project was derived from surveys of 1008 peasant-artisan domestic units in twenty communities in three districts: Ocotlán, Tlacolula, and Centro. In addition, separate interviews were conducted with a sample of sixty-nine intermediaries and shop operators in Oaxaca City and with thirty-one merchant-embroiderers in various Ocotlán communities.

Many findings standout. All of the rural communities surveyed displayed class differentiation measured by ownership/access to land and agricultural means of production (draft animals, plow, cart) and house type. Also, all displayed some mix of agricultural and non-agricultural occupational involvement; three-quarters of the households surveyed had some craft involvement but there were non-craft households even in craft-dominant communities.

A majority of sample households included some mix of agriculture and craft participation which demonstrated that these were complementary rather than mutually exclusive economic activities regionally. *Minifundisimo* (*minfundio* is a small farm) was extreme: 24 percent of surveyed households were landless and, of landed households, 60 percent cultivated 3 hectares or less of seasonal land units. Cultivated land was mostly rainfall dependent (seasonal or *temporal*) in a ratio of 10 to 1 to irrigated land. Only 13.8 percent of landed households held land in combination with principal means of production required to work it (oxteam + plow + cart). Even those households best endowed with land and means of production (≥ 5 hectares + oxteam, plow and cart) produced only about 1,000 kilos of corn annually (approximately one-half of the annual corn need for the typical household). Rural poverty was widespread throughout the region. Less than 20 percent of households surveyed could pursue agriculture as a viable full-time, year-round option. The majority had to supplement agriculture with craft production to remain viable (Cook and Binford 1990:42–47). Hence, the ubiquitousness of "obliging need."

Regarding household demographics, and craft and agricultural involvement, OVSIP found that intensive market involvement by craft producers was often associated with continued involvement in agricultural production, not by withdrawal from it (Cook and Binford 1990:47). Also, where households were large with many small children, there was a positive reward for those able to supply the labor and capital to undertake craft production alongside agriculture. The households best able to achieve this were those with higher labor supply. Even in those cases in which petty capitalist enterprises emerged from the ranks of peasant-artisan enterprises, and the separation of agriculture and industry appeared to be underway, agriculture became indispensable to petty industrialists as a source of subsistence or cash when living and business conditions worsened.

Most significantly in comparison with the existing record, OVSIP established, against Neopopulist and Chayanovian scenarios, that some household enterprises in particular branches of production accumulated capital, enlarge their stocks of instruments of labor and raw materials, and even hired additional non-household workers in order to expand output. There was definitive evidence of petty capitalist development within petty commodity household enterprises in some branches of production. The absence of such development reflected factors specific to particular branches of production, unfavorable household demographics, or the appropriative role of intervening intermediary capital – but only exceptionally did it reflect the lack of individual agent motivation or aspiration.

Politics and Political Culture

Musical sounds that, for me, are distinctively Mexican are not of guitar-accompanied *mariachi* or *corridos* (folk ballads) or unaccompanied marimba, but of bugles accompanied by drum roll that are heard as part of the reveille ritual at military barracks (*cuarteles*) throughout Mexico. These sounds are typically followed by strains of the Mexican national anthem "Mexicanos, al grito de Guerra…," alluding to battle cries in Mexico's wars to defend its homeland from foreign invaders.

I heard these martial sounds many times in Oaxaca when residing in lodgings in the vicinity of the Santo Domingo complex (once a Dominican monastery and now the site of the INAH Museum) which also quartered an army battalion in the center of Oaxaca City. An even more spectacular experience of the martial sound, for me, was from a room in the Majestic Hotel facing the Zócalo in Mexico City directly across from the Palacio Nacional. Every morning guests in those rooms are awakened by the sounds of the military drum and bugle corps playing reveille and marching out into the Zócalo from its quarters within the National Palace.

Those martial sounds conjure up a thread of despotism or of State vs. People opposition that was initiated with the emergence of the earliest state formation in pre-Hispanic Mesoamerica. This opposition was represented at the time of the Spanish conquest by the Tenocha (Aztec) empire ruled by the Triple Alliance of Tenochtitlan, Tetzcoco, and Tlacopan from the central Valley of Mexico – today's *Distrito Federal* known as Mexico City. Carlos Fuentes described this despotic thread as "the unbroken line of succession of power in Mexico: Aztec Emperor – Spanish Viceroy Republican Señor Presidente" (Fuentes 1969:5; Cook 1981). Such sounds, or some semblance of them, would have been familiar to Oaxaca Valley's indigenous villagers in the colonial and early independence periods when their daily routines were interrupted by external governmental interventions involving armed contingents of soldiers and militia with "trumpets blaring and flags raised (*clarines y banderas enarboladas*)" to administer justice, capture prisoners, resolve boundary disputes, or address other grievances (Cook 2014:192).

Malinowski in 1940–1941 could hear such martial sounds at dawn from his lodgings in the Hotel Modelo on the corner of Oaxaca City's main plaza (zócalo) within hearing distance of reveille at the Santo Domingo army barracks. It might have evoked in him memories from his European past as a Pole with a privileged upbringing in the Astro-Hungarian Empire but, by 1940–1941, as "a cosmopolitan humanist dedicated to the fight against totalitarianism" (Young 2004:xxii). Perhaps, the sounds served to remind him of the contrasts between old world and new world despotisms.

If the more plebian B. Traven had lodged in the same hotel he would have done so clandestinely. In response to the martial sounds, he might have looked over his shoulder to see if authorities were on the prowl for him – assuming that he was, in fact, before arriving in Mexico, the Bavarian anarchist, Ret Marut, still fearful of police-military apprehension due to his revolutionary activity against the German state. Traven would have had the same reaction to such sounds in Mexico City, in Tamaulipas, or in Chiapas (Cook 1995) which he surely heard.

Since Mexico's success in defeating militarily in 1867 the ill-fated French incursion to restore monarchical rule, the only potential foreign threat to Mexico's sovereignty was the United States. Despite the post-Civil War capacity and Manifest Destiny-driven motivation of the US to complete a take-over of Mexico, and two early twentieth-century invasions of Mexican territory, a full-scale invasion was wisely avoided. It appears that the US after WWII lost its appetite for territorial expansion, and found alternative strategies to penetrate Mexico through a combination of private investment and public diplomacy. Such a combination of strategies had already been successful during the Porfiriate (1877–1910) (Hart 2002).

Mexico's present and future loss of sovereignty will not be due to military invasion by the US.

Regrettably, in contemporary Mexico, the sounds of police-military intervention on behalf of state power and governance (*gobernación*) are, on occasion, those of tear gas canisters and bullets fired to quell riots or mass-protests as in the 1968 "Tlatelolco massacre" (Cook 2017c). These same sounds may arise during periods of martial law (*toque de queda*), as they did in Oaxaca City for several months in 1977 during a period of popular unrest (Cook 1984c:73).

The non-lethal bugle sounds of reveille are a reminder of a military presence in Mexican daily life that conflicts with patriotic themes of protection against invading national enemies. In Mexico, national defense is a pretext for internal security: The army is, in effect, an instrument of the state in its governance of its own people. The well-publicized narco-wars of the twenty-first century illustrate this.

In the concluding section of *Markets in Oaxaca* Diskin and I flirted abstractly with political themes implicit in the notion of "subsumption" or subordination of peasant forms of economic activity at the local and regional levels by capitalist relations of production (1976:268). Following Lenin's thesis that the struggles and antagonisms of interests typical of capitalism are present in every commodity economy and order of capitalism (1976:269), we then launched into a discussion of class relations and labor exploitation of petty commodity producers by merchants intermediaries and petty capitalist industrial employers (1976:270–275). But we did not move this discussion into one addressing political power and local and regional politics.

In the final chapter of the revised version of my doctoral dissertation (Cook 1982), I attempted to further elaborate on the class relationships, and their political implications, in the regional commodity economy by employing case studies of several industries. I also introduced a discussion of various peasant, worker, and student movements engaged in protests against abuses of power in the private business and governmental sectors, and of private interest groups protesting against alleged government abuses (1982:382–388). This effort was less abstract but still lacked ethnographic case studies. It did cover a period of political turmoil in the middle to late

1970s that resulted in a period of martial law and the resignation and exile of the university rector, Felipe Martínez Soriano, a leader of the Worker, Peasant, Student Coalition.

One of my most-inspired forays into political cultural discourse was my article in *Latin American Perspectives* (1984c) in a section entitled "Politics, Social Consciousness, and Small Industry." Around that time I was most impressed with the platform of the *Partido Mexicano de los Trabajadores* (PMT) and their candidate for Presidency, Ing. Heberto Castillo, a very articulate, astute petroleum engineer-politician of the independent left whose political propaganda was designed by none other than the famous caricaturist, Eduardo del Rio ("Rius") – my favorite Mexican intellectual. I still have hanging on the wall of my home office a framed PMT poster that circulated ca. 1987 with classic Rius prose: "*Hace un chingo de años, los indios eramos bien chingones ... ¡Cuauhtemoc era el gran chingón! Pero llegaron un chingo de gachupines y los muy hijos de la chingada hicieron mil chingaderas y chingaron a los indios ... ¡ Y nos llevó a todos la chingada.*"

Rius cleverly condensed Mexican history through the use of a cultural-historically-infused vocabulary built around variations of the verb "chingar" (to fuck) which has been employed by writers like Octavio Paz (1961: esp. Ch. 4) and Carlos Fuentes (1969) among many others. This term and its iterations is the quintessential identifier of Mexican vernacular discourse and has been exhaustively recorded in the *Chingonario* (Montes de Oca Sicilia 2010) which contains 200 pages of evidence of its inventive usage in Mexican slang. The best-known derivative term is "*La Chingada*" which alludes derogatorily to the Indian noblewoman-translator-mistress of Hernán Cortés, the Spanish conquistador, who bore him an illegitimate mestizo son – the mythical 'First Mestizo'. Known by the nickname of "La Malinche" or Doña Marina, she has arguably been metamorphosed in the collective unconscious of the Mexican people, or at least in popular culture, as the symbolic "Mother" of all *mestizos*.[11]

The PMT was the only political party of that period which actually had a section in its platform targeting voters from the ranks of small-scale rural and urban industrial commodity producers. I was impressed. It did not seem to be a factor in Oaxaca politics at the time but the following statement suggests that there might have been a niche for it (Cook 1984c:72): "Since

Oaxaca over the past few years has had its share of incidents in the ongoing crisis of the Mexican state, it is only fitting at this juncture to comment briefly on some of the political implications of my analysis of rural industry and social differentiation. With regard to the struggle between social classes and class fractions for hegemony within the party-state apparatus, and especially with reference to revolutionary socialist politics directed against the capitalist regime and the rule of the *Partido Revolucionario Institucional* (PRI) ... the following patterns seems to emerge from Oaxaca's recent political history: Support in the countryside for radical action comes from sectors of the population that have either a current or past involvement in highly capitalized agricultural operations (e.g., haciendas) or development schemes (e.g., irrigation projects). Invariably outbreaks of rural radicalism revolve around struggles over land tenure (and use) and related conditions (credit, crop subsidies, availability of farm machinery), and they have the support, collaboration, and often leaders of urban groups."

Female Labor, Inflation Crisis, and the Household Economy

The gender division of labor was of interest in the metate industry but the role of women was restricted to product finishing and marketing activities. However, in many other craft industries like weaving and embroidery female labor was both central and complementary. For example, in palm plaiting of mats (*petates*) and baskets (*canastas*) women were almost exclusively the plaiters of dried palm strips cut and supplied by males; and in backstrap loom weaving women were predominant over men as weavers. By contrast, in treadle-loom weaving men were the weavers and women were mostly involved in the processing of raw materials, or in the case of the garment industry using treadle-loom woven cotton thread, women were seamstresses. In the embroidery industry some men but mostly women did the embroidering, and both genders were involved in marketing.

A major focus of OVSIP was on comparing gender roles in the division of labor of craft household enterprises across several branches of production and industries, especially regarding the specific labor performed, the re-muneration (or not) for it, and customs and attitudes about gender roles (Cook and Binford 1990:152–189; Cook 1990a; Cook 1993). As it turned out, the unwaged or relatively low-waged role of female household labor proved to be decisive in the transition of household enterprises in two craft industries, namely, treadle-loom weaving and brickmaking to petty capitalism through a process of what I called "endofamilial accumulation" (Cook 1984a and 1984b; Cook and Binford 1990).

In 1982 the Mexican economy suffered a currency devaluation crisis which led to massive unemployment and hyperinflation, all exacerbated by September 1985 earthquake. Unemployment rose from 5 percent in 1982 to 12 percent in 1983 and continued to rise thereafter. This was worsened by record levels of underemployment. Inflation rates rose from an average of 80 percent annually from 1982 to the end of 1986, with an annual rate for the latter year officially reported to be near 106 percent (Cook 1984b:56–57), the highest ever recorded in the nation's history.

In November, 1985 during a sabbatical, I went to Oaxaca to research the impact of the crisis on a selected sample of households that had partici-pated in OVSIP. This is the only time in my career that I was compelled by external "crisis" events to re-visit previous research sites and interviewees. On the basis of re-reading the results of this study I am convinced of the merits of such "crisis"-related research, even if not intended to support possible ameliorative policy interventions.

The relatively short research effort was greatly facilitated by the avail-ability of the OVSIP files and by ongoing data analysis and interpretation. Given the depth and extent of the crisis, it was clear that the yet unwritten book covering OVSIP would have to include a chapter on the crisis. In that sense the 1985 research (which did yield an interim publication, Cook 1988) was designed to provide material for the concluding chapter of the book published in 1990 (Cook and Binford 1990: Ch. 7).

The mini-sample of twenty-five households for the 1985 crisis study interviews included residents of seven different communities repre-senting seven craft industries: metate fabrication, palm plaiting, treadle-loom weaving, wood carving, embroidery, backstrap loom weaving, and brickmaking. Three of these industries were organized by capitalist piecework relations and the rest by relations among self-employed petty commodity producers with varying degrees of dependency upon merchant buyers-up. I attempted to increase the representativeness of the sample to reflect differences in job position, degree of involvement in agriculture, and income/level of material well-being. The informants included men and women, self-employed and employees, poor and relatively affluent. Aside from economics, the interview also included questions dealing with the ideological and political consequences of the inflation crisis.

As anticipated most informants identified the crisis with a marked decline in their purchasing power attributed to price increases unmatched by increases in their incomes. Their responses typically included specific examples from their daily lives. For example a woodcarver explained: "Now one cannot buy anything at last year's prices. The stores no longer have fixed prices, they sell at any price they want. A half-kilo bag of soap detergent sold for eighty pesos last year, no it sells for 160. Everything is more expensive. The bus fare to town was eighty pesos, now it is 150 – almost double. There isn't anything that can be bought for 100 pesos."

About 70 percent of respondents either blamed the government or said that it was probably responsible. Businessmen and merchant intermediaries were blamed by 30 percent, mostly self-employed weavers and embroiderers who bought cloth, thread, and other materials from merchants they accused of arbitrary price gouging. A few weavers and embroiderers blamed raw material manufacturers. One of them said: "It's a question of the factories…two or three months ago I bought 200 kilos of thread. A week later the store was charging 125 pesos more per kilo than they had charged a week earlier. I said to them: 'It's impossible that prices are increasing daily by 10 percent.' 'That's the way it is,' they told me, and they show me a factory invoice. What more could I say?"

The research revealed two categories of reactive strategies employed by household enterprises to address the crisis: (1) those that impacted the reproduction of labor power within households; (2) those that impacted either the valorization of capital within petty capitalist enterprises, and (3) those that impacted the realization of exchange value within self-employed petty commodity producing enterprises.

With respect to the first strategy to counter the negative effects of inflation, household enterprises increased staple crop production (maize, beans, and squash). They also combined own-agriculture and collection of wild plant foods for auto-consumption to reduce their purchases of processed food items in stores; others simply reduced all consumer-good purchases.

The petty capitalist household enterprises (weavers and brickmakers), given their greater affluence, were able to draw upon a wider array of strategies (eight were identified) including increasing or decreasing non-agricultural production, increasing the production of cash crops, sell animals, and compensatory increases in selling prices of commodities produced by the enterprise.

The case of a weaving shop proprietor with several pieceworkers illustrates how the crisis impacted his enterprise's involvement in agriculture. In 1980 he had distributed most of his arable land to sharecroppers and was considering complete withdrawal from agriculture to devote all of his time, effort, and capital to his weaving business. The crisis changed things. According to him in 1985: "We changed our system. Now I don't give out much land to sharecroppers abut cultivate it myself. We have animals to feed and I don't get sufficient harvest from sharecropping. So, I spend more of my time in agriculture than before. We are working more seriously in agriculture now. I plan to plant tomatoes on a share basis. Also I bought another piece of land last year and planted garlic. That earned me about 150,000 pesos in profit over four months – a 50 percent profit on my investment. Last year I sold five tons of corn and bought thread with my earnings."

Although this particular respondent had turned the crisis to his advantage, others in the same branch of production were not fairing as well. Efforts to search for new markets in tourist resort areas like Cancún proved unsuccessful. Employee layoffs were widespread and several smaller weaving enterprises were forced to shutdown. This put many laid-off pieceworkers into difficult circumstances made worse by their lack of access to land or agricultural means of production, and thus unable to produce crops for auto-consumption.

Among my conclusions for the 1985 research was that although peasant-artisan enterprises in the Oaxaca Valley share similar structural characteristics, there was great variation in their access to and control over means of production, especially land. This variation was the basis for differences in their capacities to produce for own-use and for the market and affected their crisis responses.

The Oaxaca Shoot

I had met William T. Sanders who was a prominent member of the Anthropology Department at Pennsylvania State University before he contacted me in 1989 regarding participating as an academic specialist in a film project he was directing. I was impressed with his book with Barbara Price (1968) *Mesoamerica: The Evolution of a Civilization* as well as other works displaying his strong cultural ecological approach to the topic.

The film project under Sander's direction, named "Out of the Past," lasted from 1986 to 1993 and involved production of a television documentary series covering different world civilizational areas including Mesoamerica with a main emphasis on prehistory but also including contemporary ethnography. It was sponsored by the Annenberg/Corporation for Public Broadcasting Project with matching funds from several agencies including the National Science Foundation and the National Endowment for the Humanities.

Sanders wanted me to serve as an academic advisor for a film sequence covering metate production and marketing in the Oaxaca Valley. If I accepted, it would be up to me to make all the arrangements through my contacts in local communities for permission to film and to schedule the shoot which would take a week. I agreed to do this and worked out arrangements with my longtime friend and interlocutor, Filomeno Gabriél Mateo, to do the filming in his home village of San Sebastián Teitipac.

The Oaxaca Shoot took place over a week in early January 1990. The film crew was comprised of two technicians from WQED in Pittsburgh and the Shoot director, Werner Bundshuh from Cambridge Documentary Films of Boston. Each day of the week during filming, we left Oaxaca City early in the morning and returned at dusk at our hotel (Hotel Victoria) pretty exhausted from the day's shoot. Much of the filming occurred in the *Cerrito de los Metates paraje* located on the eastern side of the municipio's terrain (Cook 2014:89). Interviews with several *metateros* were filmed on location in the quarries as they worked. But we also managed to film *mayordomía* activities including a procession from the *mayordomo's* house to the church, agricultural activities (during which I elicited excellent information from Filomeno – Cook 2014:120–121), and a Sunday shoot following the metateros with their metates and manos from the village to the market in Tlacolula on *día de plaza* (market day in the periodic system) (Beals 1976).

Many hours of footage were shot filling a multitude of cassettes, only a tiny portion of which ever made the television screen in a sequence on "Artisans and Traders." That was disappointing but, at least, I had managed to extract gratuities from the director of the film crew for the municipal and church coffers of San Sebastián. Some of the footage included an interview with me by the director at the end of a long day's shoot. I was exhausted at the time and am glad that the footage was never shown. I also appeared in some of the quarry sequences, as a spectator of the above-mentioned procession, and in sequences filmed in the Tlacolula marketplace (see photos).

The real story began after the Oaxaca Shoot was long terminated and the "Out of the Past" series had been shown on television (Discovery Channel). It was apparent that a lot of ethnographically unique film footage had been wasted and, at the very least, should be made available for viewing in Oaxaca, by the involved subjects San Sebastianos themselves, and by other members of the academic community and public at large.

I communicated with Sanders by phone and in letters but could only get a vague commitment from him to do a jointly edited documentary on the *metateros* from the Oaxaca Shoot. All of that film footage was completely under his control as overall project director. He agreed with me about our obligation as anthropologists to make the footage available for showing in Oaxaca but I never succeeded in coming to terms with him before his death in 2008.

I was frustrated, although at some point I had convinced Sanders to make available to me a copy of the master tapes (which was negotiated by WQED-Pittsburgh at my request) which were in my possession at the time of his death. After lengthy negotiations involving the Department of Anthropology at Penn State, and video librarians/technicians there, and WQED-Pittsburgh I managed to have a professional-quality set of the master tapes sent to the *Instituto de Investigaciones Sociológicas* at the *Universidad Autónoma Benito Juárez de Oaxaca* in a format suited to television broadcasting there and for local video presentations.

Owing to the cooperation of David Webster at Penn State this happened a few years following Bill Sanders death in 2008. I do not think the tapes were ever edited for a public television broadcast in Oaxaca but my understanding is that a viewing of the tapes was arranged for the metateros of San Sebastian Teitipac.

Incidentally, I did not earn much of a fee for my services on the Oaxaca Shoot but I did get a free round-trip air ticket from Hartford to Oaxaca, and also got room and board paid for a week at the Hotel Victoria, one of Oaxaca City's finest where I had never lodged previously. During the several days that January before and after the Shoot, I was provided free-of-charge access to a vehicle and lodging in a vacant furnished apartment owned by a friend of mine, Arturo Solís, a well-known businessman who was proprietor of a large vehicle lubrication service on the Pan American Highway just a few blocks from the city center.

On Mesoamerican Archaeologists

As a sociocultural and economic anthropologist, a source of minor irritation for me over the years has been to be mistakenly identified as an archaeologist by almost anyone who asks me randomly what my occupation is. I typically reply to such queries, "I am an anthropologist" and the assumption on the part of the questioner is something like "Oh that's a field that always interested me, I'd love to go on digs and find all those ancient artifacts and stuff." I then try to correct them with a pat phrase like, "Well, I'm not that kind of anthropologist, I work with Mexican peasants ... blah blah blah ...". They look puzzled and utter something like "Oh." This makes me feel badly because I do not fit their "Indiana

Jones" stereotype, and when they get bleary-eyed as I attempt to explain to them what my career really entails. So, I usually avoid saying I am an anthropologist and just mumble something like "writer" or "historian" or "economist" to avoid disappointing and boring those who inquire.

Above, I discussed some details of my relationship with the archaeologist, William Sanders, and earlier mentioned one incident involving Kent Flannery and his wife Joyce Marcus. My first acquaintance with Flannery was by reading two very important articles dealing with Oaxaca (1968a and 1968b). I was quite impressed by his application of the conceptual pair, seasonality and scheduling, and his analysis of the latter as "cultural activity which resolves conflict between procurement system" in the context of Oaxaca Valley prehistory (1968:74). These are concepts that I have employed repeatedly in my work over the years.

I met Kent for the first time when I was working on the Beals "Markets Study" project and was doing fieldwork in Magdalena Ocotlán. Kent was into "caves" at the time and there was a complex of caves/rock shelters located on the northeastern side of Magdalena in the vicinity of a paraje known as *La Peña* which may (or not) have been on private property (although conceivably might have been on communal or ejido land) not far off the highway (Ocotlán to Ejutla). We walked to the site, which had a sort of prehistoric look. Kent surveyed the place but, apparently, found little surface evidence that merited follow-up. During that period, and especially with reference to the Teitipac villages, I tried to convince Kent to take a look at stone quarries or, at least, to assign a student to do some archaeological exploration at a quarry site in an effort to date the beginnings of extraction of stone for metate manufacture. But I never succeeded. This was also something that John Paddock had tried to stir up interest in during the 1960s but neither he nor other archaeologists followed up on the matter. I did finally get an archaeology student at UConn, Christy McDonnell, to undertake such a project but it ended up morphing into a broader study of residential mobility and migrant markets (McDonnell 2002). This was an interesting study but did not disclose much about the origins of metate production. For some reason the origin and evolution of metates remains understudied in archaeology. It just does not excite their interest.

After my experiences with Kent Flannery, I later met several other archaeologists working in Oaxaca in the 1970s and 1980s including Richard Blanton, Steve Kowaleksi, Laura Finsten, Gary Feinman, and Linda Nicholas (Blanton et al. 1999). Most or all of them were early members of the Society for Economic Anthropology and, on one occasion, we organized a meeting on the Oaxaca Economy at the International Conference of Americanists held in Amsterdam. I also remember meeting and hanging out with Blanton at an SEA meeting at UC-Davis on one occasion. When my NSF project was underway in the 1978–1980 period, Kowalewski and Finsten were engaged in an archaeological survey of the Jalieza region while I was working there Blanton was also engaged in his important Monte Alban project (Blanton 1978). We met and conversed casually about their findings on occasion, and formally so at the Amsterdam meetings.

My main frustration in conversations with my Oaxaca archaeological colleagues over the years was my failure to convince them of the analytical value of considering artifacts like metates, pottery, and other durable craft products as commodities which embody use, exchange, and symbolic values. Their avoidance of commodity economics was strange to me in view of their very inventive and imaginative pattern of borrowing from the repertory of social theory to suit their diachronic interpretative interests and their explanations of structure and process (Cook 2004:279–289; Blanton and Feinman 1984). They seemed to insist upon maintaining boundaries between reciprocal, redistributive, and market exchange relations, and to view commodity circulation as requiring pricing in money terms.

I had occasion twice in my career to comment on articles by archaeologists according to the *Current Anthropology* format (Cook 1975, 1983). While I agreed with Payson Sheets's assertion that it is "audacious for the archaeologist to claim to have discerned ancient mental ideals" I criticized him for failing "to understand that technology implies a dialectic between material and ideological processes and is a crucial component of economic infrastructure." I had not yet fully realized the potential of Marx's commodity concept but rejected Sheets's oppositional thinking pitting the "ideational order" against the "phenomenal order" and defended my position by quoting Leslie White's concise view of the ax as both object and an attitude or sentiment with regard to its use (Cook 1975:381). In opposition to Sheets's current of thought, a field of "cognitive archaeology" has emerged to which Joyce Marcus and Kent Flannery, among others, have contributed thoughtfully regarding ancient Zapotec religious beliefs, rituals, and symbolism. Their work is based upon analysis of glyphs and other symbolic stone inscriptions on materials from their own excavations in combination with available ethnohistorical and linguistic sources. Their work involves empirically informed speculation, perhaps, but is no longer audacious.

Kowalewski and Finsten considered the complex record of continuous human occupation over a period of at least 12,000 years in the Oaxaca Valley as one of "evolutionary continuity." They circumvented the discontinuity represented by the Spanish conquest which set in motion forces that led to the emergence of capitalism. I agreed that evidence of continuity could be found in subsistence practices where seasonality and scheduling have been important throughout regional history. I observed villagers collecting tree legumes and prickly pears just as their ancestors had done for millennia. An exclusive emphasis on continuity between pre-historical and historical periods, and that discrete elements or patterns may be bridge those periods, hinders our recognition that historical forms of social existence in which those discrete elements or patterns are embedded were significantly transformed by Spanish conquest and colonization (Cook 1983).

Even though Kowalewski and Finsten emphasized continuity, they would not deny that a major discontinuity in the Oaxaca Valley civilizational process had emerged by 1500 BC when plant domestication and sedentarization had irreversibly transformed the region's formerly nomadic hunter-gatherer economy. Nor would they deny that another major discontinuity was the emergence of hierarchical polities associated with the reordering of the social form of production and reproduction, a process which presumably had occurred by 500 B.C. but which fluctuated in scale and organization in a bewildering cycle of invasions and internecine strife down to the Spanish colonization. This "tributary" period beginning around 500 B.C. and lasting into the sixteenth century, with its contesting centripetal and centrifugal tendencies, was clearly discontinuous with the period of autonomous farming villages.

The anthropological and historical record from the Oaxaca Valley shows that in pre-Hispanic times industrial products, though often circulating as objects of trade or tribute with exchange value, were also imbued with sacred, ritual, social, and collective meanings. Kowalewski and Finsten recognized that the exchange values of those commodities did not carry price tags and, more often than not, that their exchange was a means of acquiring other commodities for consumption purposes or achieving social of political ends. Those exchanges, however, meant that exchange value was being realized and, even in the absence of general purpose money, there is no reason to discount operative standards of commensurability derived from generalized knowledge of labor-time equivalency and resource scarcity.

Max Weber's thinking regarding the realization and possible accumulation of exchange value in barter economies ruled by calculation in kind suggests to me the possibility of "superior equivalences" in the pre-Columbian Mesoamerican economy – that is profit-like increments of exchange value for quantities of qualitatively similar commodities transferred between producers (Weber 1978, I:101; Cook 2004:133). It is not idle speculation to propose that in the evolution of the Mesoamerican economy, prior to the emergence of regional systems of market exchange for commodities bartered at negotiated rates, there was commodity circulation by barter and reciprocity – in addition to redistributive tribute flows (Cook 2004:164–172, 2006:187–190).

CHAPTER 7

Traven, Handmade Bricks, and the Texas-Mexico Border

The Rio Grande Valley of deep south Texas is truly separate and distinct from the rest the state – and even from that part above it to the north but south of San Antonio. Even most Texans who have been there agree that it's a whole other world. The reasons for the detectably different existential look and feel of Valley life lie in history and geography. First off, it is not a valley but a river delta. The designation "valley" came from late nineteenth-early twentieth–century land developers who used the term "Magic Valley" to lure Midwestern farmers to relocate there on the railroad system out of St. Louis, Missouri completed in 1904 (Cook 1998:23–24). This project was successful and resulted in a few decades in a massive transformation of land tenure, use, and settlement patterns associated with demographic increase, urbanization, and ethno-political upheaval. This was largely an Anglo-American project to establish an Anglo agro-business culture with native Mexican labor. There was, of course, an emergent ethno-class structure that left some people of Mexican descent as landowners and as upper- or middle-class business owners – but political power for decades after the major towns along the railroad line were built – like Harlingen in Cameron Country and Mercedes, Weslaco, Donna, Pharr, McAllen, and Mission in Hidalgo County – remained mostly in the hands of the Anglo-Texan settler minority. Social life in the towns was originally segregated – Mexicans lived either north or south of the tracks which typically ran through the middle of downtown, or in dispersed *colonias*; and Anglos lived to the opposite side of the tracks or in large residences near their fields (Rubel 1966:Ch. 1).

Aside from the obvious cultural clashes between the Anglo newcomers and the Mexican natives, most notably language (English vs. Spanish) and religion (Protestant vs. Catholic), there was the nearby river border and the nation of Mexico on the other side which had larger, better-established urban populations in the border region in the early twentieth century to supply migrant laborers to the Texas labor market. Even before bridges were built, the river was easily crossed by boat, or wading, or swimming. Mexicans were on both sides and Mexicans born on the Texas side of the border had relatives on the other side; and the relationships were continuous despite efforts by the US government to control immigration during the twentieth century.

The Mexican people of the border after 1848 continued life as participants in a web of connections protected geographically from regular and sustained interventions by distant off-border power centers in Washington DC and Mexico City, or by even lesser nodes of power in state capitals or large cities like Austin, San Antonio, and Houston in Texas or Tampico or Monterrey in Tamaulipas or Nuevo Leon, Mexico. Life pretty much developed on its own after the mid-nineteenth century – until disrupted on the Texas side by the "Magic Valley" project, and the Mexican side after 1910 by the Revolution against the regime of Porfirio Díaz. Decades later came the civil rights and farmworker unionization movements in the 1960s, the NAFTA project in the 1990s, and the post 9/11 border security and immigration control crisis in the early 2000s and continuing to the present. The twentieth century encompassed transformative changes in LRGV economic, social, and cultural life. Despite all these changes daily life in the region remains characterized by a strong family-centered orientation and extended family relations, many of which reach across the border into Mexico.

The Lower Rio Grande Valley (LGRV) of 2020 would hardly be recognizable to those who lived there in 1920. It remains a delta but the course of the river has changed through natural meanders and flood-control measures. Agriculture has been mechanized, once new town sites have become urban sprawls connected by a freeway traversing all of Hidalgo County from west of Mission through McAllen and Weslaco, and Cameron County from Harlingen to San Benito and Brownsville. Several bridges now span the river at various points starting in the southernmost bi-national metropolitan area of Brownsville-Matamoros to beyond the largest one of McAllen/Hidalgo-Reynosa. The latter area is also a major hub in the Mexico-US-Canada common market arrangement with a vast Free Trade Zone full of maquiladoras, warehouses, and offices, and exhibiting ceaseless movement of container-hauling trains and trucks. Clashing with this activity, reflecting international cooperation and diplomatic harmony, is a controversial, massive construction project to build a steel-reinforced concrete high wall between Mexico and the United States. The wall, combined with the intensification of militarized policing and immigration enforcement, has the effect of disrupting the human circulation and sociocultural ties that have historically bonded the two sides of the border region. Consequently, bi-national citizenship and loyalties are strained; ethnic, national, and class divisions are exacerbated; and language and identity become related in a new, more urgent way.

Even though being Mexican or of Mexican-descent has been problematic in Anglo-dominated Texas since the nineteenth century, it is even more so in the opening decades of the twenty-first century. In the 1990s and early 2000s during my research on the border brick industry, repatriated Mexican brick molders, then either in retirement or still working in Reynosa, would tell me honestly and shamelessly things like "Me fuí de mojado" ("I went over as a wetback) or "Todos eramos mojados" ("We were all wetbacks") with reference to their earlier work experience in brickworks on the Texas side of the river. Yet, on the Texas side of the border, on multiple occasions, I heard the term "mojado" used by Tejanos with insulting reference to anyone who drove badly, misbehaved publically, or dressed or looked sloppy or unattractive. It was spoken and intended as a slur. Those Tejanos or Mexican-Americans in the LGRV who no longer speak Spanish, who embrace their American identity, and who have negative views about Mexico and Mexican migrants, may now be having second thoughts about their attitudes given the dark turn in US Mexico relations.

Jim Wessman knew of my study of handmade brick production in Oaxaca (Cook 1984a) and in 1985 sent me a clipping of a newspaper article on the handmade brick industry in Nuevo Laredo in the Albany newspaper (via the Dallas Times Herald) by a reporter named Patrick McDonnell

(1985). The article caught my attention for two reasons. First, I had no prior knowledge of the existence of the handmade brick industry on the Texas-Mexico border; and, second, it reported that the bricks were used to construct houses, commercial buildings and other projects on both sides of the border. The indication that border brickmaking was a bi-national industry involving Mexican producers and Texas buyers provided a second rationale for a comparative study with the Oaxaca Valley industry which produced brick strictly for local and regional markets.

My interest in border studies research was shared by Joe Spielberg Benítez, who was born and raised in the Lower Rio Grande Valley and was a specialist in the culture and history of that region. As a native son of Donna, Texas and a student of anthropology at the University of Texas, he had been an informant and field assistant for William Madsen's and Arthur Rubel's Hidalgo County project (Madsen 1964; Rubel 1966). I had maintained contact with him from the time we were both on the Michigan State anthropology faculty. By 1980 at UConn, I had developed and taught on a regular basis a course on Latino Studies organized around a comparison between the Puerto Rican and Texas Mexican experiences. As it turned out, handmade brick would connect my Oaxaca research on small-scale commodity production to my Texas-Mexico border studies interest, and provided an opportunity to benefit from Spielberg's social network and knowledge of his homeland.

Intrigued by the brickmaking activity so dramatically described in McDonnell's article, in 1987 I traveled to Laredo/Nuevo Laredo with Spielberg to reconnoiter the brick industry, and we also traveled the border area from Laredo/Nuevo Laredo downriver to the Rio Grande Valley for the same purpose. We confirmed that on the Mexican side of the river in the state of Tamaulipas from Nuevo Laredo to Matamoros, there were many areas of artisanal brickmaking like those described by McDonnell in Nuevo Laredo. Collectively, between 1950 and 1980, these areas had captured a substantial share of the Texas brick construction market (which, incidentally, is one of the largest in the US). Also in 1987 I spent a few days in El Paso/Ciudad Juárez to reconnoiter the handmade brick industry there which I had learned about from informants in Tamaulipas (Cook 2001:6–8).

I realized that it would prove rewarding and challenging from an economic anthropological perspective to study a labor-intensive industry of small enterprises in Mexico which had competed successfully in a US market dominated by large-scale, capital-intensive enterprises among which were some of the world's largest brick manufacturers like Acme Brick, US Brick, and Boral Brick. The 1987 trip led to a systematic pilot study during the summer of 1993 with the stimulating and fruitful collaboration of Joe Spielberg as we surveyed the lower Rio Grande/Rio Bravo region together daily. The collaborative pilot study led to a proposal to the National Science Foundation that funded my year-long solo project in 1995.

Among many border crossing incidents I experienced over the decades involving overzealous and uncompassionate US immigration officers, one that stands out for its ironic twists involved Joe Spielberg. At the end of our summer pilot project on the border brick industry in 1993, Spielberg and I had my vehicle packed and ready for departure to San Antonio. Our last stop had been to the residence of Joe's aunt and uncle's house in Donna where he was staying. Joe had arranged for his uncle, a local grocer, to acquire for him several vacuum-packed packages of dried *chorizo* (sausage) of Mexican manufacture. They had to imported clandestinely since the US had, at some point, imposed an embargo on imported pork products from Mexico. Joe had a particular fondness for these chorizos which he liked to mix and eat with his scrambled eggs for breakfast. The chorizos were well-packed and placed among clothing in Joe's suitcase.

Before picking-up Joe, I had been contacted by a brick industry informant in Reynosa regarding copies of certain photos or other documents that were available for me to pick-up prior to my departure. So, we crossed the border, drove to the ladrillera, picked up the materials, and headed back to the Reynosa-Hidalgo bridge to cross the river once again and head to San Antonio. Neither of us gave a second thought about the possibility of a baggage check since we were accustomed to crossing the border daily, sometimes more than once, without baggage checks. Well, this time it did not turn out that way. Joe, as I recall, was sporting his porkpie hat – which he referred to as his "spic" hat, and we had luggage in the back seat, so we were directed to the inspection station rather than permitted to drive straight across as day tourists, businessmen, or resident locals.

Joe and I looked at each other and saw the future: The inspector opened Joe's suitcase, immediately found the carefully wrapped packages, and asked what they contained while proceeding to unwrap them. Joe simply replied that they were his favorite chorizos that he had purchased. The inspector checked carefully and confirmed that chorizo was a Mexican-made pork product and, as such, was illegal to bring into the United States. Much to the inspector's chagrin, Joe and I broke out into uncontrollable laughter and we could not stop. The already contraband chorizo had been confiscated the second time around. It would be the Chicano INS inspector who would enjoy it with his scrambled eggs the next morning – not Joe back in East Lansing!

We were finally permitted to move on to the next inspection station – this one belonging to the State Controller of Texas to check alcoholic beverage purchases in Mexico. Before entering the bridge I had stopped to purchase some Havana Club añejo rum for later enjoyment. Unfortunately, I had bought l liter over the limit and, right there in front of us, the agent opened the bottle and dumped its contents onto the ground. Texas revenue agents at border crossings enjoy doing this to assert their authority and for the amusement of Texas taxpayers. Joe and I had yet another reason to laugh, and to engage in a contest of stringing together vulgarities in two languages, all the way back to San Antonio. By the way, Joe Spielberg won the epithet –spinning contest – he had an unmatched bilingual vocabulary of epithets and a uniquely dramatic comedic flair for expressing them (Spielberg 1974).

Despite being located in quite different physical environments 800 miles apart, the brick production landscapes in the lower Rio Grande/ Rio Bravo corridor and in the Oaxaca Valley share common characteristics apart from their location in or near periurban zones. The border corridor spans a river delta which supplies clay, sand, and water necessary for brick production. Consequently, brick production is predominantly located in the riverine zone. In the Oaxaca Valley, brick production is located in communities adjacent to Oaxaca City, where most of the brick is sold, and on agricultural land with relatively high water tables and clay soil – both of which derive geologically from activity of the Atoyac River.

In Oaxaca and the border area of Tamaulipas, *ladrilleras* all have on-site wells (*pozos* in Oaxaca or *norias* in Tamaulipas) necessary for preparing clay for molding. The presence of wells is one among several distinguishing elements shared by un-mechanized ladrilleras throughout Mexico that constitute Mexican brick culture (Cook 1998:288 n.2).

One striking difference between the Oaxaca and border brick industries lay in the larger scale and degree of mechanization of many *ladrilleras* in Tamaulipas. My interest in the brick industry in the Oaxaca Valley was triggered by its ecologically interactive process of production resulting in a gouged landscape in the fields and telltale smoke rising from the kilns during firing. Also, I was attracted to the brick industry there because of its petty capitalist organization. Bricks were produced in privately owned brickworks with either absentee or worker-owners employing wage labor on a piece-rate basis. This contrasted markedly with the production of other craft commodities in the Oaxaca Valley where family labor, not wage labor, was the mainstay of production (Cook 1984a).

The border brick industry presented even more spectacular evidence of environmental impact simply owing to its larger scale and investment in mechanization, including the use of mechanical diggers which were not used in Oaxaca. Also, its reliance on labor-saving mechanization was more pronounced and advanced than it was in Oaxaca. The reason for this difference was the much greater market demand and elevated output and capital investment levels of the Tamaulipas brick industry. It was much larger in terms of number of enterprises, personnel, and geographical dispersion than the Oaxaca Valley industry. At its peak in the 1960s and 1970s it had more than 100 enterprises, many of which had fifty or more employees.

Finally, the twentieth-century border brick industry was primarily, if not exclusively, organized in response to a demand from the Texas masonry construction market generated by the growth of urban settlements on the Texas side of the border – especially Laredo and downriver in the Rio Grande Valley in cities like McAllen, Harlingen, and Brownsville – and, after World War II, by rapid population growth and related masonry construction booms in major off-border cities like Corpus Christi, San Antonio, and Houston. So, the border brick industry, unlike that of Oaxaca, provided a setting for research on cross-border, cross-national business culture, entrepreneurial styles, business organization, ethno-national re-lations, and politics.

My research disclosed that in Laredo and downriver in the Rio Grande Valley there was an historical rift in brickmaking activity. During the nine-teenth century and until the 1950s, handmade brick production tended to occur on-site or in commercial brickworks, usually with Anglo-Texan proprietors, located on the Texas side of the river but employing almost exclusively Mexican-descent workers, a majority of whom were undocu-mented migrants from Mexico. This pattern was disrupted only by peri-odic shifts in US immigration policy that temporarily reduced the flow of Mexican workers or, as occurred in 1953–1955 with "Operation Wetback," forced the repatriation of undocumented Mexican workers. The result was the shutdown of brickworks on the Texas side of the river and their reloca-tion to the Mexican side. In turn, this led to a boom in brick production in the greater Reynosa area, and to a permanent end to brick production on the Texas side of the border (Cook 1998, 2010).

In 1993, during a routine reconnoiter of a riverine brick production zone in Reynosa, I stopped to engage in conversation with an individual seated on a stack of brick on a flatbed trailer. The conversation revealed that he was Antonio "Toño" Reynoso the owner-operator of the brickworks in which the trailer was parked. After explaining to him my experience with brickmakers and other artisans in Oaxaca and my plans for a comparative study on the border, I asked Toño how his brick business was doing. His thoughtful and surprising response was that his business suffered from the same problems as those experienced by Oaxaca basket makers as expressed by an author whose name he could not recall.

I was instantly dumbfounded because I knew the story and the author, B. Traven, and I realized that opportunity (or the gods of an-thropology) had just worked in my favor. He then remembered Traven's name and I told him that I would look for a copy of the story for him to read, and that after he had had time to do so, we could discuss the matter in more detail. This resulted in a long-term relationship involving many visits to the Reynoso brickworks, access to company archives, and several tape-recorded interviews, with Toño and other members of his family, including his son, Antonio, his older brother, Sebastián, and with many of his employees. It also resulted in extensive research into Traven's work, particularly his views on craft production and capitalism, and into various dimensions of artisanal piecework industry especially as related to labor-management relations regarding wages, productivity, and output (Cook 1995).

The specific parallel that Toño saw between his own situation as a brick industry employer and Traven's New York City-based entrepreneur and would-be buyer-up of large quantities of miniature Oaxacan baskets, revolved around the seemingly illogical relationship (from the employer's viewpoint) between wage increases and worker productivity – namely, that increments in piece wages did not result in corresponding increases in output. Rather, workers tended to produce the same output despite higher wages. Traven's would-be entrepreneur failed to get higher output despite offering higher prices for the Oaxaca artisan's baskets.

Toño had the same experience with brick hand-molded by hired piece-workers; he paid them for molded batches of 1,000 brick and, to his chagrin, found that paying them higher piece rates per thousand did not yield higher daily outputs. In fact, they would tend to mold about the same number of brick daily rather than increase daily output to earn more money. They were content to earn more for making the same number of brick rather than working longer to make more brick to increase their daily earnings (cf. Traven 1966:73–88; Cook 1998:158–160).

In the Oaxaca Valley, brickmaking had the same advantages as the metate industry for quantitative data gathering and analysis, as well as for illustrating linkages between all phases of the economic process. But unlike the metate industry, which was characterized by independent household production, the handmade brick industry also displayed petty capitalist organization in which worker-owner units regularly combined family labor with the employment of wage labor by piece-rate – thus exemplifying, together with treadle-loom weaving, "piece-work capitalism" in the Oaxaca Valley economy (Cook 1984a:199). Also, unlike most of the small-scale industries producing utilitarian craft commodities in the Oaxaca Valley, the brick industry sold its products mostly on-site to urban builders, and not through the regional periodic marketplace (*plaza-mercado*) system (Cook 1984a).

In the 1990s, as I conducted research on the handmade brick industry on the Texas-Mexico border, I formulated the concept of "Mexican brick culture" (1998:288 n.2; 2011:5–6; 2004:17 n.10) as an extension of my concern with cultural elements in the production, exchange, and use of commodities like metates and bricks. This concept compensated for my relative neglect of cultural elements, especially related to consumption, in my earlier research on commodity production in the Oaxaca Valley. It also reflected my reading of trendy literature addressing cultural/symbolic dimensions of consumption in contemporary capitalism that resulted in my focus on "commodity culture(s)" (Cook 2004) in which metates and bricks served as examples.

Shortly after my 1998 book was published, I was contacted by the editor of *The Journal of the West*, Robin Higham, to guest edit an issue on the border. I accepted his offer, assembled a group of contributors, and the issue was published in 2001 under the title of "The Mexican Connection in the Southwestern Borderlands – Trends and Prospects." Since I was directing UConn's Institute for Puerto Rican and Latino Studies at the time, and had a travel budget and no teaching obligations, I traveled again to El Paso-Ciudad Júarez and then down the border to Brownsville/Matamoros, stopping at several border crossings in between (Laredo/Nuevo Laredo, Los Ebanos/Díaz Ordaz/ Progreso/Nuevo Progreso) to monitor border crossing traffic, converse with officials, and take photographs. Several photos and maps were selected to illustrate my introduction to the issue which also made reference to my brief case study of the unique trans-border brick industry in the twin cities of El Paso-Ciudad Júarez.

In the opening paragraph of the introduction to that collection of article, a contrast was posed between the international boundary and the "border" as a metaphor for "connectedness" of Mexico and the United States which, paradoxically, originated in a "disconnection by conquest through the 1836 to 1845 Texas rebellion and annexation, the US-Mexico War of 1846 to 1848, and a subsequent transference of the Mexican territories of Texas, Arizona, and California (among others) to US sovereignty through the Treat of Guadalupe-Hidalgo in 1848" (2001:5). Following the Gadsden Purchase of the New Mexico territory in 1854, the US-Mexico border region was configured as we know it today. So, the complicated and contradictory meanings hidden within the simple term "border" derive from the nineteenth-century disconnection by conquest and expansion, sanctioned by the ideology of Manifest Destiny, that transformed Mexican territory into the United States' Southwestern Borderlands.

Also, I delineated several challenges to our understanding of the complexities of the United State-Mexico border as an international political boundary with distinctive geographical features, and as a historical zone of relations, transactions, and movements involving diverse peoples, commodities, and cultures. One challenge was to understand these complexities by identifying local and regional particularities that diversify and segment the Borderlands. Another was to deal with the impact that the North American Free Trade Agreement (NAFTA) and global capitalism will continue to have in transforming the border/borderlands and our perceptions and understanding of them. These and many other issues were addressed in my introduction and the other articles in the collection.

Another matter that I raised was that of time perspective and the anthropo-geographic vision of the border region prior to the arrival of Europeans as an area impacted by multiple encounters, migrations, inventions, and diffusions involving sedentary and nomadic Amerindian peoples and cultures. The critical prehistoric civilizational axis then was located in what is today central Mexico as the core of Mesoamerica. Accordingly, I argued that the Southwestern Borderlands was a critical space joining the northern and southern spheres of a North American civilizational process spanning several millennia – migrations and movements during most of that time span were relatively unencumbered by state-imposed boundaries or barriers (Cook 2001:5–6).

Today, xenophobia, racism, and extreme right-wing politics have invaded the Borderlands. The Republican Party of Texas, long associated with the defense of private property and water rights and resistance to the exercise of the right of eminent domain by the federal government, has hypocritically embraced President Trump's "Wall" project. It has done so even to the point of not contesting federal seizures of ranch land north of the Rio Grande for wall construction. The Texas governor has eagerly assigned state police and national guard units to assist the US Border Patrol in defending the border against illegal alien intrusions. It seems that racial

Anglo-Saxonism and the specter of the "white scourge" (Foley 1997) is alive and well in the early decades of the twenty-first century (Horsman 1981; De León 1983; Montejano 1987; Cook 1998:222–227, 239–240).

On December 17, 2005 at 9:30 a.m. I was approaching the Pharr-Reynosa International Bridge to return to the US after spending a few days in Reynosa as a guest of the municipal government. I went to Reynosa to share with the government the results of my past and continuing research on the handmade brick industry located in their municipality. In a line of traffic at a stop light not far from the entry road to the bridge, I bought a copy of El Mañana, Reynosas's leading newspaper, from an itinerant vendor. I was anticipating a long, snail-paced, frustrating crossing, although not as long as the two-hours I actually experienced. A large, bold-faced two-word headline in the newspaper immediately caught my attention: AMURALLAN FRONTERA (They are walling the Border). The bylines read: PROYECTAN BARRERA DE 283 KILOMETROS DESDE LAREDO A BROWNSVILLE (They propose a Barrier of 283 kilometers from Laredo to Brownsville). Prominently spaced below these lines was a large map of the border indicating the position of three sections of the proposed wall: in California and Arizona, New Mexico-Texas and, finally, a 227-mile-long section from Del Rio to Brownsville which would encompass the specific area I was about to cross between Reynosa, Tamaulipas and Pharr, Texas.

I knew immediately, of course, the identity of the "They" referred to in the newspaper: the US House of Representatives that includes members who allegedly represent the best interests of residents in my congressional district in central and south Texas. Certainly not on this vote did they do so!

During the first two decades of the twentieth century, as a consequence of unrest generated by the Mexican Revolution beginning in 1910, US troops invaded Mexico, either under pretext of capturing bandits, securing ports (e.g., Tampico and Veracruz), or securing the border from alleged German (WWI) saboteurs and subversion. According to many historians, Mexico was lucky to escape that period of its history with its sovereignty and territory (what was left of it after 1848) intact. During the last decade of the twentieth century, neoliberal technocrats and business sectors launched, and got ratified by Congress, a legislative project known as NAFTA (North American Free Trade Agreement) for the purported purpose of integrating the economies of the US, Mexico, and Canada into a common market system, ultimately to resemble that of the European Union. We were assured at the time that NAFTA represented a long-term formula for the common good of all three countries.

At the turn of the twenty-first century, in the aftermath of the 9/11 terrorist attack, right-wing extremists, in direct defiance of the spirit and intent of the North American Free Trade Agreement, rallied around the banner of border security and migratory regulation to attempt stem the flow of threatening hordes of migrants from south of the border. It is not surprising, then, that in this atmosphere of xenophobic backlash, in December 2005, a divided US Congress approved start-up funding for the "walled border" project.

It was almost as if the infamous "Iron Curtain" and "Berlin Wall" did not teach a majority of members in Congress a lesson. Walls do not solve long-festering political, economic and cultural conflicts. Informed, realistic, and flexible policy-making and diplomacy does. Neither of these has been evident in the area of post-9/11 US-Mexico relations to address the issue of undocumented, job-seeking Mexican citizens or Central Americans who flow into US labor markets undersupplied by job applicants who are US citizens. And certainly not with regard to asylum-seekers from violence-ridden Central America.

One reasonable proposal to address these admittedly thorny and complex issues would be to resurrect the Bracero Program to coordinate the needs of US employers and Mexican/Central American workers for temporary or seasonal employment. Another would be to retool existing statutes dealing with pathways to permanent work status and citizenship and the issue of asylum-seekers. Easier to propose than to accomplish, unfortunately (see Heyman 1998, 2014, 2012).

In 2005, I was still willing to convince myself that a majority of US citizen-voters were sufficiently enlightened to realize that the proposed "Great Wall of the Border" was nothing more than a passing phase of Congressional garrison-state mentality, and did not reflect an informed and enlightened legislative process. I viewed the proposal as "the most ill-conceived, retrograde, and shameful pieces of legislation ever to issue forth from the LOWER chamber of the US Congress" (Cook 2008:2). I never envisaged in my wildest dreams that such a repugnant project would be embraced by a US presidential candidate of a major party, much less that such a candidate would be elected in 2016 and proceed to waste untold billions of US taxpayers money on a patently xenophobic project. It is a shame that this ill-conceived project emerged too late to enable Trump's Border Wall to have been constructed of Mexican handmade brick. That, at least, would have led to a more "Mexico-friendly" outcome.

CHAPTER 8

Global Change, Information Overload, and Trends in Economic Anthropology

Disjunctive Discourses

Whichever side one took (or not) during the years of the formalist vs. substantivist controversy, or whatever position one developed in reaction to it or by reading about it in its aftermath, it can be argued that the field of inquiry identified during the second half of the past century as "economic anthropology" has differentiated into a cacophony of disjunctive discourses in the early decades of the twenty-first century. There has been an encyclopedic project devoted exclusively to economic anthropology (Carrier, ed. 2012) and another more comprehensive project with eighty-nine separately authored topical articles in the field (*The International Encyclopedia of Anthropology*, 2018). Although both encyclopedias have review essays of the field itself, these somehow do not help to harmonize the cacophony or adequately explain it but, rather, simply suggest guidelines for negotiating it and, essentially, take the cacophony as given (it is what it is). There is probably nothing else that can or should be expressed on the matter.

It is not unreasonable to propose that the cacophony is the result of competitive searches by individual scholars for innovative and ambitious theoretical and problem orientations, or of pragmatic adaptation to reduced research funding and access to foreign research sites, and/or the availability of an open-ended array of previously neglected, less exotic objects of study. Perhaps, in retrospect, the field was too arcane, too narrowly defined, and too wedded to foreign objects of study for Euro American anthropologists, and was less accessible than it should have been for other anthropologists. Also, the effort to build a guild-like consensus on scope and method issues, as was implicit in the agenda of participants in the formalist-substantivist controversy, was naïve. Then, as now, it was a field of inquiry which was idiosyncratic and unsystematic in its mode of contributing to existing knowledge about economic activity, and in its competitive, unscientific mode of transmitting such knowledge inter-generationally among practitioners.

This may not be a fatal flaw for the field in light of the verdict of a prominent philosopher of social science that theoretical approaches in economic anthropology are not falsifiable, and that "quantity and quality of empirical content, together with logical precision and clarity, must play the key role in evaluating theories for which conclusive proof or disproof is lacking" (Cook 2004:6–7; cf. Little 1986, 1989, 1991). The most recommended and rewarding approach is modified empiricism, revolving around the interplay between theory and fact but unbound to a rigid rule regarding observational confirmation or refutation of knowledge claims (Little 1989:24). This is about as far as we can go in devising rigorous standards for evaluating scholarly contributions to the field.

It is hard to sustain interest in tedious scope and method issues in an empirical, fieldwork-oriented discipline, albeit one which had greater pretensions, a tradition most recently followed by Hann and Hart who plead the case "for an economic anthropology that is able to investigate … 'human economy' anywhere in time and space, as a creation of all humanity" (2011:x). They do so in an interdisciplinary spirit, a commitment to a "world history" and global economic perspective, and to an expansive view of the human economy as involving the "satisfaction of all human needs" (2011:2–3, 8). This seems to me to be a substantivist equivalent to the extreme formalist concept of economy as embracing all choice-making and, as such, is useless for purposes of designing methodologically-sound, sharply-focused empirical investigation in ethnographic economics. Tellingly, it has been proposed at a time when the narrow field itself has blended into a broader fields of inquiry with various labels and drawing upon many social science disciplines.

Informed by twentieth-century notions of collective scientific procedure and progress, it could be argued that the comparative study of economic activity requires a new dialogue about its present and future course, particularly in view of accelerating capitalist transformation of the planet and the profound reconfiguration of peoples and cultures trad-itionally studied by anthropologists. Under such conditions, the need for conceptual clarification, theoretical readjustment, and programmatic reassessment and proposals for new directions would seem to be urgent. Unfortunately, such interventions, however well-intentioned, have had little measurable effect in the past. This is demonstrated by the fact that anthropologists who study and publish about economic topics today do so from many different theoretical perspectives, orientations, and vocabularies which originate in discourses in fields like sociology, political economy, human geography, cultural economy, and political ecology rather than in economic anthropology.

This trend was already underway at the time of my research in Oaxaca in the 1970s which drew heavily on the literature from the debates between neopopulists and Marxists in early twentieth-century Russian agrarian studies which was renewed in Mexican agrarian studies in the 1970s and focused on class differentiation (Cook and Binford 1990:15–22). In re-reading my preface to the 1990 book addressing that aspect of the research, it is clear that it represented a conscious detachment on my part from the cultural anthropological tradition that viewed Oaxacans as "bearers of par-ticular variants of indigenous ethnicity or 'traditional' culture" in favor of a perspective that viewed "Oaxacans as exemplars of types of socioeconomic conduct or as embodiments of particular social types, class relations, and class interests" (Cook 1990"xii). This was viewed as a "dangerous" approach by ethno-populists like Stefano Varese (Esparza 2020:320). Later I would partially, if critically, redirect my attention to substantive cultural-historical issues in anthropological discourse, to currents in twentieth-century eco-nomic anthropology, and Mexican studies (e.g., Cook 2004, 2014) – but without downplaying social differentiation to highlight consciousness of indigenous identity.

Indicative of the disjunctive swings in social science research is Jorge Hernández-Diaz's recent response to my request for sources to update my understanding of changes in the social differentiation of rural Oaxacan communities in two districts, Tlacolula and Ocotlán, covered in my 1970s research: "Well, the situation here is getting more difficult with each passing day. As if the pandemic weren't bad enough, there is also an increase in violence and illicit activities, and a government that daily reveals itself to be authoritarian, ridiculously inefficient and stupid. In these circumstances the countryside and the peasantry are no longer the same as they were when you saw them in the 1980s. Many in the valleys of Tlacolula and Ocotlán have begun to cultivate marijuana and other illicit crops. A large number of them have left for your country, and in part they continue to sustain the economy here and in Mexico generally. Last year they remitted 36 billion dollars, and this year are on track to do the same. The curious thing about all this is that studies like those that you and Bartra did are no longer conducted in Mexico. It would be good to do them again – that sociological view is necessary."[12]

At least I am in good company in the museum of forgotten social science research in Mexican studies. Of course, Roger Bartra's analysis was of national agrarian datasets whereas mine was strictly regional in scope and based on the OVSÍP dataset. Nevertheless, our approaches shared an orientation originating in early twentieth-century Russian agrarian studies focused on class differentiation and household reproduction. Short of culling unreliable government censuses, there is no possibility of updating our understanding of social differentiation and household reproduction in the Oaxaca Valley since the social science data to do so do not exist. There are many reasons why research like mine (and Bartra's) was not precedent-setting in terms of agrarian research in Mexico and the Oaxaca Valley but these are beside the point. Without follow-up studies we are prevented from ascertaining through systematic empirical research what changes have actually occurred since the 1970s at the community level in two key districts within one of the key areas of indigenous peasant-artisan socioeconomic life in Mesoamerica/Mexico.

Rigorous discussions of scope and method imply collective participation to achieve consensus among practitioners regarding fundamental concepts and principles. These have been supplanted since the 1980s by individualistic drives for originality and innovation, often linked to interdisciplinary quests to address or solve problems or grievances resulting from the depredations of capitalist market economy as evidenced in environmental degradation, labor exploitation and segmentation, poverty, income inequality, outsourcing, financial chicanery and mismanagement, and so on. This pattern has been exacerbated under conditions of accelerated global change in which divisions of labor and specialization, commodity markets, and wealth acquisition and distribution are reconfigured over ever diminishing time spans. Categories of actors merge, disappear, or reappear in new forms and their performances alter accordingly.

Under these conditions, would-be knowledge producers, probably best described as discursivists, are left scrambling to identify objects of study and, when they do, to improvise new approaches and methods of investigation to understand perplexing problems of massive complexity and scope. Their mobility mimics that of the constantly shape-shifting moving objects of global commodity economy they attempt to study. Value theories are churned out that have thinkers from Adam Smith, David Ricardo, Karl Marx, and Alfred Marshall spinning in their graves and scratching their heads while doing so – their tightly-reasoned theories are critiqued and discounted as a new hybrid theory of "value" writ large is fashioned to embed economy in society at the cost of diminishing economic materiality and rational calculation (Collins 2017:17–24). Only Karl Polanyi is probably smiling from above as his murky concept of socially embedded economy seems to have generated much of the recent theoretical critique (Collins 2017:24–26). Admittedly, this is the discursive milieu where Polanyi belongs, not in the one that found him somewhat out of place in the 1960s formalist-substantivist controversy which was methodological or heuristically-oriented around ethnographic research, and not directly related to the critique of capitalism's creative destructiveness.

Fields like anthropological political economy and cultural economy entail either critiques of capitalism or of theories about it, and spin-off formidable arrays of neologisms and conceptual frameworks. Typically these privilege either financialization or consumption over material production, and focus on "networks of human and nonhuman agents that bind the globe together in ways never seen before in human history" (Gregory 2014:53). Financialization, and concomitant changes in monetary systems and information technology, have placed risk and uncertainty in the saddle to complicate economic calculations by individuals and enterprises, their results, and efforts by academics to interpret and understand them. Critical energies are now public policy-oriented and directed against grandiose ideological targets like neoliberalism rather than against esoteric discipline-bound discursive targets like formalism or substantivism.

The unsettling economic disorder described above is the subject of work by the inventive meta-theorist, Arjun Appadurai. In a series of widely read publications he posited imaginary global-wide systems of "-scapes," ethno-, media-, techno- finance- and ideo-, with imagination as the key element in all forms of agency (Appadurai 1990, 1996, 2013). This scenario has become a sort of Durkheimian social fact as the principal element in a new complex, overlapping, disjunctive, and commoditized global order which is ceaselessly mobile.

To say the least, there is no easy fit between such discourse and the reality it represents, and the conceptual repertory and knowledge production agenda of mainstream economic anthropology as it developed and was practiced during most of the twentieth century. Changing economic reality was assumed as a given then but it could be argued that its discourse was skewed toward methodological issues from an ethnographic "site as given" (in situ) perspective which assumed "emplaced" economic life (Greenberg and Heyman 2012:261). This is a relative and temporal matter: Ethnography would be a fruitless endeavor if change or movement precluded the assumption of some degree of stability in social occupancy and structure, at least for a generation. A larger question becomes if the ethnographer cannot assume relative emplacement during T1 in a longitudinal, intergenerational study like mine in Oaxaca how could change be empirically demonstrated to have occurred by T2?

In the early 1980s, the economic anthropologist, Keith Hart, drawing upon Marx's thinking about the nature and development of the commodity and commodity economy in humanity's economic life, provided the theoretical framework for subsequent discourses like Appadurai's (Hart 1982; cf. Appadurai 1986). Commoditization was conceived as an evolutionary process in a division of labor "which embraces ever-widening circles of humanity in a single nexus of commodity production and exchange" (Hart 1982:38). But it was also a process that involved the progressive abstraction of social labor and the detachment of human economic activity from its material context (i.e., its dematerialization), revealing it to be a fully social but abstracted quantity. As such it was measurable as "computerized transactions which represent human subjects as numbers in information-processing machines" (Hart 1982:41). It is not surprising that this line of reasoning was a precursor to Keith Hart's treatise on money and finance in the computer age (Hart 2001).

A critical challenge for economic anthropology grounded in the study of regional and local economies is to clarify how collective local knowledges have been penetrated or transformed through inevitable interactions with the "-scaped" system – especially those circulating in the digitized media and governmental apparatuses accessible to the public (Appadurai 1990:299). Although Appadurai's culturalistic scheme is built around the landscape metaphor, the actual land- or nature-scape and humanity's interaction with it is absent. Likewise, there is no "labor-scape" – indeed, the indexes for his 1996 and 2013 books contain no listings under the labor category, nor under "work." This is not surprising given his focus on the historical trend toward rationalization and dematerialization of the commodity economy and the emergence of computerized information systems by which labor is remunerated, audited, and made accountable. This intensifies labor exploitation and, hence, increases surplus value appropriation by capital (i.e., profits), while simultaneously intermeshed with other value appropriations through a proliferating variety of fictional commodities in financial and consumer markets monitored by a white-collar proletariat and represented as numbers on a computer screen.

The logically-sound and historically-grounded nature of the commodity-focused evolutionary process outlined above, complicates the comparative analytic task of traditional economic anthropology (cf. Hart 1982:43). Considering the high level of abstraction of Appadurai's theorization of the system of global flows of people, commodities, and information, it presents formidable operational obstacles for empirical research in economic anthropology. It might be agreed, for example, that agents in a posited "financescape," wheeling and dealing in derivatives, futures and other fictive creatures of cyber-spatial markets are just as caught up in the material consequences of their decisions as are fishers, miners or factory assembly-line workers. So, there is no escape for any such agents from the benefits and consequences of the mental and material dialectic embodied in commodity production.

There is a lack of uniformity and a specific evolutionary element in the commoditization process, however, which means that localities and regions are differentially transformed by it. Consequently, there are spaces in the global economy where real commodities are still produced in low-tech fashion by actual workers whose labor power is only partially commoditized. These spaces still provide fertile ground for empirical investigation by economic ethnographers.

Also in play in the modern world are forces which have little to do with directional, evolutionary processes like commoditization but, rather, reflect shorter-term, more capricious processes emanating from the politics of international policy-making and ideological interventions. These result in irrational exclusions of certain countries or peoples from the normal conduct of economic affairs. This is notably exemplified in the Western hemisphere by the case of Cuba which for some six decades, owing to its socialist revolution, has been seen as a pariah by the United States and, consequently, has been forced to conduct its economic life without normal access to standard institutional resources of global capitalism. This has been compounded by its own clumsy state-managed interventions to control market participation.

The result has been a deformation of Cuban economic life, causing a severe decline in the domestic manufacture of consumer commodities but promoting an innovative popular response expressed through a system of porterage, under the guise of personal foreign travel. This porterage links the satisfaction of consumer demand in Cuba to the supply of foreign-manufactured consumables through an unofficial, informal system of itinerant trading partners/intermediaries who travel to several countries of the Latin American-Caribbean region to acquire consumables in demand in Cuba. This transactional system in which commodity economic behaviors are merged with or disguised as non-commodity social ones (e.g., of kinship or confidence) calls to mind a sort of Malinowskian Kula trade which has been designated anthropologically as the "Mula" trade (Cearns 2019) – borrowing a popular term in Latin America for drug couriers (*The Economist* July 4, 2020:26). . Except for a lack of hard data, this is an exemplary case study in ethnographic economics of twenty-first-century economic realities.

Some recent studies privilege ethnographic fieldwork and their objects of analysis range the gamut of sites where "economic" activities occur – from exchanges, auction houses, small town businesses, and offices to assembly plants, craft shops, sweat shops, agricultural fields, or dance festivals; or where ideas or policies about economic matters are discussed (e.g., Alvarez 2012; Appadurai 2013:243 n.13; Collins 2017; Pied 2019; Müller 2020). The economy as an object of analysis is essentially conflated with actual capitalism and its institutions, and value is viewed from cultural circulationist perspective rather than a labor-centered productionist one. The best of these studies, however, combine fieldwork with a balanced analysis of production and marketing as exemplified by Alvarez's work on the Mexican mango and Persian lime export industry (2012). His study also explains how the fate of a series of small to medium agricultural producers and marketers in Mexico is determined by internationally negotiated common market agreements and, more particularly, by specific policy decisions made by the US Department of Agriculture (2012:66–69).

Another research direction, more attuned to the computer age and cyber or IT-culture wars in hardware and software design and production and their interaction, is illustrated in the recent study by Luis Felipe Murillo (2020) of what he calls "hackerspace networks." His research methodology is described in accessible language as combining multisited ethnography, participant observation, and interviews with computer engineers, programmers, and activists who participate in an international network of community "hackerspaces" (2020:208). One of his case studies in Shenzhen, China describes an "experiment with gifts and commodities" which illustrates "how gifts become commodities and how, conversely, commodities shift to the register of the gift while maintaining their capacity for reverse transformation and differential valuation" according to Chris Gregory's scheme (1982). Murillo provides an empirical demonstration of the process through the "curious trajectory of a product, the Crazyflie" – a remote-controlled quadcopter (2020:217).

Clearly, the process described is wholly one of commoditization in which intellectually creative labor is engaged by capital with machinofactory and assembly labor to create products like Crazyflie quadcopters. As such, the application of the commodity-to-gift conversion scheme seems inappropriate. The process is clearly transactional, involving flows of information, expenditures of labor power, social relations between different types of agents and, at some point, payment of wage bills – but, throughout, deployments of capital, payments of interest, and earning of profits. As a commodity itself hacker labor is not gifted, it is simply competing for material rewards in an open market.

In all fairness to Murillo, he does not consider his research as economic anthropology but as representing the "anthropological study of technology and politics" (2020:207). To qualify as an economic study, data would have to be provided about hackers' livelihoods and about the specific enterprises (e.g., the Crazyflie firm and its subcontractors) that finance those livelihoods, that is, data regarding labor processes, relations of production, and distribution of exchange value. In an economic study, factory workers who manufacture and assemble microelectronic products could not simply be "invisible participants in the flow of exchange" and innovative hackers could not be invisible independent or sub-contracted agents in the "network" (Murillo 2020:217, 219). It seems that, in this case, factory workers and computer hackers alike are real members of a visible precariat and/or of a visible proletariat vis-à-vis an invisible IT capital.

Another notable recent ethnographic intervention in cyberspace is Beltran's innovative study of hacker-entrepreneurs and hackathons linking Mexico and the San Francisco Bay area (2020). His fieldwork explores how his subjects navigate seemingly contradictory domains: a hacker world aimed against capitalism and an entrepreneurial world that embraces capitalist practices (2020:489). His analysis reveals a great deal about the post-2000 Mexican political-economic landscape and the role of disenchanted young people in it.

Applied Economic Anthropology and the Anti-market Mentality Revitalized?

Some economic anthropologists had governmental and "NGO" roles in the heyday of twentieth-century developmentalism – including none other than Ann Dunham (2009), US president Barack Obama's mother.

My own experience in collaborating with the Mexican government with regard to village artisans was much less positive than Dunham's in Indonesia (Cook 1981). But, unlike Dunham and, apparently, increasing numbers of economic anthropologists since who are full-time staff members of non-academic institutions or agencies involved in development or other kinds of work (Wilk and Cliggett 2007:15), I was simply an independent academic researcher collaborating on a volunteer basis with a Mexican government agency.

There are calls for economic anthropology to deal directly with "questions of overwhelming significance for our species' stewardship of the planet" (Hann and Hart 2011:174), especially as part of a calculated counter-movement to Neoliberalism (Dale 2010:ch. 6 and conclusion) and the search for possible alternatives to "capitalist realism" and "business ontology" (Fisher 2009). These are hard to reconcile with the discipline's typical "bread-and-butter" focus on more easily operationalized and less ambitious theories conducive to systematic empirical investigation at the local level. Such ambitious research agendas echo Polanyi's deeply alienated call for massive re-enculturation (a "reform of our consciousness" – Polanyi 1968) of modern Homo sapiens to replace its "market mentality" created by the "great transformation" (i.e., the rise of industrial capitalism) with a more humane, socially-conscious (pre-commodity or post-commodity?) mentality. Such a re-enculturated mentality would, of course, have to be fostered by (or proceed simultaneously with) a vaguely-defined societal alternative to capitalist industrialism. An ambitious agenda, indeed, which in any case is surely beyond the purview of empirically-grounded economic anthropology and more appropriate for speculative political philosophy or moral economics (Carrier 2017).

Polanyi's linkage of his visceral dislike of the society created by industrial capitalism to a reformist, utopian vision was supported by his idiosyncratic reading of the anthropological and historical record of pre-market, non-market, and subsumed-market economies. He encountered ways of life in those contexts which, to him, were not illustrative of Adam Smith's postulation of "a certain propensity in human nature ... to truck, barter, and exchange one thing for another" (1937:13) or in which the "motive of gain" was "natural" (Polanyi 1957:269), and which might provide the basis for a new post-capitalist social organization of the human economy along democratic lines in which "the problem of industry would resolve itself through the planned intervention of the producers and consumers themselves" (Polanyi 1968:77). Actually, somewhat less utopian initiatives of the kind Polanyi envisaged have emerged in recent years in the United States and have been studied through innovative ethnographic fieldwork by the economic anthropologist Jane Collins (2017).

My preference is to look to Marx rather than to Mauss or Polanyi to find an antidote to neoliberal discourse and policies, the often inhumane and destructive consequences of which are undeniable. Most of what I learned in Mexico suggests the possibility that Adam Smith may have been right regarding assumed behavior of human agents, certainly regarding commodity circulation, except for claiming their "innate" or "natural" rather than their "postulated" and "cross-culturally detectable" (and empirically verifiable) nature. To the extent that Polanyi and the substantivists argue that such behaviors do not arise from subjects' DNA but from their socially-constituted commodity cultures, they are right. Marx, however, is the indispensable source for inspired and incisive thinking about the creativeness and destructiveness of commodity economy, and for appreciating the centrality of the commodity concept in understanding human economic life.

I would add "acquire" and "consume" to Adam Smith's "truck, barter and exchange" to complete the range of posited universal propensities of agents in the economic life of commodity economies. The painful truth may be that neoliberalism taps more deeply into the cultural and behavioral reservoirs of commodity economy than its critics are willing or able to accept (Collins 2017:158). It goes without saying, however, that the unintended consequences of neoliberal discourse and projects, not to speak of the selfish exercise of agency, perversely exacerbate real-life manifestations of the "dark side of commodity economy" (Cook 2004:84). Fortunately, even when neoliberalism is constitutionally inscribed as it was during the regime of Pinochet in Chile in 1980 so as to guarantee free-market operating conditions even in traditional social areas like health, education, and social security, it can be subject to subject constitutional reform movements which seek to restore social rights and limit market privatization (Bonnefoy 2020; The Economist October 24, 2020).

Maldevelopment in Central Texas

San Marcos, Texas, where I have resided for the past twenty years, lies at the southern tip of the "Black Waxy Prairie" (named for its rich, black, sticky soils) at the point where the "Hill Country" escarpment begins. The triangle-shaped region (or soil belt) extends for some 300 miles, starting at a point not far from the Arkansas border northeast of Dallas and ending at a point southwest of Austin near San Marcos, and ranges from 25 miles wide in its southernmost portion to 75 miles wide in the extreme northern portion. Its southern portion is on the eastern side of the I-35 corridor between Austin and San Antonio – one of the highest growth areas in the US during the last decade.

Part of this prairie region, in Bell County north of Austin, was the object of a long-neglected ethnographic survey published by Oscar Lewis in 1948. The following characterization by Lewis of Bell County then would have also applied to an eastern strip of Hays County of which San Marcos is the county seat and to adjacent Caldwell County (Lewis 1948:1–2): "The diversity within Bell County is in large part due to its marginal position which has exposed it to two distinctive influences, that of the "cotton South" and the "cattle West." As in the South, cotton has dominated the economy and has made a deep impression on the life and customs of the people. But the plantation system, which was the core of Southern culture, never took root. This, together with the early importance of stock raising as against cotton growing, was responsible for the development of cultural characteristics distinct from those of the Deep South. Indeed, King Cotton never reigned alone in Bell County. The tradition of the cowboy has come down from the early days when stock raising was the major occupation, and today every schoolboy knows that the Chisholm Trail ran through the center of the county. Unlike the Deep South, there was no leisure class to romanticize cotton farming, and it could at no time compete with ranching in capturing the imagination of the people as an ideal way of life."

This insightful characterization set the stage for Lewis' history (from settlement in 1834) and ethnography of Bell County which included ample data and analysis of multiethnic landlord-tenant relations and land use; the historical trend was from predominance of cotton culture and cattle raising to mixed farming and cattle raising – which characterizes the rural portions of Bell County (also eastern portions of Hays County and all of adjacent Caldwell County) to this day. Lewis' pioneering work on ethnoclass relations involving landowning whites and black and Mexican tenants (a few sharecroppers) was expanded and deepened by Neil Foley's landmark study *The White Scourge* (1997). The 6,000 acre Martindale Ranch in Caldwell County, historically one of the region's largest producers, has been subdivided and its lands now lie outside the town of Martindale founded by the ranch-owner in 1855 and located only a few miles east of San Marcos. Today, the building once housing Martindale's cotton gin has been converted to a restaurant for locals and tourists. Abandoned commercial buildings in the town itself, often used for movie and television film purposes, were purchased by a retired Washington D.C. lobbyist for rejuvenation. Some gentrification has occurred but commercial rejuvenation has lagged behind.

A telling metric of regional change is demography. When I studied at the University of Texas in 1955–1957 the population of Austin was somewhere between 132,000 and 186,000, the census figures for 1950 and 1960. When I moved back to Austin in 2000, the population had increased to 1,250,000; in 2019 it had grown to 2,227,000 – averaging a 33 percent increase over two decades. Figures for adjacent Hays county immediately to the south of Austin/Travis county spanning the IH-35 corridor are even higher: 61 percent increase between 2000 and 2010 and 46.5 percent increase between 2010 and 2019. The current estimated population of Hays County which includes my home town of San Marcos is 230,000. These demographics imply a stunning transformation of the natural and built environment of the region since the mid-twentieth century – a process that has intensified in the twenty-first. For someone who grew up here in the 1950s, it is barely recognizable today.

Portions of the southernmost area of the "Black Waxy" in Travis and Hays Counties have been targeted by major developers who have captured investment capital from a diverse number of global sources – especially in Asia and the Persian Gulf sheikdoms. These developments were foreshadowed by the construction of highway 130, a toll road, that cuts a swath right through the middle of the southern portion of the Black Waxy just east of Martindale and connects to IH-35 north of Austin and with IH-10 east of Seguin about 25 miles north of San Antonio. One of these projects, just east of Austin's Bergstrom International Airport, is known as the "Circuit of the Americas" which is a mega-entertainment complex featuring a 216 mile-long Formula One racetrack with stadium and non-stadium seating for 300,000 racing enthusiasts – a percentage of whom are celebrity and anonymous multi-millionaire and billionaire jetsetters from around the world.

The second development project is in its early stages and is centered in the area between San Marcos and Kyle in Hays County to the east of I-35 and in the western portion of the "Black Waxy." It involves a Canadian real estate investment company, Walton Development and Management, dedicated to well-researched, long-term (fifteen to twenty years) but speculative land development schemes. These are funded by attracting money capital from investors world-wide through a network of "capital raising offices." The collected capital is then deployed in systematic land acquisition in target areas (in this case land in the "Black Waxy" now only marginally suited to farming and ranching due to soil depletion, drought, and other factors). Separate land parcels have been acquired and consolidated by this development company which now owns twice the acreage once held by the 6,000 acre Martindale cotton ranch. The consolidated land has been subdivided into a series of mostly residential tracts; subcontractors have been (or will be) hired by the Canadian firm to build tract infrastructure (roads, sewerage, underground utilities). Once this infrastructure is in place, tracts will be sold to other companies (developers or builders) for further development. When this process is completed a portion of the old "Black Waxy" will become part of the gigantic urban sprawl with subdivisions like "Camino Real," "Caldwell Valley," and the "Cornerstone," (already built) that will, within a decade, fill the entire Austin-San Antonio I-35 corridor (Collins Walsh 2014).

A more recent and highly-publicized project now underway is the Tesla gigafactory on 2,100 acres in the Del Valle area just east of Creedmoor where as a teenager I went on a night-time hunt for treed raccoons and skunks with another boy and his dog on his parent's farm who were church acquaintances of my parents. The Tesla electric-car plant is expected to employ 5,000 workers and will trigger industrial and retail spin-offs (Novak 2020) to generate even more jobs. Also, to its credit, it will be dedicated to producing environmentally-friendly vehicular commodities that one day will hopefully displace the carbon fuel-guzzling and -spewing kind long preferred by Texas drivers.

I doubt that it ever occurred to Oscar Lewis that an adjacent portion of the farm and ranch region he surveyed in the 1940s would experience this level of urbanization and transformative economic development. The question now becomes whether present and future Oscar Lewises will play any role whatsoever in studying it.

Now that anthropology is fully-engaged in the study of global capitalism, my answer would be a qualified "yes" simply because of the region's unique role in cotton culture and in Texas economic history – especially regarding the transformative change outlined above. Coming up with a specific research problem and feasible proposal and research plan will, however, be challenging – especially for a lone investigator. The best options, in my opinion, might include a study of the long defunct Martindale Ranch as a representative ethnographic case study focused on changes in multiethnic class relations and land use patterns. Case studies could also be designed for the other three examples, namely, the Canadian investment company's land development project, the Circuit of the Americas Formula One racetrack project, and the Tesla gigafactory project. All of these development projects involve creative destruction financed by a diverse array of investors that displaces and eliminates previously existing modes of existence and livelihood to replace them with new modes attuned to global markets.

The anthropological study of the transformative implications of these development projects will encounter formidable obstacles like research problem definition, issues of theoretical approach, methodology, and so on. The land development project could involve the study of subcontracting chains, including recruitment and roles of Mexican migrant construction workers. The Circuit of the Americas and Tesla case studies would surely require technical and, considering their global ramifications, international collaboration to be fully realized. These possible projects will be viable only through an interdisciplinary team approach and will present challenges the application of ethnographic methodology.

We still have to ask ourselves a question from the knowledge production standpoint: Why economic anthropology instead of investigative business journalism or applied economics or cultural geography or sociology? This kind of question never came up back in the 1960s, 1970s, and 1980s when I was working in the Valley of Oaxaca, Mexico or in the 1990s and first decade of the 2000s when I worked on the Texas-Tamaulipas border. Villages and regions in Oaxaca were simply assumed to be legitimate objects of ethnographic or anthropological research. In the case of the Texas-Tamaulipas border, even though I first became informed about the handmade brick industry by reading a newspaper article, there was never any question in my mind as to whether or not an ethnographic study, informed by economic anthropological theory, could be conducted on the topic. After all, I had already completed and published such a study in Oaxaca and even had the good fortune of a favorable review of it in an anthropological journal (Isaac 1986). The border project, given the wide geographic dispersal of the brick industry on both sides of the river border between Mexico and the United States, did provide formidable challenges for a solo fieldworker

Owing to the writings of the cultural geographer David Harvey (1982, 1990, 2018) and, most recently, of his student, Andy Merrifield (2020), we are better informed about Marx's analysis of the capitalist mode of production which highlighted the ongoing and existentially profound impact on land and labor of capitalists' inherent drive for monetary gain – a process that Marxists identify as valorization. According to Merrifield (2020:57): "Capital was Marx's fargazing, a condition, he thought, where all countries were headed, his image of everybody's future. He sketched the historical and geographical mission of the capitalist mode of production, with its need to create industrial cities, to move mountains, to dig canals, to connect everywhere, to nestle everywhere." Hence, in the late twentieth and early twenty-first centuries in places like central Texas and the lower Rio Grande/Rio Bravo border, massive capital-intensive projects have reshaped natural landscapes – pastures for livestock and agricultural fields have been obliterated and replaced by a vast assortment of manufacturing and assembly plants (*maquiladoras*), warehouses, residential subdivisions and big-box commercial centers, and even a sprawling Formula One racetrack complex. Needless to say, the driving force motivating this ceaseless transformative activity is capital accumulation through the capture of myriad, interconnected streams of rent, interest, and profit – all encompassed by the simple formula of $M - M^{1\cdots} \ldots M^{nth}$.

CHAPTER 9

Commodities and Unresolved Issues of Theory and Analysis

By the time I taught my last seminar in economic anthropology at the University of Texas-San Antonio in 2004, I took the liberty of fashioning my own concept of commodity derived from Marx's contribution to classical thought on the subject by adding a third element of symbolic value to the mix of exchange and use value (Cook 2004:126, 136–154 et. passim). This heuristic modification of the commodity concept enabled me to argue that in economies like that of the Zapotecs in the Oaxaca Valley where many products circulate into and through markets, as well as into and through ceremonial circuits according to reciprocity-based or redistributive activities, their value content – either use, exchange, or symbolic was realized according to social context or relations through which they circulated. Their commodity status remained constant, but the values realized through circulation were conditional.

My fieldwork revealed that particular commodities could be gifted, sold for cash, or bartered. Gifts were simply commodities that were transferred without concern for an immediate equivalent return. They were transferred to symbolically reinforce or represent bonds between giver and recipient – thus, realizing their symbolic value. Those same commodities may have been produced or purchased or received in barter by their givers in prior transactions in which exchange value was realized. Or, after being received as gifts by a recipient, they may have been stored for future use, put to immediate use, or exchanged. Their commodity status remained unchanged by the different sites in their circulation; or, for that matter, when they were out of circulation as heirlooms or museum pieces. Only the realization of their inherent value elements changed. Another way of expressing this is to assert that all gifts are commodities; commodities are "gifts" only conditionally, when gifted, but not finally and forever.

Godelier Revisited

Maurice Godelier, when considering the difficulties economists had in including unpaid domestic labor by women in their analyses of capitalist economies, warned against making a theoretical fetish of the commodity. He implied that by so doing meant that economic services were not assigned monetary values and hence were eliminated from economic analysis, even though female domestic labor in our economy and in "primitive" or pre-capitalist economies is economic. Such an analytical elimination defies substantive economic reality because female domestic labor is necessary to social reproduction in all economies; and to commodity production itself that involves male domestic labor. He then drew a generalized conclusion that a "reality may be economic without being a commodity" (1972:283).

In another publication written at the same stage in his career, and specifically focused on his New Guinea fieldwork, Godelier introduced the notion that wealth items in "primitive" non-capitalist, non-market economies, as exemplified by the Baruya, have a double nature as commodities and non-commodities, and can circulate as currencies or gifts as well as utilitarian goods (1971). This parallels Malinowski's earlier interpretation of another Melanesian economy that of the Trobriand Islands and emphasizes the opposition between two materialized economic forms: commodities and gifts. Godelier's interpretation, unlike Malinowski's functionalism, is informed by sophisticated Marxist and structural-functional theoretical schemes but the outcome is quite similar: Melanesians inhabit economic worlds quite different organizationally and culturally from those of, say, Euro American capitalism of the nineteenth and twentieth centuries. Commodities are produced and circulate in all of these worlds but only in market-integrated capitalism do they dominate economic life, whereas in kinship-integrated or religiously-integrated societies, they are subordinated or subsumed. In the latter contexts, individual agency is socialized and encumbered by a complex entanglement of cosmological and consanguineous norms and beliefs.

There are two problems with Godelier's analysis. First, his analysis of the production and circulation of Baruya wealth items is heavily functionalist in the sense that the same item functions as a commodity in one situation but not in another – so its nature seems to shift conditionally from commodity to gift and back again (Godelier 1971:53). My preference is to recognize that the commodity nature of such items does not shift according to function. Properly defined as embodying exchange, use and symbolic value through its manufacture, such items are by nature commodities, and their potential value content – exchange, use, or symbolic – is realized in their circulation.

A second problem arises from Godelier's insistence that labor is not a commodity in economies like the Baruya because "it was never transformed into commodities which could be exchanged for other commodities" (1971:53). This has a double meaning: (1) in-kind labor is not a commodity even when it is embodied in a product which is bartered for a different product; and (2) wage labor is absent in the Baruya economy so that labor time or work has no price equivalent. From my perspective, labor power embodied in products like salt or a whole variety of products made by the Baruya that serve as means of production (stone adzes), weapons (e.g., bows and arrows), or valuables (e.g., pig's tooth necklace, cowrie necklace, headdresses) and which are bartered for salt, is a commodity. If it were not, the exchange value of such products could not be realized through transactions. Also, Godelier himself noted that specialized salt manufacturing labor is remunerated by wages in kind (i.e., salt bars). Labor, therefore, is a commodity in the Baruya economy (Godelier 1971:59–61; 2004:5).

Godelier, again like Malinowski, seeks to move from the particularities of his ethnographic case study to the universalities of human experience. In Malinowski's case the passage is from Trobriand fieldwork into the realm of elaborating a scientific theory of culture in which the economy is an integral element. In Godelier's case, the passage is from Baruya fieldwork, the realm of primitive or simple commodity economy, into that of advanced commodity economy and actual capitalism. This comparative method also served Marcel Mauss in his quest to understand the dynamic opposition he posited between gifts and commodities in the history of humanity's economic life. But, Mauss' oppositional thinking was less informed by Marx than is Godelier's. For Godelier the opposition between gift and commodity, is less rigid that it was for Mauss and clearly is informed by Marx's dialectical method. But, Godelier, still equivocates regarding the opposition between commodities as gifts and commodities as non-gifts. His equivocation on this matter exposes a failure to break with Maussian oppositional thinking.

Godelier's overall focus, however, is on commodity economy – its origins, evolution, and present condition. This clearly reflects his intellectual debt to Marx, as does his recognition that scientific knowledge production begins with "the complex forms if they are to discover the content and sense of the simple ones" (Godelier 1977:165; Eiss and Wolfe 1994).

Commodity and economic identity, it bears emphasizing, are not bound to corporeality. The non-corporeal is commoditizable and, therefore, is economic. Baruya narratives, names, and forms of thinking, associated with material heirlooms, are economic commodities in the same sense as are token instruments, represented as computerized digits, traded in present and future time, on a long or short basis by hedge fund traders, to generate profit in actual capitalist financial markets. The commodity in its currently evolved condition provides insights into its implications in a less evolved one.

Godelier, from early in his career, was clearly profoundly inspired by Marcel Mauss's comparative study of the value of things. More recently, he has been energized by Mauss's post-World War I concern with private philanthropy as a means to overcome deficiencies in redistributive government transfer payments to alleviate income inequality in liberal capitalist economies. Accordingly, Godelier applied a version of Mauss's musings about gifting to a critique of the foundational social-contractual disjunctures in actual capitalism between market economy and legal-constitutional institutions necessary for social reproduction (1999:1–9, 208–210; 2004:8–15). Material things embodying human labor and circulating through barter or reciprocity or market exchange are transmuted into either non-circulating symbolic material objects or mostly immaterial objects like "narratives, names, forms of thinking" (1999:200).

But Godelier injects into Mauss' musings some of his own, derived from his Baruya field work focused on religious notions of the "sacred" (symbolic, imaginary) alleged to make material things unalienated and inalienable so that "the men who manufactured" them are simultaneously (and paradoxically) present and absent (Godelier 2004:18–19). Hence, in the context of actual global capitalism objects circulate (or not), and, accordingly, are alienable, inalienable, or alienated in a dizzying mix of commodities, gifts, and sacred objects. I would like to say that this complex discourse makes sense to me in terms of my effort to interpret the value of things in past and present Mexican economic life but I am hard pressed to do so.

Godelier may be flirting here with a theoretical fetishization of the gift – concrete examples of which he studied in New Guinea as sacred, precious, and currency objects (1999:ch. 2). His arguments can be construed as denaturing and dematerializing economic realities of the Baruya, and transmuting them into proxy vehicles for re-moralizing neoliberal capitalism a la Mauss vis-à-vis post-WWI liberalism. Perhaps this is where his earlier journey" towards a renovation of the idea of "economic rationality" has led him (Godelier 1972:303–319) – the exposure of the sacred or the *mysterium tremendum* (Bell and Werner 2004:xiv) – which in this instance translates into the *kwaimatnie* "bundles of seemingly unspectacular objects" which are products of Baruya labor and exemplify the ultimate irrationality of their exercise of substantive rationality (Godelier 2004:xiv).

The larger truth may be that even in a purportedly comparative discipline like economic anthropology which claims to take survey of all the world, the influence of the fieldwork experience is paramount in shaping our thinking. Godelier's thinking about commodities in general, informed by reading the specialized literature and being born and raised in a commodity economy, is skewed to favor his interpretation of data collected during his fieldwork on the relevant particularities of non-market Baruya economy, society, and belief systems. In similar fashion, my thinking on the topic has been skewed to reflect the results of my research on Zapotec and mestizo peasant-artisans in Oaxaca and on Mexican brick industry workers in Tamaulipas, all participants in different regional formations of the Mexican capitalist economy. In short, anthropologists are peculiarly susceptible to entrapment in an ethnographic cage in our attempt to relate the particular to the universal. Fortunately, for some of us, Marx's method provides guidelines to reduce skewed interpretations of the relationship (Carver 1975).

CHAPTER 10

An Uncertain Future for Economic Anthropology

Hann and Hart (2009, 2011:166–174) propose renewing an engagement with Mauss and Polanyi to counter the perpetuation of *homo economicus* and to find the "missing link between the everyday and the world at large" as their remedy for malaise in economic anthropology. For me, the missing link is the "commodity" in all of its forms and iterations as Hart ably demonstrated in his exemplary dialectical exposition of Marx's analytical use of the concept (Hart 1982). Within this conceptual framework, informed by related ideas from the work of Max Weber and from several twentieth-century ethnographers, starting with Bronislaw Malinowski, the entire gamut of world historical commodity production is on record along with the theoretical tools to accommodate the study of subject agency and decision-making together with social relations and cultural meanings (Cook 2004:Ch.5). For me an engagement with the contributions of Polanyi and Mauss were thought-provoking but not analytically useful.

The Hann-Hart proposal for reconsidering the meaning of economy by pursuing Gudeman's (1990:139–159) "house" versus "market" opposition dissolves in areas like Mesoamerica/Mexico with ancient commodity and market traditions where peasant-artisan domestic units have long been hybrid forms of kinship and enterprise (Cook 1987; Cook 2004:165–172, 220–221). Even as subalterns in redistributive tributary systems, national and regional capitalist economies, and local reciprocity systems, commodity production and the realization of commodity value in market exchange in ancient Mesoamerica and modern Mexico by peasant-artisan household enterprises were and are critical to their livelihood. Market-mediated exchange is simply a particular variation of commodity culture(s). In other words, products, objects, goods, artifacts, or anything made with human labor, including that labor itself, is a commodity by virtue of containing use value that is potentially realizable through exchange and consumption. This approach rests upon a reconstituted concept of commodity, and a corresponding view of the general process of commodity valuation involving the differential realization of exchange, use, and symbolic value (Cook 2006:187–190; cf. Cook 2004:165–172). Polanyi-Mauss currents are reflected here in concerns with reciprocity, redistribution, and symbolic value – but the driving architecture is from Marx and Weber.

Chris Gregory (2005:892) has observed that economic anthropology has two "sacred" field sites – one in Melanesia, the other in Central America. He generously credits me with having synthesized one hundred years of economic thought and ethnographic analysis from the Central American/Mexican site, and emphasizes the "need for a comparable synthesis from the other 'sacred' site in Melanesia" (2005:893). Even a larger need in the process of building the "necessary foundations for a revitalized economic anthropology for the twenty-first century" (Gregory 2005:893) is to reconcile the separate currents of economic ethnography: one from Melanesia (and other areas of Oceania and Asia) that has focused on so-called primitive and tribal peoples with weak or marginal market traditions, and the other from Mexico/Central America that has been predominantly focused on postcolonial indigenous peasantries with strong market traditions. One obvious framework for undertaking this comparative project would be through a rigorous, flexible, and imaginative application of the Malinowski-Polanyi conceptual scheme of reciprocity, redistribution, and barter/market exchange informed by a Marxist commodity-focused theoretical orientation. This might promote clearer understanding of the gift vs. commodity opposition and, perhaps, place limits on its relevance.

This situation draws our attention to an opportunity lost with the premature death of Malinowski in 1942 before he could complete his Oaxaca research which held the promise of being foundational to the development of comparative economic anthropology. If Malinowski had lived long enough to complete his Oaxaca project, he probably would have drawn comparisons with his earlier work on economic life the Trobriand Islands. We can only speculate about the results of such a comparison but surely they would have further documented his view that economic activities like material production and exchange were functionally interrelated in shifting ways with non-economic relations like kinship and religion; and that economic organization and performance involved individual agency as well as group engagement. There is every reason to believe that he would have drawn upon his recognition of the broader sociocultural ramifications of the notable presence of pre-Hispanic grindstones in twentieth-century markets as paralleling the role of many commodities he had studied previously in the Trobriand economy and the Kula trade.

The fact that the contrasting ethnographic endeavors focused on indigenous market economics in Mexico and marginal market economics in Melanesia have not been addressed comparatively in recent decades represents a sharp break from the precedent set in the 1930s when comparative projects like Thurnwald's (1932) or Herskovits' (1940) were more comprehensive in scope and never ignored available data from any of the world's major culture areas pertaining to central topics like production, ownership and property, trade, markets, barter, gift and ceremonial change, money, and so on. These single-authored comparative projects of earlier generations contrast with twenty-first-century projects like Carrier's multi-authored *Handbook* (Carrier, ed. 2005), Hann and Hart's (2011) book, and individually authored comparative studies like Graeber's (2001, 2011) that, inexplicably, exclude coverage of publications pertaining to the major culture area of Mexico/Central America.

The blunt truth is that in terms of the comparative spatio-temporal understanding of economic life, despite all of the subsequent theoretical and conceptual innovations and refinements, accumulation of ethnographic data, and ideological debates, the 1930s works by Thurnwald and Herskovits remain analytically useful. When understood on their own terms, these contributions remain sources of valuable explanations and researchable hypotheses which, arguably, are as relevant as those than can be gleaned from later generations of economic anthropologists. It is not the case that progress has been lacking in improving our understanding of economic life on the periphery of capitalism since the 1930s but the record of empirically demonstrating that progress is imperfect and less clear that it should be – except for a few areas like gender roles.

There is no longer a divide in economic anthropology between "tribalists" and "peasantists" that segmented economic anthropology discourse at least as much than the formalist vs. substantivist divide did in the 1960s and 1970s. A more important divide probably separates "old worlders" from "new worlders" – British and French anthropologists seem still to focus most on ex-colonial areas of their countries' imperial past; and, also, between those who focus on their own countries and materials written in their own language, and those who study foreign countries and consult materials written in the host countries' languages. With some exceptions, this seems to be the case, for example, in Mexican anthropology and other social sciences where there is typically little citational evidence of familiarity with non-Mexican, non-Spanish language sources.

Progress toward eliminating these and other divisions in the field should also occur from the conduct and publication of topical surveys/ explorations by specific themes (e.g., rural industry, tenancy, markets, specific commodities). A recent example of such a study which sets a good precedent is by Mike Chibnik (2011) on the issue of choice and decision-making. Once such a literature is in place I think we all would be able to agree that the field had indeed matured in a way to satisfy LeClair and Schneider's vision, and to meet ideals of scientific progress which can only be achieved through informed, conscientious collective effort. Given the vast literature now available in the economic anthropological field, no single scholar can be expected to produce a grand synthesis; that will require a better-designed and more-inclusive collaborative project than any undertaken to date.

I agree with Graeber that fundamental issues discussed in the formalist-substantivist debate "have not been resolved" (2001:12). Hann and Hart (2011:163) concur that "basic issues concerning the definition of economy and the theories and methods that anthropologists should use to investigate it were never resolved." I was among those who attempted to draw these issues "vigorously to the attention of other anthropologists" (ibid. cf. Cook 1974a) in the 1960s and 1970s. But, according to Hann and Hart, in the present century economic anthropologists "… have practically ceased to exist as an intellectual community" (2011:98).

This seems to be a consequence of anthropologists shedding their preoccupation with "primitive" and "non-industrial" societies and recognizing that we are living in one world unified by capitalism. The result has been a shift in the location of research back to the Euro American heartlands of the discipline (Hann and Hart 2011:142). New research topics include the material culture of consumption at home, industrial and other forms of work, capitalist development, and corporate capitalism and finance. Another issue still confronting economic anthropology today is that of "levels of integration" – a problem that has bedeviled modern anthropology (Wolf 1982:14–15). When one views the external social world from the bottom up, that is, starting with localities, then sub-regions, regions, nation-states, continental and sub-continental formations, and, finally, the entire planet, the concept of "one-world capitalism" (Hann and Hart 2011:142–162) requires empirical demonstration in specific studies. From the perspective of my work in villages, towns, and regions of southern Mexico, and in the state of Tamaulipas along the US border, the top-down influences are not uniformly discernible; they can be assumed but not easily demonstrated. Even when they are demonstrable, they may not be central to the dynamics of local or regional economic life.

Two illustrative cases from my work in Mexico come to mind. After spending more than a year and a half in the field observing un-mechanized and semi-mechanized production of hand-molded brick in an around Reynosa, Tamaulipas – and interviewing many dozens of brick molders and other workers, worker-owners, and owners – it became clear that the border industry mostly producing brick for the Texas and Louisiana construction markets was characterized by a more highly internalized business model of introducing labor-saving/productivity increasing mechanization wherever possible and of expanding and modernizing plant size to accommodate increased output. This was in direct contrast to the brick industry in the periurban zone of Oaxaca City where un-mechanized production supplied a local construction market (Cook 1984a). In short, the border industry was more driven by incentives derived from a wider (i.e., local domestic plus Texas and Louisiana) capitalist market.

In a special case of a three-generation family enterprise that had evolved from an un-mechanized household labor-only status to a semi-mechanized, predominantly hired-labor status, I had been impressed by a capital-saving strategy of in-house improvisation regarding invention and maintenance of physical plant and equipment – including all machinery, transport vehicles, and so on. Cash capital expenditures were mostly reserved for labor, not for plant or equipment where family labor was dominant. However, after a young, college-educated, highly entrepreneurial family member became a full partner in the enterprise, the capitalization strategy shifted gears and became more driven by wider market participation. Inspired by his reading of my first book (1998) on the border brick industry which included a section on his family's enterprise this individual traveled widely in Mexico, South America (his wife is Argentinian), and the United States to visit brick factories and suppliers of brickmaking machinery. He also started reading Searle's (1956) classic history of brickmaking (which I had given him) to get ideas for making innovations in his firm's production technology and layout.

On I recent visit to his factory to see for myself how some of these innovations were impacting production, I was shocked to learn that he and his father had just returned from an excursion to China expressly for the purpose of researching and buying new equipment for their plant. His father is the same man I had interviewed twenty-five years earlier in the middle of his modest, mostly un-mechanized plant (except for a flatbed truck and a backhoe) when he made a comparison of the difficulties of "mass production" shared by artisan basket makers in Oaxaca as discussed in B. Traven's famous story and small-scale handmade brick producers in Reynosa (Cook 1995, 2011). In short, on the basis of the above narrative the "one-world capitalism" thesis seems to have found empirical verification in one case of a US-Mexico border brick manufacturer.

The second case pertains to my research in the Valley of Oaxaca, Mexico on the metate industry involving peasant-artisan producers in four separate localities (Cook 1982, 2014). For most of its history, probably dating to the Pre-Hispanic period, the quarrying and stonecutting technology employed in this industry involved the use of stone, wooden, and steel tools. Stone and wooden tools predominated in the pre-Hispanic and early colonial periods; stone tools were displaced starting in the mid-sixteenth century by steel tools adopted from the Spanish colonizers but some wooden tools were still in use in the early twentieth century. From that time on innovations in tool technology were few but focused exclusively on the repertory of steel tools. The only non-technological evidence I found in the twentieth century of change in the metate industry were restricted to work organization (the formation of workshops in combination with out-work) and marketing (increased capitalization of merchant/intermediary businesses) (Cook 2014:chs. 3–4).

About a decade ago I initiated correspondence with colleagues in Oaxaca regarding the disposition of several videotapes derived from the Oaxaca Shoot described above. My intention was to stimulate the involve-ment of some of Oaxaca *licenciatura* students in a project to edit and show these tapes in the local community where they had been filmed and, if possible, to undertake a new video documentary to update developments in the metate industry. Those efforts succeeded and the documentary was updated. Upon viewing the update, I was excited and surprised to see a sequence involving the use of an electric grinder to cut-out and shape me-tates from solid blocks of stone. Knowing the pragmatism and deliberative reasoning that is part-and-parcel of Oaxaca commodity-market culture, the move to mechanize a process traditionally done with steel hand tools (which had long ago displaced stone tools) was, in itself, not completely surprising. But I never expected market conditions to sustain the increased cost of mechanization – albeit in a market not solely dependent on utili-tarian demand for metates to grind foodstuffs but significantly driven by a ceremonial demand for metates as bridal gifts.

In Oaxaca, I had met requests from woodcarvers over the years, to bring them mechanical cutting and sanding devices and wood burning instruments, for their use in manufacturing a variety of wooden utensils. I had done likewise with regard to safety improvements (e.g., goggles, gloves) for kiln-burners in the brick industry. Later, I focused quite a bit on problems of labor-saving mechanization and other innovations in the border brick industry. Also, as it turns out, prior to viewing the updated Oaxaca metate industry video, I had been involved in discus-sions in Texas regarding the uses of particular cementitious materials as additives to clay in the manufacture of hand-molded brick. All of these experiences coincided in promoting the idea that, yes, the day may come when metates in Mexico were molded rather than carved from natural, quarried stone.

I communicated with Jorge Hernández-Díaz in Oaxaca expressing this idea in my reaction to his students' video showing the use of an electric-powered grinder. He responded by expressing amazement that I had also mentioned the possibility of molding technology in the future of the metate industry. He had just learned that, in fact, metates made of molded cementitious materials simulating natural stone, were being produced and sold in the state of Puebla near Mexico City! Hence, rapid change in an industry deeply rooted in indigenous commodity economy, albeit within Mexican capitalism. Herein lies the possibility for yet another updated study of metate-making focused on the introduction of mechanized technology in an industry that still in the 1980s epitomized traditional peasant-artisan production persisting relatively unchanged in an economy experiencing social differentiation and capitalist development (Cook and Binford 1990:74).

The paradox here is that metates should be on the list of endangered commodities – that is, those which are no longer indispensable for utilitarian purposes and, therefore, are on a permanent downward demand trajectory. Since the mid-twentieth century, there have been alternatives to processing corn by manual stone-grinding in the form of hand-operated metal grinders, mechanically-driven stone grinders and, even, mechanically mass-produced ready-to-eat tortillas. By all odds, the combination of labor-saving alternatives to grinding corn on metates, and opportunity-cost logic on the part of indigenous female subjects, squeezed more than ever by pressures to reduce unremunerated household reproductive chores toward income-generating activities, should have resulted in a sharp decline in demand for and supply of metates. Surprisingly, systematic empirical data on metate output and sales from the 1960s and 1970s showed increases rather than declines, and my unsystematic observations of market activity in 1990 and again in 2004 suggested continuing increases in these variables. This "against-all-odds" scenario seems to defy utilitarian logic but not the logic of commodity value. The continuing demand for metates seems to reside significantly in their flow into the market and then into circuits of ritual gifting and of the reproduction of female identity in the indigenous Zapotec *usos y costumbres* regime (Cook 2014:291–293; 356n3).

Since thought, like all human activities and humanity itself, evolves, it is perfectly reasonable to assume, along with Karl Marx, that the development of capitalism in Europe was simply a transformative moment in the development of humanity's economic life. Because of this Marx reasoned that the analysis of the elements and processes of capitalism would necessarily illuminate fundamental elements and processes of universal economy and, even more, of each and every particular concrete economy of record. Despite cultural differences, for Marx, humanity has many particular histories that belong to a common universal history. From this world-historic perspective comparative economic anthropology is conceived as being "able to investigate ... 'human economy' anywhere in time and space, as a creation of all humanity" (Hann and Hart 2011:x, 164).[13]

I have argued that Marx's conceptualization of artifacts as commodities, an exercise he undertook as a first step in his analysis of money capital and the capitalist mode of production, provided a platform for a theory of value applicable to the entire range of humanity's economic life (Cook 2004:105, 121–154; 2006:187–190). Since the mid-1970s the labor theory approach to commodity value has been central to my research on commodity production in Mexico – most notably with regard to metates (1976b; 2004:229–234; 2006b:190–191; 2014:289–293) and bricks (Cook 1984a, 1998, 2011). I have done so not as an article of faith but because it provides the best explanation of the data I have collected regarding the production and marketing of the commodities studied.

It may be true that "anthropologists' preoccupation with fieldwork-based ethnography has led them to focus on present time within narrow spaces" (Hann and Hart 2011:164), although I think the best ethnographies, even dating back to Oscar Lewis' study of Tepoztlán (1951), had a broader focus. Whenever possible ethnographers have designed and conducted research in a representative sampling of local communities to account for diversity within regions, and to take account of the past as well as the present (e.g., Cook and Binford 1990; Cook 2014). Such initiatives must relegate grand theories of global economy in crisis, and the search for possible alternatives to "capitalist realism" and "business ontology" (Fisher 2009), to a back burner and focus on more easily operationalized mid-level theories conducive to systematic empirical investigation. The best economic ethnographies can be variously informed by multiple traditions of social science theory and knowledge of world history but must be conducted through cultural immersion and sensitivity, and also guided by a rigorous definition of the economic field and by a concern for the empirical demonstrability of variables deemed "economic."

There is still a vast division of labor out there in which most people on the planet are making and earning livelihoods locally in regional economies. It is not difficult to relate ethnographic findings to wider and deeper discourses, but it is doubtful that economic anthropologists will play a significant policy role in developing a new world financial and monetary system or in seeking massive redistributions of wealth in the future of global capitalism – although Keith Hart (2001) and Chris Gregory (2004) have earned consideration for such a role.

Anthropology's unique contribution to the study of economic life has come from ethnographic fieldwork – originally among so-called "primitive" or "tribal" peoples, then among peasants, artisans, and workers in the Third World. Bronislaw Malinowski casually employed the term "ethnographic economics" in his unpublished review of Herskovits' *The Economic Life of Primitive Peoples* (Malinowski 1940–1941:2; Cook and Young 2016:665) where he rejected Herskovits' complaint that ethnographers almost perversely buried economic activities in tangential cultural ones with the result of encumbering economic analysis (Herskovits 1940:39–40, 465–466; 1952:59–60, 63). Malinowski, was not opposed to detaching economic from other sociocultural elements for heuristic purposes, but he emphasized that the entire complex of interwoven sociocultural practices involved in producing, exchanging, and consuming products and commodities were "economic" and comprised the economy (Malinowski 1940–1941:7–10; Cook 2017b:238).[14]

Exhaustive documentation of macroeconomic neoliberal global policies sanctioned and financed by the World Bank (e.g., Greenberg, Weaver et al. 2012, esp. Chs. 1–3), which evolved after 1944 to foster and monitor capitalist reconstruction and development, reveal the myriad ways in which capitalists and their enterprises invent innovative schemes or instruments to appropriate surplus value. Needless to say, world economic history over centuries is replete with such examples, and market-oriented reform policies, including privatization and austerity, have been enacted by a broad spectrum of political regimes and studied by an equally broad spectrum of social scientists. For those who might be motivated to practice economic ethnography, their best recourse is to return to the historical roots of the discipline, address a whole series of unresolved issues about method and theory in the study of human livelihood, proceed with theoretically-informed fieldwork, and allow the results to point where they may.

The Covid pandemic of 2020 has greatly disrupted daily life in many areas of the world including Oaxaca as if the pace, scope, and scale of existential change already underway there since the 1990s was not disconcerting enough. Since the designation of Oaxaca's Monte Albán as a UNESCO World Heritage Site in 1987 and subsequent reconstruction and upgrading there and in other archaeological sites by the Mexican government, the Oaxaca Valley has experienced an unparalleled upsurge in national and international tourism (Brulotte 2012:60). This has resulted in nothing short of a remaking of the central district that includes Oaxaca City and Monte Alban. Old neighborhoods have been vacated and remodeled to accommodate tourists or expatriates in housing or boutique hotels; new businesses of all types and sizes have been built providing service sector jobs for displaced locals and migrants who flood into periurban *colonias* and new residential subdivisions (*fraccionamientos*) – resulting in a sprawling metropolitan area of one million inhabitants. Urban rents and real estate values (*mercado inmobiliario*) have skyrocketed and traditional barrios like Xochimilco and Jalatlaco which traditionally housed artisans now have chic residences, four star hotels, and entertainment sites for mostly retired American and European expatriates and global tourism.

The system of periodic markets (*plaza-mercados*) continues but with modifications of its twentieth-century configuration. During the initial stages of the Covid pandemic, the system was identified by the government as a "contagion hot spot" (*foco de contagio*) and was shutdown for three weeks but community participants rebelled and the suspension was lifted. By and large, the rural populations continue to attend weekly markets which now display more cheap goods from China (*chácharas*). A recent local observer of market activity described the market scene as follows: "They are a sort of hybrid where you find products of the peasants and artisans but they are dominated by informal sector merchants (*comerciantes del sector informal*) who sell clothing, tools, small domestic appliances, and so on" (Jorge Hernandez Diaz, personal communication, October 20, 2020).

My recent virtual excursion through a Google map disclosed an amazing spread of the area's settlement pattern and inventory of business sites in all directions compared with the late twentieth and early twenty-first centuries. Roads into and out of the city are dotted with a wide assortment of car dealerships, hotels, restaurants, bars, big-box stores, and so on. Housing subdivisions proliferate in periurban communities like Xoxocotlán, Santa Lucía del Camino, Atzompa, and San Jacinto Amilpas.

In view of the above, it may well be that knowledge production regarding these rapidly changing realities and their profound and interrelated existential dimensions defy time-consuming and exacting systematic social scientific inquiry. Perhaps they are fit subjects only for sardonic caricaturists, fast-working investigative journalists, bloggers, podcasters or for imaginative writers like B. Traven – and not for those who attempt to follow the trail of Malinowski.

Conclusion

What does a Red Ryder BB rifle have in common with a handmade brick? This strange question might have served as a "hook" at the beginning of this exploration but my hope is now that the reader will not find the question so off the wall or oxymoronic at its conclusion. The obvious answer to the question posed is that the two products share a "commodity" identity and, as such, entered my life – in one case as a gift for my use and enjoyment, and in the other as an object of anthropological study. I also hope that every reader of this book will now pose similar questions regarding the significance of particular valuable things in his or her own life, because the act of doing so will reflect an understanding of the pervasive role of commodities in our lives in twenty-first-century America and how that connects us to a wider and deeper history of humanity at other times and places.

In Oaxaca, I not only passed through a phase of "pot fever" but almost simultaneously contracted a longer-lasting sister-affliction "craft fever" manifested through selective and situational buying of handmade products of my liking, typically utilitarian items or well-made and aesthetically-attractive, carved, woven or molded decorative items. Years later in the brickworks of Reynosa, Tamaulipas on the border one of my informants, Jesús Ruíz Sánchez, a kiln setter and foreman, referred to the boom years of export to the Texas market as "brick fever" (*la fiebre del ladrillo*) – a phrase that for him evoked images of Texas trucker-intermediaries appearing almost daily at the region's brickworks buying-up every brick in sight, fired or unfired. There was not only full-employment but everyone was working overtime (Cook 1998: 146–158; 2011:87). In those years, demand for Mexican handmade brick originating in the Texas masonry construction market appeared to be insatiable.

All of these "fevers" expose a mix of rational and irrational behavior associated with commodity production, exchange, and consumption. This mix probably cross-cuts historically-, geographically- and culturally-bounded epochs and sections of economic life. A pre-Hispanic Zapotec jade statue from 50 BC Oaxaca, a factory-machined Red Ryder BB rifle from 1940s USA, and a hand-molded brick from a semi-mechanized brickworks in Reynosa, Mexico in 2000 have all been objects of the same human behavioral mix.

In view of the material presented above, and the introspective and critical thinking evoked in the process, what circumstances and influences do I find most compelling as pre-conditioning my decision to become an anthropologist to study those valuable things called "commodities" in a neighboring country south of the Rio Grande? My childhood experience in relocating from the cold, sooty environment of wartime Pittsburgh to the sunny, arresting landscape of San Antonio surely was an early contributing factor. I first saw there people who became for me something akin to an "exotic group" namely, people of Mexican descent who were unlike any I had seen before.[15]

There was something about the way they looked, the language they spoke, the food they ate, their music and lifestyle that caught my attention and attracted me. On the West side of downtown San Antonio on Commerce Street close to the Armour and Company branch where my father was assistant manager, were two places that caught my attention, the Buckhorn Saloon and the Mexican Market, both packed with displays of exotic goods evoking the Southwest and Mexico: leather goods like saddles, bridles, chaps, belts, holsters, boots, and, of course, Mexican jumping beans which all kids found intriguing. Colorful Mexican crafts including many shapes, sizes, and styles of ceramic ware, clothing like sarapes and shawls, wall hangings of various materials, paintings, silver jewelry, adornments and utensils of wood, leather, metal, and so on. Then there was the lilting sound of mariachi and *conjunto* music, street dancing, and the tantalizing smells and delicious tastes of a whole host of spicy foods with unusual names like tamales, enchiladas, tacos, chalupas, flautas, and a host of others, not to mention pecan pralines known as *dulces de nuez* which were the perfect dessert. In the mid-1940s I and my family of Pennsylvania "Yankees" were, to say the least, overwhelmed by the novelty of Southwestern and Mexican culture and its spectacular array of commodities. Whose curiosity and interest would not be aroused about their provenance?

I wanted to know this exotic world that was presented to me better as I grew up but considering the unique Anglo-Texan regime of Jim Crowism, rooted in an invasive, expropriative, and subjugative history of Anglo expansion in Mexican Texas, my ability to do so, except superficially and strictly as an outside tourist-like consumer, had to be postponed. All that I managed to accomplish in that direction through my formal public schooling in Texas was to take Spanish-language courses, and to have a few casual friendships with Mexican-descent fellow students, although never at their homes but at mine or in public spaces.

Later in high school and at the University of Texas, family excursions to the Mexican border to eat Mexican food in fine restaurants and buy Mexican goods in craft markets were replaced by young masculine pleasure excursions to bars, restaurants and red-light districts or "Boystowns." As it turned out, my marriage to Hilda Almenas from Puerto Rico led to periods of residence and research on that vibrant island and, afterwards, in the interior of Mexico. Even so, it was not until the 1970s, in preparing undergraduate curriculum at the University of Connecticut, that I finally undertook a serious reading of the Mexican-American and Border Studies literature. Finally, in the 1990s and the early 2000s, I expanded my research on commodities to include the handmade brick industry on the US-Mexico border which enabled me for the first time to deeply experience and explore the culture and economic life of the *Tejano* homeland and the *Norteño* border region of Mexico

I think that my upbringing in San Antonio and Austin, and my peripatetic high school experience, pre-conditioned me toward viewing the world as a sort of critical outside observer-participant from a comparative perspective. I became conscious of regional ethnic and cultural differences, of those between border Mexico and south Texas, between central and south Texas, and of nuanced differences in political, organizational, and religious cultures between states (Pennsylvania, Texas, Oklahoma, Iowa) and communities (San Antonio, Austin, Oklahoma City, Davenport).

For some reason, I developed an aversion to joining or affiliating with organizations or movements – religious, political, or otherwise – but, over the years, I have exercised my right to vote. Over nearly seven decades as a voter, I recall voting only twice for Republican Party candidates: once in

1969 in Michigan when I voted for William Milliken for governor and again many years later in Connecticut when I voted for Lowell Weicker three times as senator (1971–1989) and once as governor (1991–1995). Both were progressive, independent, honest, atypical Republicans who placed public interest over private, and who were not beholden to corporate money or corporate agendas. Aside from these two exceptions, I have voted by default for Democratic Party candidates. I have done so partly in the spirit of "the lesser of two evils" but also because Democrats for the most part are somewhat less beholden to the agendas of corporate lobbyists and donors than are Republicans, and more inclined to be supportive of the interests of workers rather than employers; and supportive of private sector regulation, progressive taxation, environmental protection, universal health care, separation of powers, checks and balances, and freedom of expression.

From an early age, I became accustomed to traveling and adapting to new milieus. All told, I think I learned more that way than if I had experienced growing-up and being educated in the same community or even the same state. Unquestionably, I have developed certain degrees of romantic attachment to particular places and to their peoples and cultures that I interacted with over the years. With a few exceptions, the more tropical they were the stronger my attachments and the fonder my memories. San Marcos, Texas became my final "home" partly due to a combination of my personal history in and familiarity with the Austin-San Antonio corridor, and to the fact that our two daughters and their families resided in nearby Austin. San Marcos is a college town, and within a few hours' drive to the border with Mexico where I was still conducting fieldwork, has a congenial climate and, last but not least, is blessed with a manageable cost of living – certainly in comparison with any location in Connecticut.

In this sense, "home" could just as easily been Puerto Rico or Oaxaca, Mexico. Texas is by no means "home" for me in the literary sense, for example, that Mississippi was for Willie Morris (2000). Given my peripatetic trajectory that sort of home was not in the cards for me. I have no regrets about that. In fact, such personal rootedness to one place probably inhibits one's capacity to exercise objective, comparative, thoughtful analysis vis-à-vis life in other places.

I had the opportunity during my junior high and high school years of exposure to my father's business world by traveling with him through central and south Texas to the Mexican border. Also, summer jobs exposed me to aspects of that world which I found fascinating but was not inclined to pursue as a career option. I was aware of my father's upward mobility in the meat-packing industry but also of his later departure without a pension from that long career through disenchantment with corporate reorganization and a new generation of know-it-all MBAs – and that made me wary and less than enthusiastic about corporate America or a business career. I was appreciative, however, of the income I was able to earn at several summer or interim jobs that I held thanks to my father's managerial positions and business contacts.

It is also true that my experiences at the University of Texas during my freshman and sophomore years, including the fraternity fiasco, but also my first exposure to critical social science discourse about economics and history, pointed me in a certain academic direction. However, I did not avail myself of formal academic counseling and my intellectual formation was mostly untutored, unsystematic, and curiosity-driven. At least, I was able to identify areas of knowledge that attracted my interest and suited my aptitude, and those which did not. My last two years of undergraduate study in Washington DC at American University reinforced my attraction and aptitude for certain approaches and subject matter in economics but also broadened my intellectual formation to include introductory politics, philosophy, literature, and art.

My job experience in New York City and my opportunity to renew graduate study in Puerto Rico in an innovative program at the University of Puerto Rico (where, among other things, I was introduced to anthropology for the first time) was career-altering. So was my formal and informal education there about life in a colonial setting and what it means for people to become foreigners in their own land. This started my long-term academic affair with a particular kind of alterity, combined with a critical gaze toward my "matrix" society (Cook 1974:805–808), the source of my enculturation – the USA. I developed an intellectual orientation akin to reverse-xenophobia by partially appropriating a radical Mexican (and Latin

American) gaze toward "Gringolandia." From that perspective "American exceptionalism" took on a different, unflattering meaning.

There is no doubt in my mind that I left Puerto Rico in August, 1963 a much different person that I was when I first arrived there. I was more aware of the unsavory consequences of US policy toward Latin America and the Caribbean, and of the complicity of capitalist business and strategic military interests in that policy. I documented and experienced as a researcher some of the existential impacts, intended or not, of many of those policies. I witnessed political reactions to those conditions, and acquired a higher degree of political awareness about their causes. I was then predisposed to expand and deepen my new understanding with more material from radical and other academic discourse. Some of my graduate student coursework at the University of Pittsburgh was undertaken strictly to satisfy doctoral program requirements, but I was also able to pursue coursework conducive to the formulation and initiation of a research agenda in the field of economic anthropology that would dominate my subsequent career.

It was one thing to negotiate the bureaucracy of a megaversity like Michigan State but quite another for a gringo anthropologist to negotiate the bureaucracy of the party-state apparatus in Mexico. Hugo Nutini had the assurance of Latino identity, upper-class savoir faire, and political indifference to easily negotiate relations within the Mexican anthropological establishment and, I am sure, in his dealing with regional and local officials. This was sort of the Malinowskian style. Admittedly, Nutini was quite sensitive and resentful – and rightly so – of being viewed, in his estimation, in patronizing or stereotypical ways by the Anglo-American anthropology establishment represented by Ralph Beals at his alma mater, UCLA, and at Pitt by George Peter Murdock and John Gillin (Williams 1993:115). I heard him express this on several occasions in discussions in Spanish with his friend, Pedro Carrasco – who shared the same experiences and views. Both of them felt more at home in Mexican academic circles than in Anglo-American ones.

From a quite different background and orientation, I had to confront different realities. As an Anglo-American or "gringo" in Mexico one must always deal with deep-seated animosities rooted in historical grievances of US-Mexico relations – which, after all, included a nineteenth-century war of Manifest Destiny in which Mexico lost half of its territory, and early twentieth-century occupations by US troops of the port cities of Veracruz and Tampico during the Mexican Revolution. Those animosities are always present – and sometimes openly so – in social interactions between Americans and Mexicans in Mexico. Visiting anthropologists have to deal with this on two levels – the bureaucratic, both in Mexico City and in the provinces like Oaxaca, and the popular sectors – that is, in relations with the public at large and those who might be or are informants.

In my experience, friction expressed through arrogant xenophobia or officiousness was more apt to occur with the bureaucrats than with the public – but tension, if not outright animosity, was often present in relations with anthropologists as well (both Mexican and non-Mexican I might add) – especially by those working on the same problems or on the same turf. If not age-old resentments tied to antagonistic international relations, anthropologists are always contentious and divided by competing ideological or scholastic loyalties or problem-foci. Thus, in villages I could be falsely perceived as or be snubbed for allegedly being a CIA operative, or in conclaves of anthropologists for allegedly being an enemy of indigenous identity and a Marxist espouser of class over ethnicity. These kinds of allegations were always in the anthropological air and one had to be prepared to deal with them.

It was possible to approach these matters in a Malinowskian way by diplomatically negotiating one's way through the bureaucracy – finding allies and supporters and avoiding detractors; or the Traven way which was to avoid, whenever possible, dealings with officialdom at all levels and even with members of one's own "guild" whenever possible. In other words, maintain as low a profile as possible – and avoid any type of attention-seeking behavior while quietly performing your job.

I employed both strategies and, fortunately, like Malinowski, I had very good luck in finding sympathetic or supportive members of the establishment who were understanding and generous with their assistance. In Mexico City there were several such individuals like Angel Palerm, Fernando Cámara, Alberto Beltrán, and, especially, Rodolfo Stavenhagen. In Oaxaca, several officials were helpful and supportive but Manuel Esparza, director of the regional center of INAH, stood out as not only providing invaluable official assistance and support but also friendship over the years. As his published record demonstrates, he did not suffer fools, although he treated them with respect so long as they did not earn his wrath through their actions (Esparza 2020). Esparza was unique in handling his job in the anthropological establishment and government bureaucracy honorably and efficiently but, also, in his recognition of its foibles, abuses, and excesses.

Ironically, pre-Hispanic objects like the jade statues excavated in San Jose Mogote by Flannery and Marcus, once they are commoditized as national cultural patrimony and placed under glass as museum showpieces, can become dangerous to the tenure of those government employees responsible for their care. According to Manuel, the large jade statue excavated by Flannery and Marcus was, at some point, mishandled by museum personnel who accidentally dropped it on the floor and, in the process, breaking one of its legs which they attempted to repair with crazy glue. The repair job did not work because it left a visible scar on the leg. Manuel then enlisted the help of a lifelong friend who happened to be a restoration specialist employed by INAH in Mexico City. He made the scar disappear but, meanwhile, had fallen into disfavor with the director of INAH in Mexico City. Word got back to the director of the technician's "off-the-books" assignment in Oaxaca and Manuel was summoned to Mexico City to explain why he had violated the official chain of command. He pleaded his case in the name of rescuing national patrimony (and sacred Zapotec culture) but the director argued that such a decision should have been made by him, not by Manuel. A few days later Manuel was fired from his job as director of INAH-Oaxaca. What better example could be found of the unlikely connections between inanimate objects embodying ancient human labor and meanings, and social life in a twentieth-century capitalist state bureaucracy?[16]

Owing to my 1965 participation in Stanford's summer field school in Oaxaca I was able to concretely visualize on the basis of my own experience the vivid descriptions and astute observations provided by Malinowski (1957) in his monograph on commodity circulation in the regional market system. For example, his frank admission of the intimidating activity confronting the ethnographer of market activity (1982:64): "The ethnographer becomes easily lost at first, and fieldwork in a market place is by no means easy. The difficulty consists in the chaos of the general picture, combined with the appalling simplicity of each concrete transaction. The chaos makes it difficult to see the woods for the trees. The triteness and finality of each individual act short-circuits any full development of problems, and in a way paralyses observation." This is vintage Malinowskian expressiveness, telling it like it is but with unique insight – which, incidentally, is less expressive in the earlier Spanish-language version published in Mexico (1957:25).

There was truth to Herskovits' claim in his 1940 book that the Malinowskian tradition in the study of non-capitalist economies manifested a sociological bias when studying economic phenomena and encumbered the analysis of the economic field with emphasis on traditional rules of social behavior, religious beliefs, and other interrelated non-economic ethnographic and psychological data. The economy, for Herskovits, should be treated as if it were an autonomous aspect of culture in the same way that art, religion, folklore, and linguistics were treated (1940:39–40, 466). Malinowski's functionalist approach, from the perspective of economic analysis, seemed to inhibit rather than promote the identification, measurement, and interpretation of core variables like cost, output, price, and allocation of rewards. Such variables were not of main concern in Malinowski's pre-Oaxaca work, nor compatible with his functionalist theory of culture. Nevertheless, they became of concern to him in his Oaxaca work which, if he had lived to finish it, might have yielded a more direct response to Herskovits' criticism than was provided in Malinowski's unpublished review of Herskovits' book (Malinowski 1940–1941:7–10).

It was evident to me in reading Traven's Oaxaca tale in Spanish as "*Canastitas en serie*" in the 1960s but, especially, when I re-read and analyzed it more carefully in its original English version as "The Assembly Line" (Traven 1993:73–88) in the 1990s (Cook 1995), that Herskovits' critique of Malinowski would be less applicable to Traven. Although Traven was unconcerned with decontextualizing the economic field for analytical purposes, his story's focus leaves no doubt about his systematic concern with economic variables like labor supply, cost, price, output, income, and market demand. For example, only five paragraphs into his story as he describes his Indian protagonist's basket making activity, Traven writes the following (1993:74): "His principal business ... was not producing baskets. He was a peasant who lived on what the small property he possessed – less that fifteen acres of not too fertile soil – yielded, after much sweat and labor and after constantly worrying over the … distribution of rain, sunshine, and wind and the changing balance of birds and insects beneficial or harmful to his crops. Baskets he made when there was nothing else for him to do in the fields … the sale of his baskets, though to a rather limited degree only, added to the small income he received from his little farm." In a few well-chosen words, Traven managed to capture the essence of peasant-artisan livelihood which he embellishes further as his story continues.

I spent decades and wrote thousands of words to document and analyze in greater detail this essential household reproductive dance partnering agriculture and craft production among indigenous peasant-artisans in Oaxaca. I was remiss in not recalling during most of that time the unique contribution Traven made to understanding the fundamental nature of that dance and for recognizing and illustrating its incompatibility with the profit-seeking dance of capitalism – despite the fundamental role of commodities in both dances. My work has demonstrated how, in exceptional cases, the two dances can converge in the form of petty capitalist production, yet Traven's scenario still holds in a majority of cases.

A focus on the trajectory of commodities is simply one way to approach the work Malinowski and Traven. It by no means provides complete coverage of the themes or subject matter that commanded their attention. Malinowski had much less to say about capitalism and capital-labor relations than Traven did and, only during his Oaxaca period, did he come to grips with the quotidian realities of peasant-artisan life in a market economy. Traven, on the other hand, devoted most of his literary career to critically portraying aspects of the class struggle between capital and labor in Mexico – especially in the mahogany forests of southeastern Mexico and in the oil and cotton fields of its northeastern coastal plains. Their distinctive visions, however, combined with anthropological knowledge available after they wrote, support the proposition that regardless of the time and setting of the economic life of humanity under consideration, the role of commodities cannot be discounted.

The concepts "commodity," "good" (or "product"), and "gift" have been with us for many centuries in economic discourse. They are associated with or evoke several different, often conflicting, philosophies, ideologies, and scientific paradigms of value. The extant literature addressing them is not only vast in extent but erudite and intimidating in intellectual content, involving as it does many of the world's greatest thinkers from Aristotle and Ibn Khaldun, Adam Smith, Karl Marx, and Carl Menger to Max Weber, Marcel Mauss, and Bronislaw Malinowski. Among contemporary scholars the work of Chris Gregory (1982/2015) is an indispensable source critically analyzing this discourse with special attention to its application in the field of Melanesian Studies. Of course, the list of other notable contributors to the discourse from the field of economic anthropology is extensive.

There is, however, an issue of false equivalency that requires scrutiny regarding the epistemological status of these concepts in producing knowledge about the production and reproduction of humanity through time and across space in our earthly habitat. If Karl Marx had not shed light on the matter in the *Grundrisse* (1971) and Volume 1 of *Capital* (1930, 1967) we might still be excused for failing to appreciate the extent of the false equivalency. But Marx demonstrated the analytical and explanatory power of the commodity concept as he dialectically dissected capitalism backwards into preceding and simpler modes of production and reproduction of human labor in the history of our species. The fact that labor and its products (or "goods") have been documented by anthropologists to be systematically gifted or redistributed in non-market economies pales into insignificance when we consider its commoditization as labor power (and surplus value) in the capitalist mode of production and its conflation with money capital as a universal commensurizer of value. Moreover, my own long-term inquiry into economic life in Mexico – one of the independent centers of humanity's civilizational development – has shown that products of human labor transferred as gifts or redistributed as tribute or rent are, in fact, typically commodities also transferrable through in-kind or money-mediated market transactions.

My argument for the heuristic superiority of the commodity concept defined as a mix of use, exchange, and symbolic value, each element of which may be structurally dominant (Cook 2006:187–190), is based upon logic, empirical observation, and analysis, not metaphysics, and is not falsifiable in the positivistic sense (Robinson 1964:27). This simple, eclectic conceptualization of the commodity has the advantage of being compatible with various antagonistic approaches like Marx's (commodity value determined by the amount of labor used in producing them) and Menger's (value of goods determined by the wants they satisfy). And, also, of having explanatory value regarding institutions corresponding to reciprocal, redistributive, and market relations – and with their shifting places in different social formations across time and space. If the focus is on the realization of value elements, these are not constant – material transfers will highlight, or balance, utility, exchange, or ideological values situationally in accordance with the social relations corresponding to them (Cook 2004: esp. Ch. 7). This may not convince those who consider the terms gift, commodity, and good/product to be equivalent "linguistic signs of quite different paradigms of value" (Gregory 2015:xxiii) but for those of us more pragmatically focused on labor, it is a compelling approach.

Endnotes

Introduction

1. According to Marcus and Flannery (1994:67–70) a pair of jade statues, one measuring 49 cm and the other 15 cm were found in offering boxes below Structure 35 at the San José Mogote site, and dated to the middle of the Monte Alban II sequence around 50 BC. They speculate that these statues could have been representations of "sacrificed elite males" (ibid. p. 69). They describe the statues as "spectacular artifacts" involving "many hours of invested craftsmanship" – but, in accordance with prevailing archaeological thinking, not as "commodities." In any case, my presumption is that these references are to the statues I saw in 1980.

2. "Culturalism" and "culturalist" are terms that identify any approach in anthropological thought that tends to break the interactive connection between agency or action from its cultural products such as symbols, meanings, or inscribed texts. Culturalism does remind us that "meanings persist beyond events" and that "symbols ... outlast and transcend the intentions of their creators" (Roseberry 1989:25) but easily lapses into a reification of those products and a de-emphasis on the process of cultural production under conditions of social differentiation. As Roseberry expressed it: "Interpretation cannot be separated from what people say, what they do, what is done to them, because culture cannot be so separated" (1989:29).

3. This document has been written as an exercise in combining (1) memory bank extraction assisted only by my publications and internet retrieval from Google searches or contact with surviving colleagues or ex-students; and (2) critically reviewing my publications and the discourses to which they contributed. In the strict sense of the word, this is neither an autobiography nor a memoir, although I do explore possible linkages between facts or incidents in my biography to my professional intellectual development. I view it as a culmination of my long-standing interest in issues of epistemology and method and my specific concern with the "epistemological situation of the economic anthropologist" (Cook 1974a:803–808).

    I admit to having shared some of the exasperation expressed by Peter Worsley in the "recall" problems he encountered in writing his memoir (2008:ix), and of the need to check sources regarding faded memories (2008:ix, 275). However, he concluded his project by stating: "I have been surprised how I have succeeded in remembering an awful lot once prompted by some detail, even if at the cost of lost hours of sleep" (2008:275). I can say the same about my experience in writing this book; however, the process of thinking about (and reconsidering) my contributions to knowledge production has taken priority over biographical details. Worsley wisely finesses the autobiography vs. memoir issue by simply using the terms interchangeably and distinguishing them from biographies (2008: ix). All three are nonfiction genres differing only in whether the author is the subject or not of the exercise.

Many personal files from the period covered are not available to me as I write this. Most files that were in my possession after relocating from Connecticut to Texas are now housed in the Scott Cook Papers at the Benson Latin American Library at the University of Texas. Those files are not yet digitally retrievable. I still had a few files remaining in my physical possession, mostly course syllabi, that will be consulted in the appropriate section of this text. Those files have now been deposited in my Papers.

While at the University of Connecticut, my files were kept in filing cabinets located in five different offices over the years – two as director of Latin American and Caribbean Studies, two as director of Puerto Rican and Latino Studies, and one in the Department of Anthropology. The files in the Department of Anthropology included all of my correspondence and other materials pertaining to my graduate students and to correspondence with colleagues.

A complete set of my Oaxaca project files were transported to my home office in Connecticut when I closed my office in Oaxaca in 1981. Some of those files, including complete sets of all the original survey questionnaires were discarded in preparation for my relocation by car and U-Haul trailer from Connecticut to Texas in August of 2000.

At UConn, files were either discarded or lost in moves between offices or, in the case of the Department of Anthropology, moved to my home office files or discarded in 1996 upon my retirement from that department at the time I became director of the Puerto Rican and Latino Studies Institute and moved into a new office in a separate building. Files pertaining to my stints as director of Latin American Studies and Puerto Rican/Latino Studies remained in the archives of those programs. I retained complete sets of files for most of my research work in anthropology, and some relevant correspondence, in my home office. However, during the relocation to Texas in 2000, following the end of my UConn employment, many of those files were placed in storage and others were hauled to Texas. Inevitably, some were lost, misplaced, or mistakenly discarded in the process of removal from storage and transport to Texas. In short, the Scott Cook Papers in the UT Benson Library probably comprise only one-half or so of my career files. Remaining portions of the files included in the Benson Library Papers consist of seven boxes or six linear feet. A detailed inventory has not yet appeared. All files concerned with my last project on border brickmaking are housed in special collections in the library of the University of Texas-Edinburg. Digital copies of many of these files were also deposited in the Benson Library.

Chapter 1   From Pennsylvania to Texas, Places in Between, and Back Again

4. The slag dumping process I witnessed with my parents most likely occurred at "Brown's Dump" in West Mifflin, near McKeesport. Reportedly, "families … would park their cars on the roadways surrounding the slag pile to joyfully witness the red glow … created by the flow of hot slag… and would gasp in awe as the molten mixture lit up the night sky" (google "Brown's Dump"). It was like viewing the "northern lights" or a spectacular fireworks show. The Google map shows this slag mountain to be relatively near to the impressive Kennywood amusement park where my parents took me on more than one occasion.

5. By 1770 the area north of the Rio Grande that would be known as the Lower Rio Grande Valley was divided into a patch quilt of contiguous landed ranch properties owned by Spanish-Mexican families, most of whom had permanent residences south of the river in urban centers like Matamoros or Reynosa. These landowning families were typically linked through marriage – including to relatively late arriving, non-Mexican/Spanish immigrants. For example, María Salomé Ballí, one of the numerous descendants of a family that settled in Reynosa in the eighteenth century from Mexico City where their Italo-German patriarch arrived in 1574, married John McAllen, an Irish immigrant, after the death of her first husband John Young, a Scottish immigrant, in 1859. The Balli-Young-McAllen role in regional economic history hinged on their ownership of the Santa Anita land grant lying 50 miles north of the Rio Grande in what is today northern Hidalgo County and explains the entanglements of the McAllen family in that history (McAllen Amberson et al. 2003). During the second half of the nineteenth century the political and economic activities of these landowning and business people laid the foundations for the early twentieth-century irrigation and urbanization ("Magic Valley") project.

6. There probably exists an experience-based, well-informed, and –written (from the perspective of single, urban Anglo-Texas teenage or young adult males) essay on the phenomenon of "boystowns" (*zonas de tolerancia* or *zumbidos*) in the second half of the twentieth century along the Texas-Mexico border from El Paso/Ciudad Juárez to Brownsville/Matamoros. If such a piece of literature has been published, I have

yet to read it. In my opinion, such an essay would have to be written in the spirit of the Ry Cooder song ("The Border" movie soundtrack) "The Old Skin Game" which highlights the lyrical phrase "A boy becomes a man in Mexico." It would have to emphasize the Mexican-side-of-the border-red-light-district experience as part of a cross- and counter-cultural excursion broader than simply "sex tourism." Many of us viewed the Mexican side of the border through romantic lenses and as a way to express our coming of age as independent young men unbound by rigid and hypocritical middle-class conventions regarding courtship and alcohol consumption; and also simply to be treated as adult men rather than as boys.

Our typical routine after crossing the border, usually in the late afternoon or early evening, was to head for the best bar-restaurants in central downtown areas that we could afford, to spend time drinking, eating, and being attended by well-dressed, courteous, professional waiters who knew that our money was as good as anyone else's. We were never able to experience this special treatment on the Texas side of the border. Only after a couple of hours eating, drinking, and being served at leisure did we look for taxi's to take us to cabarets or to the *Zonas*. In either of these settings, we could watch or associate with bevies of attractive young women, dance, and – depending on the circumstances or the establishment – have sexual encounters, if that was our intent. In any event, we could literally establish "girlfriend-like" companionship in one evening with these attractive young women without going through all of the prolonged dating rituals and attendant tribulations prevailing on our side of the border. Companionship without sex could occur with or without direct payment. We had no moralistic concerns regarding prostitution per se.

The unique Wittliff (2000) book of photographs with accompanying essays fills a gap in the literature. Unfortunately, the photos and accompanying text somewhat exaggerate the exotic, if shocking, tawdriness, vulgarity, and raunchiness of *La Zona* establishments. Consequently, it downplays the less tawdry, less shocking, and less raunchy, if still exotic, dimensions of the cross-border excursions that were at play in the total experience both outside and inside the boundaries of *Las Zonas*. In those days, it was only on the Mexican side of the border that young men from Texas could pair-up with attractive young ladies, eat, dance, drink, and be merry for several hours and, sometimes, have breakfast before hesitantly retreating to the other side.

Wittliff's translation of "Zona de Tolerancia" as "Zone of Indulgence" exposes a bit of literary license on his part and reflects the older male Texan "hedonistic customers" perspective (Wittliff 2000:107). A literal translation as "Zone of Tolerance" is more in keeping with Mexico's long-standing official national policy of regulating prostitution for public health, not moralistic, reasons; and for allowing individual states, and especially localities, to establish designated areas as special zones for brothels. Prostitutes were by no means restricted to practice their trade exclusively within such designated zones. Typically, their only legal obligation was to register with public health authorities and to get weekly medical examinations. The best discussion I have found on the subject of *zonas de tolerancia* in the border region is Arreola and Curtis 1993:106–117).

Chapter 2 Graduate Study in Anthropology at the Universities of Puerto Rico and Pittsburgh

7. In that conversation Lewis mentioned that the Italian Vittorio de Sica would direct the film. That did not happen. The film was not released until 1978 with another director – but Anthony Quinn did play the lead role. Obviously, Lewis's sudden death in 1970 complicated matters.

Here is how Lewis viewed his approach to life histories vis-à-vis Mintz's in a letter to his copy editor dated December 15, 1962 only a few months before my conversation with him: "… I am quite disturbed at your suggestion for me to break in at various points of the narrative or at the beginning or end of sections. I am inclined to reject this possibility because it would violate the form which I have slowly and patiently been building. If you want to see an example of what such a mixed style lead to look at Sidney Mintz's *Worker in the Cane*, a Puerto Rican Life History … which … is … something I want to keep away from. He even listed a few of his own questions to the informant to keep it 'scientific'. I realize this is far from what you had in mind but the very thought of going towards such a 'mixed' style, i.e., back to formal anthropology frightens me. Instead, I believe I can lick the problems you raised by a good introduction and perhaps a part two of analysis" (Rigdon 1988:237–238).

In his response to a very critical letter from Eric Wolf regarding the "culture of poverty" concept Lewis underlined the difference between his approach in the *Children of Sanchez* with the work of Ruth Benedict and Robert Redfield: "Although both of them talked and wrote a good deal about the humanistic component in anthropology, it has seemed to me that their work lacked the crucial humanist component, namely a vital concern with individuals, with the everyday reality. One does not find human beings in the work of Ruth Benedict, instead there are cultural configurations" (Rigdon 1988:231).

Chapter 4   Back East to New England: Anthropology, Puerto Rican, and Latin American Studies at the University of Connecticut

8.   According to Tuchman (2009:126–127): "After Provost Tremaine (Emmert) left Wannabe University, even the officers of the local chapter of the American Association of University Professors claimed that he had overspent … Tremaine had promised academic departments more monies than were in the budget so that when friends from other universities check on him, the Wan U professoriate would sing his praises." He may have done so but, in the case of the Institute under my direction that benefited from his strategy, the end justified the means. It was a zero-sum game. Emmert left UConn to become chancellor at LSU; then took the same job at his alma mater the University of Washington before becoming head of the NCAA in 2010.

Chapter 5   Malinowski and Metates in Four Oaxaca Communities, 1965–1974

9.   For some reason, probably just an innocent oversight, my name was not listed as one of the "field assistants" in his project, nor was any mention made of me in his acknowledgments for his 1975 book (Beals 1975:viii et passim). Beals did, however, send me a copy of the book upon publication with the following dedication on the flyleaf: "To Scott Cook whose work in the field and whose ideas about economics have been a great aid" (see Photo Appendix for copy). Also, he cited data from me at a dozen places in his text (1975:408). A copy of my field notes from Magdalena Ocotlán for 1967–1968 is deposited in Beals' Smithsonian Papers in the Oaxaca Market Studies Project files (a copy of these field notes is also in my Benson Collection Papers). Elsewhere, I have reviewed the communication between Beals and me starting in 1965 prior to my affiliation with his project in 1967–1968 (Cook 2004:32–33). In that correspondence, an agreement was reached that I would join his project, as a research associate, before completion of my dissertation write-up in Oaxaca during the late Spring of 1967. I completed the dissertation write-up in Oaxaca and then conducted fieldwork in Magdalena Ocotlán for Beals' project from July 1967 to July 1968.

Chapter 6 OVSIP, the Inflation Crisis Study and the Shoot, 1978–1990

10.   I recently had occasion to critically review a manuscript which addressed the non-monetary nature of money lodged in political and cultural regimes of value. It struck me that the author's arguments put the cart before the horse, and required more grounding in and examples of the economic functions of money which, after all, underlay and facilitated all of its non-economic implications in his/her case study. This led me to look for a source to refresh my memory about the functions of money from an undergraduate course in economics on money and banking. The source I had at hand was a primer written by Walter Neale (1976) where in one page he explains quite masterfully the economic functions of money starting with medium of exchange. He wrote (1976:7): "Medium of exchange means that money is received in payment for a good or service rendered and is later used to purchase a good or service. As a medium, money is a way-station in the exchange of goods or services sold or rendered for goods or services purchased. This function has been expressed in the formulation "Goods into Money into Goods," meaning that in this function money is but an intermediate, convenient stage in converting one kind of good into another." Clearly, in this passage Neale was euphemistically interpreting Marx's famous C – M – C circuit from volume 1 of Capital, adhering to neoclassical discourse's preference of the term "good" rather than "commodity." He then proceeds to weave all of the additional functions like store of value, standard of deferred payment, unit of account, means of payment – and even purchasing power – into his concise discussion.

11.   A rough and vulgar (translating *chingar* as the f-word in English) translation of RUIS's condensed history is as follows: "Many years ago we Indians were fucking great! Cuauhtemoc was our greatest fucking leader! But a fucking bunch of pale-faced Spaniards arrived and the sons of whores did a lot of fucking bad things and fucked over us Indians. And all of us went to fucking hell!" In my experience, the best mainstream Spanish-English dictionary treatment of iterations of the "chingar" complex is *The Oxford Spanish Dictionary* (1994: p.150). Despite its historically grounded metaphorical meanings, the term "hijo de su chingada" is employed so often in casual Mexican male banter as to convey no particular meaning other than the terms "bastard" or "son of a bitch" in casual banter among Anglo-American males. It is also prevalent in Tejano banter, as is the term "cabrón" (literally he-goat but implying cuckold and equivalent to "bastard"). Cabrón is not a fighting term in Mexico or in South Texas but it is in Puerto Rico.

Chapter 8 Global Change, Information Overload, and Trends in Economic Anthropology

12. The Spanish version of Jorge Hernández's message dated July 15, 2020 is as follows: "Pues the situación aquí se está poniendo cada vez más difícil, a la pandemia se suma la violencia, el aumento de las actividades ilícitas, y un gobierno que llegó con un gran respaldo popular, pero cada día se revela ademas de autoritario, ridículamente ineficiente y torpe. Es estas circunstancias el campo o los campesinos han dejado de ser lo que tu viste en los 80s, muchos en el valle de Tlacolula y Ocotlán se had dedicado al cultivo de mariguana y otros cultivos no permitidos. Una gran cantidad se fué a tu país, y en parte son los que siguen sosteniendo la economía aquí y en México en general, el año pasado enviaron 36,000 millones de dólares, y este año las tendencias indican que la cifra se mantiene.

Lo curioso de todo esto es que los estudios, como el tuyo o el de Bartra, se han dejado de hacer en México. Sería un buen proyecto, lástima que ya no tengo muchas ganas y tampoco energías para meterme a ese tipo de trabajo. Pero no hay que abandonar la idea para si otros la retoman, pues es necesaria esa mirada sociológica."

Recent figures on monthly remittances by Mexican citizens working in the US suggest that the annual total for 2020 may be well beyond the $36 billion for 2019. In March 2000, the total was 4.02 billion dollars vs. 2.96 billion in 2019 – a 36 percent increase (Reuters.com).

Chapter 10 Economic Change and Unresolved Issues

13. For Marx, as Terrell Carver (1975:147–148) pointed out: "The most abstract categories, though valid (in the sense that they are logical universals) for all forms of society, are nevertheless very much the products of a long historical process of development. They can only be formulated at a late historical stage when social life has become diverse and complex, and only in a developed society do they possess their 'full validity,' their full range of connotations and denotations."

14. In the same review Malinowski also referred to "primitive economics" and to "anthropological economics" which he clearly viewed as synonyms of "ethnographic economics." He did not use the term "economic anthropology."

Conclusion

15. I first heard this term in a lecture by Harry Hoetink at the University of Puerto Rico in 1961/1962. He may have coined it but, in any case, he defined it as a group "that differed physically and/or culturally, although not subjectively considered as a threat to the existing social order" (1967:139).

16. Manuel Esparza's account of this incident is from a personal communication to me dated August 12, 2020. Below are relevant excerpts in the original Spanish: "Hablas de la pieza de piedra verde de San José Mogote, quién iba a decir que tan importante hallazgo iba a ser la causa de mi despido de director del INAH de Oaxaca. Sucedió que por descuido de los museógrafos del Santo Domingo dejaron caer la pieza y se rompió una pierna, para disimular la pegaron con Kola loca pero se notaba la cicatriz. Entonces traje a … del INAH de Mexico que era muy mi amigo. Hizo todo lo que pudo para mejorar el daño. Resulta que … había caído en la desgracia de … director general, y cuando éste se enteró se encabronó todito y nos pegamos de gritos en su oficina, yo defendiendo el patrimonio y él su autoridad. A los pocos días me notificaron que estaba despedido." These incidents occurred in 1980 at the time Garcia Gastón Cantú directed INAH and Jaime Cama, Esparza's friend, was director of the *Escuela Nacional de Conservación, Restauración y Museografía* within the INAH bureaucracy.

References

Adams, John. 1996. "Epilogue: The Influences of Wendell C. Gordon." In Adams, J. et al., eds, *The Institutional Economics of the International Economy*. Amsterdam: Kluwer Academic Publishers.

Alvarez, Robert R. 2012. "Neoliberalism and the Transnational Activity of the State: Offshore in the US-Mexico Mango and Persian Lime Industry. In Weaver, Thomas et al., pp. 51–74.

Alonso, Armando C. 1998. *Tejano Legacy: Rancheros and Settlers in South Texas, 1734–1900*. Albuquerque: University of New Mexico Press.

Antler, Ellen P. 1982. *Fisherman, Fisherwoman, Rural: Capitalist Commodity Production in the Newfoundland Fishery*. PhD dissertation, University of Connecticut.

Appadurai, Arjun. 1986. "Introduction: Commodities and the Politics of Value." In Arjun Appadurai, ed., *The Social Life of Things: Commodities in Cultural Perspective*, pp. 3–63. Cambridge University Press.

—— 1990. "Disjuncture and Difference in the Global Cultural Economy." *Theory, Culture* & *Society* 7: 295–310.

—— 1996. *Modernity at Large: Cultural Dimensions of Globalization*. Minneapolis/London: University of Minnesota Press.

—— 2013. *The Future as Cultural Fact: Essays on the Global Condition*. London: Verso.

Argetsinger, Amy. 2015. "Jon Hamm was an awful frat guy. He could be a great anti-bullying advocate now." *Washington Post*, April 10, Arts and Entertainment section.

Arreola, Daniel D. and James R. Curtis. 1993. *The Mexican Border Cities: Landscape Anatomy and Place Personality*. Tucson and London: University of Arizona Press.

Baca, George. 2016. "Sidney W. Mintz: From the Mundial Upheaval Society to a Dialectical Anthropology." *Dialectical Anthropology* 40 (1): 1-11..

Bartra, Roger. 1974. *Estructura agraria y clases sociales en México*. Mexico City: Ediciones Era.

—— 1975. "La teoria del valor y la economia campesina: invitacion a la lectura de Chayanov." *Comercio Exterior* 25(5): 517–524.

Bartra, Roger and G. Otero. 1987. "Agrarian Crisis and Social Differentiation in Mexico." *Journal of Peasant Studies* 14(3): 334–362.

Beals, Ralph L. 1976. "The Oaxaca Market Study Project: Origins, Scope, and Preliminary Findings." In Cook and Diskin, eds, pp. 27–44.

Becker, Gary. 1976. *The Economic Approach to Human Behavior*. Chicago: University of Chicago Press.

Bell, Duran and Cynthia Werner. 2004. "Values and Valuables: From the Sacred to the Symbolic." In Werner and Bell, eds, pp. xi–xxv.

Belshaw, Cyril. 1965. *Traditional Exchange and Modern Markets*. Englewood Cliffs, NJ: Prentice-Hall.

Beltrán, Héctor. 2020. "Code Work: Thinking with the System in Mexico." *American Anthropologist* 122(3): 487–500.

Benítez Zenteno, Raúl, ed. 1980. *Sociedad y Política en Oaxaca 1980: 15 estudios de caso*. Oaxaca: UABJO, Instituto de Investigaciones Sociológicas.

Berle, Adolph A. and Gardiner Means. 1932. *The Modern Corporation and Private Property*. New York: Macmillan.

Binford, Leigh. 2013. *Tomorrow We're All Going to the Harvest: Temporary Foreign Worker Programs and Neoliberal Political Economy*. Austin: University of Texas Press.

Blanton, Richard E. 1978. *Monte Alban: Settlement Patterns at the Ancient Zapotec Capital*. New York: Academic Press.

Blanton, Richard E., Gary M. Feinman, Stephen A. Kowalewski, and Linda M. Nicholas. 1999. *Ancient Oaxaca*. Cambridge, UK: Cambridge University Press.

Blanton, Richard E. and Gary Feinman. 1984. "The Mesoamerican World System." *American Anthropologist* 86: 673–682.

Bohannon, Paul and George Dalton, eds, 1962. *Markets in Africa*. Evanston, IL: Northwestern University Press.

Boujouen, Norma Esther. 1990. *"Menea esas manos": Factory Work, Domestic Life and Job Loss among Puerto Rican Women in a Connecticut Town*." Doctoral Dissertation, University of Connecticut.

—— 2013. "The Puerto Rican Experience in Willimantic: A Reflective Account 30 Years Later." Keynote Speedh, Latino Migration Exhibit, Windham Textile and History Museum. Willimanic, CT, April 19.

Brandford-Calvo, Dania. 1993. *Changing Relations of Production among Paneleros and Sugar Cane Producers*. Doctoral Dissertation, University of Connecticut.

Brulotte, Ronda. 2012. *Between Art and Artifact: Anthropological Replicas and Cultural Production in Oaxaca, Mexico*. Austin: University of Texas Press.

Cardenas Salcido, Esperanza and Jorge Hernández-Díaz. 2016. "¡Ay, Mezcal, Me Volviste a Dar! Experiencias Hedonistas para el Consumo de una Bebida Destilada del Agave." In Worthen et al. eds, pp. 173–225.

Carrier, James G., 2005. *Gifts and Commodities: Exchange and Western Capitalism since 1700*. London and New York: Routledge

Carrier, James G., ed., 2012. *Handbook of Economic Anthropology*, 2nd edn. London: Palgrave Macmillan.

Carrier, James G., 2017. "Moral Economy: What's in a Name." *Anthropological Theory* 18(1): 18–35.

Carter, Keith, Dave Hickey, Christina Pacheco, and Bill Witliff. 2000. *Boystown: La Zona de Tolerancia*. New York: Aperture Foundation.

Carver, Terrell. 1975. *Karl Marx: Texts on Method*. New York: Barnes and Noble.

Cearns, Jennifer. 2019. "The 'Mula Ring': Material Networks of Circulation Through the Cuban World." *The Journal of Latin American and Caribbean Anthropology* 24(4): 864–890.

Chibnik, Michael. 2011. *Anthropology, Economics, and Choice*. Austin: University of Texas Press.

Chiñas, Beverly. 1976. "Zapotec Viajeras." In Cook and Diskin, eds, pp. 169–188.

Clark-Madison, Mike. 2003. 'A Proprietary Love'. *The Austin Chronicle*, July 4.

Coggins, Clemency. 1981. "Recent developments concerning the illicit traffic in antiquities in Mesoamerica." Paper presented at the Annual Conference of the New England Council of Latin American Studies, October 3, Brown University, Providence, Rhode Island.

Collins, Jane L. 2017. *The Politics of Value: Three Movements to Change How We Think about the Economy*. Chicago/London: The University of Chicago Press.

Collins Walsh, Sean. 2014. "Canadian Real-Estate Firm Bets Big South of Austin." *Austin American-Statesman*, Monday, November 17.

Cook, S., 1963. *Some Sociocultural Aspects of Two Revivalistic Religious Groups in a Puerto Rican Municipio*. Graduate Thesis, Interamerican Program of Advanced Social Science in the Caribbean Region, Institute of Caribbean Studies, University of Puerto Rico, Rio Piedras.

—— 1965a. "The Prophets: A Revivalistic Folk Religious Movement in Puerto Rico." *Caribbean Studies* 4(4): 20–35 (Reprinted in a slightly revised form in Horowitz, Michael, ed., *Peoples and Cultures of the Caribbean*, 1971, pp. 560–579. Garden City, NY: Natural History Press).

—— 1965b. "Review" of E. Seda Bonilla, *Interaccion social y personalidad en una comunidad de Puerto Rico*. Ediciones Juan Ponce de León, San Juan, Puerto Rico, 1964. *Caribbean Studies* 4(4): 93–98.

—— 1965c. "The Metateros of Teitipac." Field Report, Tri-Institutional Summer Field Training Program in Oaxaca, Mexico. Stanford University, Department of Anthropology. Mimeograph.

—— 1966. "The Obsolete 'anti-market' Mentality: A Critique of the Substantive Approach to Economic Anthropology." *American Anthropologist* 68(2), part 1: 323–345. Reprinted in LeClair and Schneider, eds, 1968: 208–227.

—— 1968. *Teitipac and Its Metateros: An Economic Anthropological Study of Production and Exchange in a Peasant-artisan Economy in the Valley of Oaxaca, Mexico.* Doctoral dissertation, University of Pittsburgh.

—— 1969. "The 'Anti-Market' Mentality Re-examined: A Further Critique of the Substantive Approach to Economic Anthropology." *Southwestern Journal of Anthropology* 25(4): 378–406.

—— 1970. "Price and output availability in a peasant-artisan stoneworking industry in Oaxaca, Mexico: An analytical essay in economic anthropology." *American Anthropology* 72: 776–801.

—— 1973a. "Foreword" to *Social Change and Personality in Puerto Rican Agrarian Reform Community* by E. Seda, pp. vii–xxiv.

—— 1973b. "Stone Tools for Steel-Age Mexicans? Aspects of Production in a Zapotec Industry." *American Anthropologist* 75: 1485–1503.

—— 1973c. "Production, Ecology and Economic Anthropology: Notes toward an Integrated Frame of Reference." *Social Science Information* 12(1): 25–52.

—— 1974a. "Economic Anthropology: Problems in Theory, Method, and Analysis." In John J. Honigmann, ed., *Handbook of Social and Cultural Anthropology.* Chicago: Rand McNally College Publishing Company, pp. 795–860.

—— 1974b. "Structural Substantivism. A Critical Review of Marshall Sahlin's Stone Age Economics." *Comparative Studies in Society and History* 16 (3): 355–379.

—— 1975. Comment on "Behavioral Analysis and the Structure of Prehistoric Industry" by Payson Sheets. *Current Anthropology* 16(3): pp. 380–381.

—— 1976a. "Value, Price and Simple Commodity Production: Zapotec Stoneworkers." *Journal of Peasant Studies* 3(4): 395–427.

—— 1976b. "The 'Market' as Location and Transaction: Dimensions of Marketing in a Zapotec Stoneworking Industry." Cook and Diskin, eds, 1976, pp. 139–168.

—— 1977. "Beyond the Formen: Towards a Revised Marxist Theory of Precapitalist Formations and the Transition to Capitalism. *Journal of Peasant Studies* 4(4): 360–389.

—— 1978. "Petty Commodity Production and Capitalist Development in the 'Central Valleys' Region of Oaxaca, Mexico." *Nova Americana* No. 1: 285–332. Torino: Giulio Einaudi editore.

—— 1981. "Crafts, Capitalist Development, and Cultural Property in Oaxaca, Mexico. *Inter-American Economic Affairs* 35(3): 53–68.

—— 1982. *Zapotec Stoneworkers: The Dynamics of Rural Simple Commodity Production in Modern Mexican Capitalism.* Lanham, MD: University Press of America.

—— 1983. Comment on "The Econmic Systems of Ancient Oaxaca" by S.A. Kowalewski and L. Finsten. *Current Anthropology* 24(4): 427–428..

—— 1984a. *Peasant Capitalist Industry: Piecework and Enterprise in Southern Mexican Brickyards.* Lanham, MD: University Press of America.

—— 1984b. "Peasant Economy, Rural Industry and Capitalist Development in the Oaxaca Valley, Mexico." *Journal of Peasant Studies* 12(1): 3–40.

——1984c. "Rural Industry, Social Differentiation, and the Contradictions of Provincial Mexican Capitalism." *Latin American Perspectives* 11(4): 60–85.

—— 1984d. "Pequeña producción industrial, diferenciación social y dinámica contradictoria del capitalismo provincial." *Cuicuilco (Revista de la Escuela Nacional de Antropología e Historia)*, Año IV, numero 12: 11–18.

—— 1987. Review of *Economics as Culture: Models and Metaphors of Livelihood.* Stephen Gudeman. London: Routledge and Kegan Paul. *American Ethnologist* 14(4): 784–785.

—— 1988. "Inflation and rural livelihood in a Mexican province: an exploratory analysis." *Mexican Studies / Estudios Mexicanos* 4(1): pp. 55–78.

—— 1990a. "Preface" to Cook and Binford, pp. xi–xv.

—— 1990b. *Oaxaca Shoot Audio Transcript.* Handwritten version in Spanish transcribed from video film footage from the 'Out of the Past' Project, WQED (Pittsburgh) and Cambridge Documentary Films Production (Boston). Project Director, W. T. Sanders, Department of Anthropology, Pennsylvania State University. Scott Cook Papers, Benson Latin American Collection, Austin: University of Texas.

—— 1993. "Craft Commodity Production, Market Diversity, and Differential Rewards in Mexican Capitalism Today." June Nash, ed. *Crafts in the World Market.* Albany: SUNY Press, pp. 59-84.

—— 1995. "B. Traven and the Paradox of Artisan Production in Capitalism: Traven's Oaxaca Tale in Economic Anthropological Perspective." *Mexican Studies/ Estudios Mexicanos* 11(1): 75–111.

—— 1998. *Mexican Brick Culture in the Building of Texas, 1800s–1980s.* College Station: Texas A & M University Press.

——2001. "The Mexican Connection in the Southwestern Borderlands: An Introduction." In Cook, ed., pp. 5–14.

——2003. "Struggling to Understand Complexity: The Sociocultural Anthropology of Mexico at the beginning of the Twenty-First Century." Mexican Studies/ Estudios Mexicanos 19(1): 197–235.

—— 2004a. "Cultura, mercancías y economía indígena en Mesoamerica." Public lecture delivered IIS-UABJO, Oaxaca City, June 25.

—— 2004b. *Understanding Commodity Cultures: Explorations in Economic Anthropology with Case Studies from Mexico*. Lanham, MD: Rowman & Littlefield Publishers.

—— 2005. "Cultura, mercancías y la economía indígena de Mesoamerica." *Cuadernos del Sur*, Año 11, num. 21: 35–49.

—— 2006. "Commodity Cultures, Mesoamerica and Mexico's Changing Indigenous Economy." *Critique of Anthropology* 26: 181–208.

—— 2008. "A Wall of Shame." Rio Grande Guardian. Wednesday, June 18 (article accessible on line @ www.RioGrandeGuardian.com).

—— 2011. *Handmade Brick for Texas: A Mexican Border Industry, Its Workers, and Its Business*. Lanham, MD: Lexington Books.

—— 2014. *Land, Livelihood, and Civility in Southern Mexico: Oaxaca Valley Communities in History*. Austin: University of Texas Press.

—— 2017a. "Malinowski in Oaxaca: Implications of an Unfinished Project in Economic Anthropology, Part I." *Critique of Anthropology* 37(2): 132–159.

—— 2017b. "Malinowski in Oaxaca: Implications of an Unfinished Project in Economic Anthropology, Part II." *Critique of Anthropology* 37(3): 228–243.

—— 2017c. "The 'critical current' in Mexican Social Anthropology vs. the Indigenista Establishment in the Aftermath of the 1968 Tlatelolco Massacre: An Outsider's View." *Dialectical Anthropology* 41: 305–311.

Cook, S., ed. 2001. "The Mexican Connection in the Southwestern Borderlands – Trends and Prospects." *Journal of the West* 40(2), Spring.

Cook, S. and Leigh Binford. 1990. *Obliging Need: Rural Petty Industry in Mexican Capitalism*. Austin: University of Texas Press.

—— 1991. "Petty Production in Third World Capitalism Today." In R. W. England, ed., *Economic Processes & Political Conflicts: Contributions to Modern Political Economy*. New York: Praeger, pp. 61–88.

Cook, S. and M. Diskin, eds. 1976. *Markets in Oaxaca*. Austin: University of Texas Press.

—— 1976a. "The Peasant Market Economy of the Valley of Oaxaca in Analysis and History." In Cook and Diskin, eds, pp. 5–25.

—— 1976b. "A Concluding Critical Look at Issues of Theory and Method in Oaxaca Market Studies." In Cook and Diskin, eds, pp. 247–280.

Cook, S. and Jong-Taick Joo. 1995. "Ethnicity and Economy in Rural Mexico: A Critique of the Indigenista Approach." *Latin American Research Review* 30(2): 33–59.

Cook, S. and M. Young, 2016. "Malinowski, Herskovits, and the Controversy over Economics in Anthropology." *History of Political Economy* 48(4): 657–679l.

Crisp, James E. 2005. *Sleuthing the Alamo*. New York/Oxford: Oxford University Press.

Dalton, George. 1961. "Economic Theory and Primitive Society." *American Anthropologist* 65: 1–25.

—— ed., 1968. *Primitive, Archaic and Modern Economies: Essays of Karl Polanyi.* Garden City, NY: Doubleday-Anchor.

——1971. "Introduction." In G. Dalton, ed., *Studies in Economic Anthropology.* Anthropological Studies No. 7. Washington, DC: American Anthropological Association.

De la Teja, Jesús F. 1995. *San Antonio de Bexar: A Community of New Spain's Northern Frontier.* Albuquerque: University of New Mexico Press.

De León, Arnoldo. 1983. *They Called Them Greasers: Anglo Attitudes toward Mexicans in Texas, 1821–1900.* Austin: University of Texas Press.

Delpar, Helen. 1992. *The Enormous Vogue of Things Mexican: Cultural Relations between the United States and Mexico, 1920–1935.* Tuscaloosa: The University of Alabama Press.

Diskin, Martin and Scott Cook, eds. 1975. *Mercados de Oaxaca.* México, DF: Instituto Nacional Indigenista.

Dunham, S. Ann. 2009. *Surviving Against the Odds: Village Industry in Indonesia.* Durham and London: Duke University Press.

Eiss, Paul and Thomas C. Wolfe. 1994. "Deconstruct to Reconstruct: An Interview with Maurice Godelier." *The Journal of the International Institute* (University of Michigan) 1(2), Summer.

Ellner, Steve. 2008. *Rethinking Venezuelan Politics: Class, Conflict, and the Chavez Phenomenon.* Boulder, CO: Lynne Rienner.

Esparza, Manuel. 2020. *Mi circunstancia al desnudo. Temas hablados y mudos.* INAH Centro INAH Oaxaca: Carteles Editores.

Firth, Raymond. 1939. *Primitive Polynesian Economy.* London: Routledge.

—— 1967. "Themes in Economic Anthropology." In Firth, ed., pp. 1–28.

—— 1967, ed., *Themes in Economic Anthropology.* London: Tavistock.

Fisher, Mark. 2009. *Capitalist Realism: Is There No Alternative?* Winchester, UK: Zero Books.

Foley, Neil. 1997. *The White Scourge: Mexicans, Blacks, and Poor Whites in Texas Cotton Culture.* Berkeley: University of California Press.

Fuentes, Carlos. 1969. "Viva Zapata." *New York Review of Books* XII(5): 5–12.

Godelier, Maurice. 1967. *Racionalidad e Irracionalidad en la Economía.* Mexico City: Siglo Veintiuno Editores, S.A. (First published in French in 1966 as *Rationalité et Irrationalité en Economie.* Paris: F. Maspero).

—— 1971. "Salt Currency and the Circulation of Commodities among the Baruya of New Guinea." In G. Dalton, ed., *Studies in Economic Anthropology,* pp. 52–73. Anthropological Studies No. 7. Washington, DC: American Anthropological Association.

—— 1972. *Rationality and Irrationality in Economics*. New York: Monthly Review Press.

—— 1977. *Perspectives in Marxist Anthropology*. Cambridge and New York: Cambridge University Press.

—— 1986. *The Mental and the Material*. London: Verso.

—— 1999. *The Enigma of the Gift*. Chicago: University of Chicago Press.

—— 2004. "What Mauss Did Not Say: Things You Give, Things You Sell, and Things That Must Be Kept." In Werner and Bells, eds, pp. 3–20.

Godfrey, Ellen. 1981. *By Reason of Doubt: The Belshaw Case*. Toronto/ Vancouver: Clarke, Irwin & Company Limited.

Graeber, D. 2001. *Toward an Anthropological Theory of Value: The False Coin of Our Own Dreams*. New York: Palgrave.

—— 2011. *Debt: The First 5,000 Years*. New York: Melville House.

Gras, N. S. B. 1927. "Anthropology and Economics." In W. F. Ogburn and A. A. Goldenweiser, eds, *The Social Sciences and Their Interrelations*,pp. 10–23. Boston: Houghton Mifflin.

Gregory, Chris. 1982/2015. *Gifts and Commodities*. London: Academic Press (1982) and 2015) Chicago, IL: HAU Books.

—— 2004. *Savage Money: The Anthropology and Politics of Commodity Exchange*. London: Routledge.

—— 2005. Review of Scott Cook, Understanding Commodity Cultures: Explorations in Economic Anthropology with Case Studies from Mexico. *Comparative Studies in Society and History* 47: 892–896.

Gudeman, Stephen and Alberto Rivera. 1990. *Conversations in Columbia: The Domestic Economy in Life and Text*. Cambridge University Press.

Hamnett, Brian R. 2006. *A Concise History of Mexico*, 2nd edn. Cambridge, UK: Cambridge University Press.

Hann, Chris and Keith Hart. 2011. *Economic Anthropology: History, Ethnography, Critique*. Cambridge: Polity Press.

Hann, Chris and Keith Hart, eds. 2009. *Markets and Society: The Great Transformation Today*. Cambridge, UK: Cambridge University Press.

Hart, John Mason. 2002. *Empire and Revolution: The Americans in Mexico since the Civil War*. Berkeley: University of California Press.

Hart, Keith. 1982. "On Commoditization" In Esther N. Goody, ed., *From Craft to Industry: The Ethonography of Proto-Industrial Cloth Production*. Cambridge: Cambridge University Press, pp. 38–49.

Hart, Keith. 2001. *Money in An Unequal World: Keith Hart and His Memory Bank*. New York: Texere.

Hernández-Díaz, Jorge. 1987. *Café Amargo: Crisis y diferenciacion social entre los Chatinos*. Oaxaca: IIS-UABJO.

—— 2001. *Reclamos de la Identidad: La Formación de las Organizaciones Indígenas en Oaxaca* Oaxaca City, Mexico: UABJO.

—— 1991. "Ethnic and Class Relations in Oaxaca, Mexico. PhD dissertation, University of Connecticut.

—— 2007. *Ciudadanias diferenciadas en un estado multicultural: Los Usos y costumbres en Oaxaca.* Mexico City: IIS-UABJO-Siglo XXI.

—— 2016. *Artesanías: Urdiendo identidades y patrimonias para el Mercado.* Mexico: Juan Pablo Editores.

Herskovits, Melville J. 1940. *The Economic Life of Primitive Peoples.* New York: Knopf.

Heyman, Josiah McC., 2014. "Illegality and the US-Mexico Border: How It Is Produced and Resisted." In C. Menjivar and D. Kanstroom, eds, *Constructing Illegality in America: Immigrant Experiences, Critiques, and Resistance,* pp. 111–135. New York and Cambridge, UK: Cambridge University Press.

—— 2012. "Constituting a 'Perfect' Wall: Race, Class, and Citizenship in US-Mexico Border Policing." In P. G. Barber and W. Lem, eds, *Migration in the 21ˢᵗ Century: Political Economy and Ethnography,* pp. 53–74. New York and London: Routledge.

—— 1998. *Finding a Moral Heart for US Immigration Policy: An Anthropological Perspective.* American Ethnological Society. Monographs in Human Policy Issues. Washington, DC: American Anthropological Association.

Heyman, J. McC. and Howard Campbell, 2009. "The Anthropology of Global Flows." *Anthropological Theory* 9(2): 131–148.

Higgins, Benjamin. 1956. "The 'Dualistic Theory' of Underdeveloped Areas." *Economic Development and Cultural Change* 4(2): 99–117.

—— 1959. *Economic Development: Problems, Principles, and Policies.* New York: W.W. Norton.

Hoetink, Harmanus, 1967. *Two Variants of Caribbean Race Relations: A Contribution to the Sociology of Segmented Societies.* Oxford, UK: Oxford University Press.

Hollandsworth, Skip. 1991. "The Greek Way." *Texas Monthly,* March.

Horowitz, Michael M., ed. 1971. *Peoples and Cultures of the Caribbean.* Garden City, NY: The Natural History Press.

Horsman, Reginald. 1981. *Race and Manifest Destiny: The Origins of American Racial Anglo- Saxonism.* Cambridge, MA: Harvard University Press.

Howell, Signe. 2018. *Ethnography.* University of Oslo. Cambridge Encyclopedia of Anthropology (online version –www.anthroencyclopedia.com).

Isaac, Barry L. 1986. Review of Peasant Capitalist Industry by Scott Cook. *American Anthropologist* 88: 476–477.

Kane, Eileen. 2010. *Trickster: An Anthropological Memoir.* Toronto: University of Toronto Press.

Lauria-Perricelli, Anthony. 1989. *A Study in Historical and Critical Anthropology: The Making of the 'People of Puerto Rico.'* Doctoral dissertation, New School for Social Research, New York.

LeClair, E. E., Jr, 1959. *A Minimal Frame of Reference for Economic Anthropology (Revised).* Troy, NY: Rensselaer Polytechnic Institute.

—— 1962. "Economic Theory and Economic Anthropology." *American Anthropologist* 64: 1179–1203.

LeClair, E. E., Jr, and H. K. Schneider. 1968. "Introduction: The Development of Economic Anthropology." In LeClair and Schneider, eds, pp. 3–13.

—— eds. 1968. *Economic Anthropology: Readings in Theory and Analysis.* New York: Holt, Rinehart and Winston, Inc.

Lenin, V. I. 1964. *The Development of Capitalism in Russia.* Moscow: Progress Publishers.

Lewis, Oscar. 1948. *On the Edge of the Black Waxy: A Cultural Survey of Bell County, Texas.* St. Louis: Washington University Studies, New Series, Social and Philosophical Sciences, No. 7.

—— 1966. *La Vida: A Puerto Rican Family in the Culture of Poverty.* San Juan and New York: Random House.

Little, Daniel. 1986. *The Scientific Marx.* Minneapolis: University of Minnesota Press.

—— 1989. *Understanding Peasant China: Case Studies in the Philosophy of Social Science.* New Haven: Yale University Press.

—— 1991. *Varieties of Social Explanation: An Introduction to the Philosophy of Social Science.* Boulder: Westview Press.

Littlefield, Alice. 1976. *La Industria de las Hamacas en Yucatan, Mexico: Un Estudio de Antropología Económica.* Mexico, DF: Instituto Nacional Indigenista.

Lippert, Julius. 1930. *The Evolution of Culture.* Translated and edited by George Peter Murdock. New York: Macmillan & Co.

Madsen, William. 1964. *The Mexican-Americans of South Texas.* New York: Holt, Rinehart & Winston.

Malinowski, Bronislaw. 1940–1941. Review of the *Economic Life of Primitive Peoples*, by M. J. Herskovits. Typescript, 9 pp. in Malinowski Papers at the London School of Economics.

—— 1961. *Argonauts of the Western Pacific.* New York: E. P. Duttton and Company.

Malinowski, Bronislaw and Julio de la Fuente. 1982. *Malinowski in Mexico: The Economics of a Mexican Market System.* Edited and with an Introduction by Susana Drucker-Brown. London: Routledge and Kegan Paul.

Marcus, George E. 1995. "Ethnography in/of the World System: The Emergence of Multi-sited Ethnography." *Annual Review of Anthropology* 24: 95–117.

Marcus, Joyce and Kent Flannery. 1994. "Ancient Zapotec Ritual and Religion: An Application of Direct Historical Approach." In Colin Renfrew and Ezra B. W.

Zubrow, eds, *The Ancient Mind: Elements of Cognitive Archaeology*. Cambridge, UK: Cambridge University Press.

Marx, Karl. 1904. *A Contribution to the Critique of Political Economy*. Chicago: Charles H. Kerr.

—— 1930. *Capital*, Vol. 1. New York: E. P. Dutton (Everyman's Library).

—— 1967. *Capital*, Vol. 1. New York: International Publishers.

——1971. *The Grundrisse*. Edited and translated by David McLellan: New York: Harper and Row, Publishers.

Mauss, Marcel. 1954. *The Gift: Forms and Functions of Exchange in Archaic Society*. London: Cohen & West. Originally 1925.

McAllen, Amberson, Mary Margaret, James A. McAllen, and Margaret H. McAllen. 2003. *I Would Rather Sleep in Texas: A History of the Lower Rio Grande Valley and the People of the Santa Anita Land Grant*. Austin: Texas State Historical Association.

McWilliams, Carey. 1948 [1968]. *North from Mexico: The Spanish-Speaking People of the United States*. New York: Greenwood Press.

Meek, Ronald L. 1967. *Economics and Ideology and Other Essays*. London: Chapman and Hall.

Mintz, Sidney, 1960. *Worker in the Cane*. New Haven: Yale University Press.

Montejano, David. 1987. *Anglos and Mexicans in the Making of Texas, 1836–1986*. Austin: University of Texas Press.

Montes de Oca Sicilia, María del Pilar. 2010. *El Chingonario: Diccionario de Uso, Reuso y Abuso del y sus Derivados*. Mexico, DF: Editorial Lectorum.

Morris, Willie. 2000(1967). *North Toward Home*. New York: Vintage Books.

Müller, Juliane. 2020. "Webs of Fiesta-Trade: Chinese Imports, Investment and Reciprocity in La Paz, Bolivia." *Critique of Anthropology* 2: 238–263.

Murillo, Gerardo (Dr Atl). 1922(1980). *Las artes populares en México*. Mexico City: Instituto Nacional Indigenista.

Murillo, Luis Felipe R. 2020. "Hackerspace Network: Prefiguring Technopolitical Futures?" *American Anthropologist* 122(2): 207–221.

Neale, Walter. 1957. "Reciprocity and Redistribution in the Indian Village: Sequel to Some Notable Discussions." In Polanyi et al., eds, pp. 218–236.

—— 1976. *Monies in Societies*. San Francisco: Chandler & Sharp Publishers, Inc.

Novak, Shonda. 2020. "The Tesla Effect: Automaker's Gigafactory Could Offer Unprecedented to Transform Del Valle." *Austin American-Statesman*, Sunday, August 9, p. 1 and A 19.

Nutini, Hugo, 1965. "Some Considerations on the Nature of Social Structure and Model Building: A Critique of Claude Levi-Strauss and Edmund Leach." *American Anthropologist* 67: 707–731.

Palerm, Angel. 1982. *Antropología y Marxismo*. Mexico, DF: Editorial Nueva Imagen.

Paz, Octavio. 1961. *The Labyrinth of Solitude*. New York: Grove Press.

Pérez, Ricardo. 2005. *The State and Small-Scale Fisheries in Puerto Rico*. Gainesville: University of Florida Press.

Pied, Claudine M. 2019. "The Revolution Will Not Be Paid: The Politics of Small Town Entrepreneurial Economic Development." *Critique of Anthropology* 39(4): 439–457.

Plattner, Stuart, ed. 1989. *Economic Anthropology*. Stanford University Press.

Polanyi, Karl. 1968a [1944]. "Our Obsolete Market Mentality." In Dalton, ed., pp. 59–77.

—— 1968b. "Anthropology and Economic Theory." In Morton Friend, ed. *Readings in Anthropology, Vol. II Cultural Anthropology*, pp. 215–238. New York: Crowell.

Polanyi, Karl, Conrad M. Arensberg, and Harry W. Pearson, eds. 1957. *Trade and Market in the Early Empires*. Glencoe, IL: Free Press.

Richardson, Chad. 1999. *Batos, Bolillos, Pochos, and Pelados: Class and Culture on the South Texas Border*. Austin: University of Texas Press.

Rigdon, Susan M. 1988. *The Culture Façade: Arts, Science, and Politics in the Work of Oscar Lewis*. Champaign-Urbana: The University of Illinois Press.

Ríos Méndez, Isnoel. 1988. *An Ethnographic Study of Intracultural Variation among High School Students of Mexican Descent*. Doctoral dissertation, Stanford University, School of Education.

Robinson, Joan. 1964. *Economic Philosophy: An Essay on the Progress of Economic Thought*. Garden City, NY: Anchor Books, Doubleday & Company, Inc.

Roseberry, William. 1978. "Historical Materialism and the People of Puerto Rico." *Revista/Review Interamericana* 8: 26–36.

—— 1983. *Coffee and Capitalism in the Venezuelen Andes*. Austin: University of Texas Press.

—— 1989. *Anthropologies and Histories: Essays in Culture, History, and Political Economy*. New Brunswick and London: Rutgers University Press.

—— 1996. "The Unbearable Lightness of Anthropology." *Radical History Review* 65: 5–25.

Rubel, Arthur J. 1966. *Across the Tracks: Mexican-Americans in a Texas City*. Austin and London: University of Texas Press.

Sahlins, Marshall D. 1972. *Stone Age Economics*. Chicago: Aldine-Atherton.

—— 1976. *Culture and Practical Reason*. Chicago: University of Chicago Press.

Seda, Eduardo. 1964. *Interaccion social y personalidad en una comunidad de Puerto Rico*. San Juan: Ediciones Juan Ponce de León.

—— 1970. *Requiem por una cultura: Ensayos sobre la socializacion del Puertorriqueno en su cultura y en ambito del poder neocolonial*. Rio Piedras, P.R.: Editorial Edil..

—— 1973. *Social Change and Personality in a Puerto Rican Agrarian Reform Community*. Evanston, IL: Northwestern University Press.

Schneider, Harold K. 1974. *Economic Man: The Anthropology of Economics.* New York: The Free Press.

Searle, Alfred B. 1956. *Modern Brickmaking.* London: Ernest Benn.

Spielberg, Joseph. 1974. "Humor in a Mexican-American Palomilla: Some Historical, Social, Psychological Implications." *Revista Chicano-Requeña* 2: 41–50.

Stavenhagen, Rodolfo. 1971. "Decolonizing Applied Social Sciences." *Human Organization* XXX, 4: 334.

Stephen, Lynn. 1991. *Zapotec Women.* Austin: University of Texas Press.

Steward, Julian and Louis Faron. 1959. *Native Peoples of South America.* New York: McGraw-Hill.

Straus, Murray A. 1968. "Communication, Creativity, and Problem-solving Ability of Middle- and Working-class Families in Three Societies." *American Journal of Sociology* 73(4): 417–430.

The Economist. July 4, 2020, p. 26, "The Americas: Cuba; Neither mulas nor moolah."

Thurnwald, Richard. 1932. *Economics in Primitive Communities.* London: Oxford University Press.

Traven, B. 1956. *Canasta de cuentos mexicanos.* Translated from the English by R. E. Lujan. Mexico City: Cia General de Ediciones, SA.

Traven, B. 1966. *The Night Visitor and Other Stories.* Chicago: Elephant Paperbacks, Ivan Dee, Publisher.

Tuchman, Gaye. 2009. *Wannabe U: Inside the Corporate University.* Chicago and London: University of Chicago Press.

University of Connecticut. *El Instituto: Institute of Latina/o, Caribbean, and Latin American Studies.* Posted on April 18, 2019.

Weaver, Thomas, James B. Greenberg, William L. Alexander, and Anne Browing-Aiken, eds. 2012. *Neoliberalism and Commodity Production in Mexico.* Boulder: University Press of Colorado.

Weber, Max. 1978. *Economy and Society: An Outline of Interpretive Sociology.* 2 vols. Edited by Guenther Roth and Claus Wittich. Berkeley: University of California Press.

Werner, Cynthia and Duran Bell, eds. 2004. *Values and Valuables: From the Sacred to the Symbolic.* Walnut Creek: Altamira Press.

Wessman, James W. 1982. "Antropología y Marxismo, Angel Palerm." *Journal of Anthropological Research* 38(3): 329–330.

—— 1981. *Anthropology and Marxism.* Cambridge, MA: Schenkman Publishing Company.

Wharton, Clifton R., ed. 1969. *Subsistence Agriculture and Economic Development.* Chicago: Aldine.

Wilson, Brian. *Sects and Society.* Berkeley: University of California Press.

Williams, Melvin D. 1993. *An Academic Village: The Ethnograpohy of an Anthropology Department*. Ann Arbor, MI: Melvin D. Williams.

Wittliff, Bill. 2000. *Boystown: The Zona de Tolerancia*. New York: Aperture Foundation.

Wolf, Eric R. 1982. *Europe and the People without History*. Berkeley: University of California Press.

Worsley, Peter. 2008. *An Academic Skating on Thin Ice*. New York and Oxford: Berghahn Books.

Worthen, Holly, Jorge Hernández-Díaz, and Charlynne Curiel, eds. 2016. *El Valor de las Cosas: Aspectos sociales y culturales de la producción y el consumo*. Mexico: UABJO-IIS, Juan Pablo Editor.

Young, Michael W. 2004. *Malinowski: Odyssey of an Anthropologist 1884–1920*. New Haven and London: Yale University Press.

Printed by
CPI books GmbH, Leck